Praise for Worldly Women

"In *Worldly Women* the authors, Caroline and Sapna, make a convincing argument for having more females participate in the global work process. They have gathered up-to-date materials for going beyond anecdotal evidence. Females bring something to the party that is unique to them, making the expatriate job more fulfilling. Bravo!"
~ **Fons Trompenaars, author of Riding the Waves of Culture**
Fons Trompenaars, cross-cultural expert, is ranked in the Thinkers50 2011 listing as one of the top 50 most influential management thinkers alive. He was voted one of the top 20 HR Most Influential International Thinkers 2011 by HR Magazine.

"When you add it all up there are plenty of books out there supporting female expatriates as the "trailing spouse". Finally - here is a book that puts the professional woman in focus and takes you through the challenges from both the personal, family and business perspective. A must read for any woman who has an interest in an international career. *Worldly Woman* is a great read - packed with great stories and tons of practical advice. Read, enjoy and conquer the world".
~ **Deanna Rasmussen, Head of Global Mobility, Deutsche Post - DHL Supply Chain**

"*Worldly Women* is a must-have tool for any women considering or in the process of an international assignment. I wish I had information like this 15 years ago when I was considering an international assignment. The good news is that I now have this blueprint to share with women I coach about their careers. I will provide this book to every woman we send on an international assignment!"
~ **Jennifer Gardner, Vice President Human Resources, Highlights for Children, Inc. (Including Highlights International). Formerly a Talent Firm Director with Deloitte**

"This book brings together useful and important information for female expatriates."
~ **Neelie Kroes, Vice President of the European Commission**
Neelie Kroes, a European political powerhouse, has made the Forbes' - The World's 100 Most Powerful Women list multiple times in the past decade.

"A core competency of the leaders of tomorrow is deep global experience. *Worldly Women* is a groundbreaking book focused on how women approach this challenge and opportunity. I recommend this book for all women (and men too) seeking to chart their global leadership path."
~ **Mike Dulworth, President & CEO, Executive Networks, Inc. and author of The Connect Effect**

"*Worldly Women* represents a tremendous contribution, and should be required reading for all students of international business. Female students need it to help optimize their expectations and preparation for their future role in our global economy. Male students, as future managers, need it to help them overcome an unfounded yet persistent prejudice against women serving as expatriates—a prejudice that is not only unfair to women but also renders uninformed organizations at a great disadvantage in the global war for talent."
~ **Dr. Charles M. Vance, author of Managing a Global Workforce and management professor at Loyola Marymount University**

"*Worldly Women* will inspire and motivate you and serve as your guide to develop a toolkit of behaviors to be successful as an expatriate."
~ **Mirella Visser, Center for Inclusive Leadership, author of The Female Leadership Paradox**

"*Worldly Women* is a great read filled with ground breaking research, meaningful stories, and hands on exercises for women who want to enrich their professional and personal lives by entering the international arena."
~ **Prof. Holger Ernst, PhD, Chair for Technology and Innovation Management, WHU, Otto Beisheim School of Management**

"Excellent research of 62 female expatriate experts. The authors, both HR professionals on foreign assignments themselves, intertwine excerpts from interviews in a logical and easy to read manner, backed up with many relevant studies. An absolute 'must-read' for women considering a foreign assignment! But, not just for women - also a 'must-have' for HR-professionals to motivate their female employees to see the benefits of an international assignment."
~ **André Kuperus (Global Nomad), Regional Sales Director, Ford Motor Credit Company**

Sapna Welsh
Caroline Kersten

How to Expatriate with Excellence

Worldly Women

The New Leadership Profile

How to Expatriate with Excellence

Sapna Welsh
Caroline Kersten

Foreword by Harriet Lamb

www.LeverageHR.com

Worldly Women - The New Leadership Profile How to Expatriate with Excellence

Copyright © 2013 by Sapna Welsh and Caroline Kersten.

All rights reserved. No part of this book may be used or reproduced by any means, graphic, electronic, or mechanical, including photocopying, recording, taping or by any information storage retrieval system without the written permission of the publisher except in the case of brief quotations embodied in critical articles and reviews.

iUniverse books may be ordered through booksellers or by contacting:
iUniverse
1663 Liberty Drive
Bloomington, IN 47403
www.iuniverse.com
1-800-Authors (1-800-288-4677)

Editor: Thomas Welsh
Cover design: Patricia Mensinga
Design and production of interior: Janet Hannah

Disclaimer: All of the WiSER's quotes in this book are based on their real-life expatriate experience and were shared during personal interviews. The views of the WiSER represent their own personal opinion, not those of the organizations they have been or currently are employed with. This book aims to provide useful information and ideas primarily to women considering working and living abroad or women interested in accelerating their careers. Readers of this book are responsible for consulting professional advisers for personal, legal, financial or other counsel tailored to their individual circumstances. LeverageHR.com, the authors, editor, contributors, publisher, sponsors, designer, distributor and promoters will not be held accountable for any errors, omissions or damages arising from information contained in this book.

Because of the dynamic nature of the Internet, any web addresses or links contained in this book may have changed since publication and may no longer be valid. The views expressed in this work are solely those of the author and do not necessarily reflect the views of the publisher, and the publisher hereby disclaims any responsibility for them.

ISBN: 978-1-4759-8301-2 (sc)
ISBN: 978-1-4759-8302-9 (ebk)

Library of Congress Control Number: 2013906539
Printed in the United States of America
iUniverse rev. date: 05/13/2013

Dedicated to our children

Dhillon, Kareena, and Devan
Bente and Britt

"May the world be your playground"

Contents

- **Foreword** 1
- **Preface** 4

Section I - The World is your Stage 7

1. **'Worldly Women' your Time is Now** 9
   - The world needs expats 10
   - Organizations need expats 13
   - Women are the answer 16
   - Circle of women 20

2. **Nothing Ventured, Nothing Gained** 25
   - Personal rewards 29
   - Potential risks 33

3. **The Culture Club** 39
   - Navigating cultural differences 40
   - Cultural dimensions 44
   - To adapt or not to adapt? That is the question 51

4. **Recipe for Success** 63
   - Do you have what it takes? 64
   - The female factor 79
   - Look before you leap 82

Section II - WiSER Competencies
(Women in Senior-level Expatriate Roles) 89

5. **Bells and Whistles** 91
   - Warning whistles - Barriers to women moving abroad 91
   - The bell curve - It is different for female expatriate leaders 100

6. **Self-awareness** 113
   - The international gold standard 116
   - Mirror, mirror on the wall 118
   - The journey to self-awareness - tips 124

7. **Conscious Imbalance** **133**
   A positive definition 134
   Maintaining imbalance - tips 138

8. **Operating Outside your Comfort Zone** **149**
   "Elastigirl" 151
   Managing stress 152
   Make it comfortable - tips 155

9. **Active Career Management** **163**
   Take the driver's seat 164
   Strategic networking 165
   Hit the bullseye - tips 174

Section III - Succeeding in Your International Assignment **183**

10. **The Roller Coaster Ride** **185**
    Fasten your seatbelt 186
    Enjoy the ride 193
    Welcome back riders 203

11. **Your Debut** **209**
    First impressions 210
    The power of words 211
    Creating your masterpiece 217

   Epilogue **226**

   Bibliography **227**

   Appendices **234**
   Appendix A: Research details 235
   Appendix B: WiSER profile 239
   Appendix C: Organization profile 244
   Appendix D: Interview questions 246
   Appendix E: Two promising paths 248
   Appendix F: Acknowledgments 250
   Appendix G: About the authors 251

Foreword

In this book, authors Caroline and Sapna encourage women to actively manage their careers, seeking an expatriate assignment as a conscious move to develop themselves as future leaders. There is much advice in here that would have benefited my younger self as I bumbled along. It's a secret that I only dare tell now: when younger, I considered finding a rich Scottish sheep farmer with a castle who threw plenty of parties: the optimistically named 'gin and tonic career option'. But no tartan laird appeared to sweep me off my feet. So I went for the total extreme, the 'brown rice' option, following my commitment to contribute to social justice. I have lived and worked in India and Germany and today have my dream job leading a global organization working with hundreds of people across the world. But I always squirmed at the interview question about how you see your career developing in 10 years' time. I had never thought that far ahead!

Expatriating is a tough gig. I've been there and it isn't easy to keep going with the normal demands of home and work, while at the same time closing things down in one country and then opening them all up again in another—from tax authorities to banks, dentists to doctors, renting a house, storing your furniture, schools and childminders, kindergartens and language classes... Not to mention making new friends. It's like putting all the usual challenges of being a working mother on steroids. There are the endless, painful moments when every time you try to start a meeting and impress your new colleagues—knowing how important those first weeks are—your phone rings with an urgent home problem; embarrassed, you just don't know how your new colleagues view such interruptions. Likewise, every time you try to settle down to a game with your kids, work is on the line with an urgent problem. You feel you have to respond in case they have different expectations here. And you constantly feel guilty about both worlds—you need your new office to accept you, and you need to help your kids settle in. Like so many women, I seem to have won the right to feel permanently exhausted and endlessly guilty.

And yet and yet and yet... every tedious, stressful moment is more than outweighed by the sheer exhilaration of learning about new cultures and new ways of working and living — experiences that stay with you and shape you forever. When I was a child, in the heyday of 1960s, my father was sent to India to establish a Formica factory, whose laminated tops still decorate many an Indian tea shop! That experience of living overseas was a defining feature of my upbringing and meant that as soon as I left school, I went to work in India, returning again later. I confess that as a teenager and then young job applicant, I over-played having lived in India, believing that it made me more interesting. I am sure that it is why I have embraced opportunities to work overseas and why today I work at Fairtrade International as my small contribution to ending global injustices and poverty. Every time I step off a plane and smell the warm, humid air of an airport in India or Kenya, I am still swept with excitement and the power of a thousand associations. And equally, each experience of living and working abroad builds a woman's skills to work with, understand and manage people from around the world.

Reading this book, I realized that I have been badly in need of following Caroline and Sapna's number one rule about being 'self-aware', in order to improve your performance at work, in particular if you move to a new culture. Personally, I have too often learned that on the job. For example, people in Germany address each other much more formally, while in Latin America personal relationships are the key to success, and I still blush hot red remembering how jokes that brought the house down in English, met stony silence in translation; now I am much more tentative in my humor until I have found the mood of an international audience. Today, as CEO of Fairtrade International, I am much more self-consciously considering through which strategies and in which ways I can effectively lead people working for Fairtrade across the world. For sure, what worked for me when I led the Fairtrade movement in the UK, needs very different ways of working at a global level.

As Caroline and Sapna underline, leading teams overseas is not about changing your personality, but about adapting your natural style — that has worked so well for you at home — to the new culture where you now live and work. So, they recommend, you should defend your core values and be flexible about nearly everything else.

But I have scored better against their call for women to grasp opportunities, to search out 'conscious imbalance'. When we had our second child, my partner got a job in Germany with Deutsche Welle and I was happy to leave my job in London and move. Within a few months, I had landed the job with Fairtrade International which is based in Germany. Building the Fairtrade movement in the UK and globally became the defining feature of my career.

Sapna and Caroline are enthusiasts for women working overseas. They argue that there has never been a better time for women to get such overseas opportunities as companies increasingly operate at a global level and are looking for global leaders who have experience managing teams across the world. They say, find a job you love and if the chance comes to move overseas, why not embrace it? They encourage women, not to try to have everything in perfect equilibrium, but rather to look for those 'best ever' times of full engagement and passion. They stress the importance of thinking carefully about whether a move overseas is the one for you, and then planning every step of the way. If you take the plunge, the book outlines some of the pitfalls to avoid and the best steps to success—at work and at home, moving out and coming back home, including, of course, making sure that your family is happy too.

Global leadership is different from national leadership. And to date, all the studies on global leadership have been done with the male majority. So, it is indeed time for such new thinking about women becoming global leaders, so they can confidently shatter all those glass borders to take up those great job opportunities overseas.

Harriet Lamb
CEO Fairtrade International

Preface

When thinking of leaders, we often recall famous political or business leaders. Big names may spring to mind such as Nelson Mandela, Golda Meir, Steve Jobs, Oprah Winfrey, or Richard Branson. These leaders can be described as strong and dedicated. They were dedicated to their cause, whether it be integrating people or influencing the thinking and mindset of a society. The words creative and inspiring are an understatement when describing some of these leaders, considering that their innovations are profound - putting technology in everybody's hands or working to enable any person to venture beyond our planet. Memorable leaders have found themselves at the right place, at the right time in history. For example, if Oprah Winfrey had lived fifty years prior in the US, could she have propelled her career in the same way and have had the same influence? These leaders were visionaries. They saw possibilities for a different future that most people did not see.

Popular misconceptions would lead us to believe that good leaders are famous leaders. To the contrary, good leaders can be found everywhere. They may differ in style, approach, and personality, but good leaders all focus on meeting the needs of the people or the organization they are leading. The "new leadership profile" further emphasizes the importance of possessing an international perspective in order to lead effectively. We are at the right place and the right time in history for women to pursue international opportunities and prepare to become tomorrow's global leaders.

This book examines the topic of female leadership in the international environment during a critical period of intensified globalization, a threatening shortage of talented global leaders and the rise of women's influence in the world. Most of the research conducted on topics such as expatriate assignments, global leadership competencies, and managing international transitions has focused on the traditional male expatriate. Our goal is not to produce yet another volume of research on these particular topics. Rather, we focus on an in-depth examination of shared behaviors that contributed to the success of senior-level expatriate women. As a woman considering an international job, you will have an opportunity to determine if you, too, possess the characteristics needed to succeed in an international setting. Organizations will have an opportunity to determine if they have incorporated assessment and development of these characteristics, in order to build their female, international talent pool.

Worldly Women combines the expertise of the authors, along with practical tips and tools, and humorous, courageous stories of female, expatriate experts from around the world to prepare women for their global leadership journey.

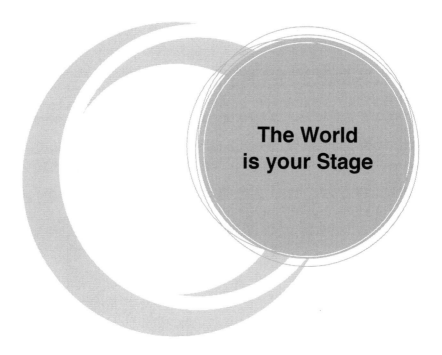

Section I

'Worldly Women' your Time is Now

"Women hold up half the sky"
~ Mao Tse Tung

"My mother would say, 'With your skills, with your languages, you can become the personal assistant of a CEO', but she couldn't quite imagine that I would become the CEO myself."
~ WiSER Flavia

Have you wondered how to:

- Explore the world?
- Learn another language?
- Travel and visit people you know around the world?
- Have 1000 LinkedIn connections that you actually know?
- Propel your career?
- Position your experience more individually?
- Boost your financial prospects?
- Be your best?
- Lead the world of tomorrow?

It is all possible, and the answers lie within.

History is filled with stories of bold explorers, who challenged existing notions and endured hardship to discover new lands and new treasures. Bartolomeu Dias circumnavigated the southern point of Africa, thus opening up lucrative trading routes from Europe to Asia. When most people thought the world was flat, Christopher Columbus wanted to sail the world in search of India, but instead he found America. Exploring the world is challenging and requires a large dose of courage and vision and a dash of madness. You may find what you are looking for, but you are bound to find the unimaginable.

Over time, societies have become more politically, economically, and socially interdependent. Advanced technologies have innovated transportation and communication, making exploring the world available to virtually anyone willing to take the bold step. Technology has made our world much smaller than it used to be. We can buy products overseas, which are delivered to our doorsteps within a couple of days. We can apply for jobs at the other end of the world. We can communicate with a growing number of "friends" on different social media platforms. The world is literally at our feet.

Globalization creates new markets and increases opportunities for economic growth, innovation and cooperation. An imperative for the future is global connectedness. "Collaboration will be the watchword as companies and governments share costs and knowledge to remove barriers to mobility and manage regulation" (PriceWaterhouseCoopers 2010). Global collaboration will create a fluid environment where employees move freely between countries.

Organizations are expanding their businesses across borders and the number of multi-national corporations is rising. The economic power of these corporations is enormous and still growing. In 2009, it was reported that, of the world's 150 largest economies, 59 percent are corporations (Keys and Malnight 2010). Beyond corporations, global NGOs (non-governmental organizations) wield substantial influence in global affairs and often have budgets matching GDPs of small countries (Karajkov 2007). As a consequence, our workforce is becoming more global, and this trend, if anything, has gained momentum in recent years.

The world needs expats

Initially, the impacts of globalization were limited to primarily working in international teams from your home country. As globalization intensifies, the number of jobs which require relocation to another country has steadily risen, and it will continue to rise as a result of global workforce trends.

There is a startling workforce skills gap on the horizon. "To sustain projected growth, the USA alone needs twenty-five million more workers by 2030, Europe will need twenty-four million more workers", and by 2020, China will need to double its talent base to sustain projected growth (World Economic Forum 2011, 6). There are three widely held reasons for the expected skills gap at a global level.

1. First, there is an aging workforce combined with lower birthrates in developed countries. By 2050, most G7 and BRIC countries will have more than doubled their populations aged over sixty-five. The world requires 2.1 children per woman to replace the dying population. Although the birthrate has fallen below this figure before, this happened only at times of war and famine. Never before in history has the birthrate dropped below the current 1.3 in southern and Eastern Europe. At this rate, experts in population demographics predict that a country's population would be cut in half in 45 years, literally changing the face of that nation (Shorto 2008).

2. Second, all eyes are looking toward the newly emerging high growth economies, which are employing growing numbers of workers. Frequently looked at groupings include the BRIC countries (Brazil, Russia, India, China) which are high risk/high growth economies. Recent listings of countries with major growth rate, based on GDP real growth, include Mongolia, Turkmenistan, Ghana, Qatar, Panama, Zimbabwe, China and Iraq (CIA 2011). "New 'capital' cities will emerge as business hubs according to size of local working age populations and new revenue streams" (PriceWaterhouseCoopers 2010).

3. Third, domestic labor forces increasingly do not have the skills required for the jobs available. Similar to the industrial revolution of the past; developed countries have undergone a technology revolution where they can produce more food and higher living standards with less manpower. This renders old skills unneeded and requires a more educated workforce to continue to be productive.

   Uneven access to education throughout the world is leaving potential workforce candidates unprepared. For example, only 25 percent of Indian professionals and 20 percent of Russian professionals are currently considered employable by multinational firms. Educating large, capable populations who would otherwise be engaged in unskilled labor could result in a situation where talent meets needs. There is a potential shortage of medium skilled workers in developing economies, of high skill workers among advanced economies and China, and surplus of 90 to 95 million low skilled workers around the world (McKinsey 2012).

The war for talent will be "fast and furious", as many organizations across the world struggle to fill positions, let alone key positions.

One solution to the skills gap is labor migration. Collectively, international migrants could make up the world's fifth-largest nation (Migration Policy Institute 2009, 12). Common sense would tell us to match the migrants to the nations who have a need for millions of workers. Unfortunately, the solution is not so simple. Currently, much migration is unintentional and does not focus on matching skilled and suitable workforce candidates to jobs. Conversely, expatriation is intentional migration, matching skilled workers to jobs.

There are several well renowned groups that assess and report trends in global labor migration. According to a new report by the Economist Intelligence Unit, the movement of expatriates around the globe is set to remain strong, despite the impact of the global recession. Brookfield Global Relocation Services (Brookfield GRS) publishes an annual report, which is one of the industry's most reliable sources of global relocation data and trends. Their 2012 study showed that 64 percent of responding companies indicated that their number of expatriates had increased in 2011 (an increase of 43 percent compared to 2010) and 63 percent expected that number to further grow in 2012 (2012, 9). "While the number of employees on international assignments has remained relatively stable over recent years, the percentage of global nomads (employees who move from country to country on multiple assignments) has increased" (Mercer 2012). The report further revealed that most companies are neglecting Western markets in order to send expatriates to developing markets such as India, Africa, and China.

For the purposes of this book, the term expatriate is defined broadly as "someone who has left her home country to live and work in another country for an extended period of time" (Vance, McNulty and Chauderlot 2011). We further defined an "extended period of time" as an international position requiring relocation for twelve months or longer outside of one's home country. The international or expatriate assignment (interchangeable terms) is either self-initiated or offered by the employer. The expatriate may be "responsible for business in a single nation, a region or the world" (Catalyst 2000, 4). We have intentionally refrained from further defining the term expatriate and have elected not to include points such as benefits packages, retirement packages, guaranteed or non-guaranteed employment upon return, and so forth. This decision was based on our determination that these types of variables do not have an impact on shared behaviors for success on an international assignment.

Organizations need expats

With the globalization of our economies, the number of international roles that require relocation is steadily rising. As a result, the number of employees on international assignments has continued to increase over the recent years. When we examine the upward trajectory of international assignments over the past 30 years, the increase is striking. From 1970 to 1990, international assignments were mostly initiated by global organizations based in western developed nations. These were the original and traditional expatriates, leaving their home nation for up to five years to bring domestic knowledge and processes to foreign locations and they were paid handsomely to do so. From 1990 to 2010, new markets opened up around the world, offering new revenue streams for predominantly western companies. Many of these emerging markets were the same nations that offered low cost labor, leading to the rise of offshoring. In addition to the traditional expatriate, there was a parallel growth of international (virtual) work teams, requiring travel, short-term rotations and technology to support communication and cooperation.

Looking at expatriation today and tomorrow, expressions like "overseas assignments" are antiquated. The connectedness of the world is becoming seamless. In this world, Levi's jeans are manufactured in China, popularly worn in India among teenagers who are drinking Coca Cola produced in the US, where Americans are eating fast food like KFC, and Pizzahut which are owned by Yum!, a Chinese company. In Europe, traditional local coffee houses are facing competition from Starbucks who gets his coffee from South-American coffee farmers, who are coming together to gain a voice and marketing ability through FairTrade which is based in Germany. The mobility of products, services and people is fluid. In this connected world, expatriates are the new "normal" workforce. Numbers clearly illustrate this trend. The number of locations where organizations send their expatriates, has increased from an average of 13 countries in 1998, to 22 locations in 2009 and projected to reach 33 by 2020 (PriceWaterhouseCoopers 2010).

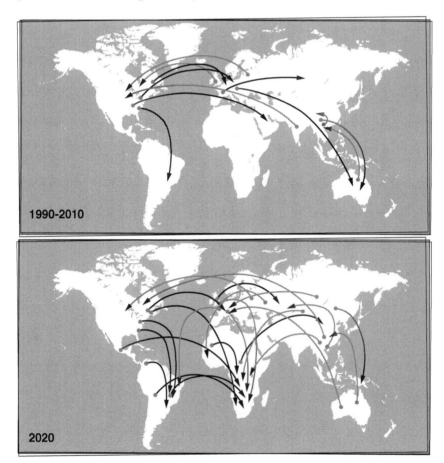

Increasing expatriate movement (based on PriceWaterhouseCoopers 2010)

As per Mercer (2008), the growth of the number of expatriates, regardless of the recession, has been driven by companies' desire to be globally competitive. Remaining competitive in an international arena requires organizations to have leaders and staff members who possess a "global mindset", meaning, they can get results in different cultural situations and adapt to local markets. Therefore, employers are looking for people who want to advance their careers through international experience, since it is through the crucible of foreign assignments that employees stretch themselves and acquire valuable skills they wouldn't have gained otherwise. However, companies cannot confidently fill international assignments because they lack a bench of talented global leaders who can fill these roles. Significantly, women are woefully underrepresented on this bench. As history shows, organizations often make damagingly deep cuts in regards to talent management decisions during times of recession. This leaves them less equipped to take advantage of the opportunities that come with the economic recovery. "The future is in the global market, and companies need to retain people who are going to help them make an impact in that global market. A lot of the people who are being repatriated have the unique advantage of having that global experience and perspective which will be invaluable on the upturn" (Woodward 2009).

In order to gain and sustain competitive advantage, international mobility is key for companies and organizations that operate in the global economy. As a result, international assignments become an important aspect of global leadership development programs. Where working in various geographies used to be a "nice to have", it is becoming a "must have" on the career ladder of international firms (Mercer 2012). Four in five executives believe a stint overseas can improve a worker's chances of career progression (Hyslop 2012). This is the crux of the new leadership profile. Organizations with a strong "talent mindset" understand the value of leveraging employees with a "global mindset" and therefore, expatriate talent as a development tool, rather than a costly staffing tool. ROI is often a topic of discussion when expatriate assignments are assessed, because international assignments are approximately three to five times more expensive than an assignee's domestic salary. However, many organizations have neither accurate information, nor a valid mechanism in place for measuring the ROI of expatriates. This makes it difficult to quantify the benefits and therefore easy to focus solely on costs involved. "For companies that want to grow on a global scale and gain experience in the international business arena, expatriate assignments are a necessary investment in a long-term strategic goal" (Krell 2005).

For a global leadership development program to be successful, the organization must not only send employees for longer periods of time on expatriate assignments, but also prepare them for assignments in advance, and retain this talent by repatriating or moving these employees again through a well-managed method. It is the flow of the acquired skills back into the organization that makes such employees especially valuable. Why shouldn't one of those employees be you?

Women are the answer

All women pursuing an international career, your time is now. Women are playing an increasingly important role in the world. We see more women at the top, in political roles, in executive roles, and in positions of influence. There are more women in the "top 100" lists of Forbes most wealthy, powerful, influential people, more women who defy traditional role models, and more options and choices for women to manage professional lives than ever before. The changing role of women can be discerned in business sectors throughout the world.

The tipping point for women to fill their share of expatriate leadership positions is here. The idea of a tipping point was popularized by author Malcolm Gladwell (2002), who used it as a new lens through which to view trends and the ebb and flow of social waves. How did Harry Potter become a worldwide phenomenon overnight? How did Twitter become a powerful platform exerting great influence on consumer's deciding on products, services, and political and social opinions? "The tipping point is the moment of critical mass, the threshold, the boiling point" (Gladwell 2002, 12). For example, during the 1990s, the use of cell phones grew. First, only a few people had them, then more and more, as cell phones got smaller and cheaper, and the service improved. The tipping point was reached in 1998. Experts state that the tipping point is reached when something gains the critical mass of 17 percent. In other words, once 17 percent of the population used cell phones, the remaining majority wanted to buy one as well and "suddenly" everyone had a cell phone. Similarly, we are witnessing the tipping point for women to fully participate in global leadership ranks. Currently 17-20 percent of all expatriate roles are held by women (Brookfield 2012, 10). So, at this point, women in expatriate roles are at the "tip", or the moment of what appears to be sudden change.

Women expatriates are an optimal solution for organizations who want to develop a bench of competent global leaders to remain competitive. The need is there, forces are at play to move women into executive roles, women are available, educated, and possess many global competencies in abundance. Woman expatriates are an ideal answer for several reasons:

- Companies with women on the executive committee achieved a return on equity of 41 percent higher and an EBIT that was 56 percent higher than that of companies with no women on their executive committees (McKinsey 2010, 7).
- Having at least one female director on the board appears to reduce a company's likelihood of becoming bankrupt by 20 percent, and having two or three female directors lowers the likelihood of bankruptcy even further (Credit Suisse 2012,19).
- More than 70 percent of purchasing decisions are made by women. Not only do they decide on the typical female items such as clothes, household appliances and furniture, they are also very influential in many purchases typically considered to be male items, such as cars and PCs (McKinsey 2007, 10).
- Companies with mixed executive committees score better on organizational effectiveness and innovation (McKinsey 2010, 7).
- Boards with three or more women perform much better in terms of governance than companies with all-male boards (Credit Suisse 2012, 18).
- Women represent 55 percent of college graduates worldwide. Simple math demonstrates that there are potentially more women with higher education degrees and, presumably, workforce preparation than men to fill workplace roles – and this includes expatriate positions (Moore 2010).

Companies with a high share of women in top executive positions (mixed leadership) are economically more successful and achieve high profits, which are above average (McKinsey 2010). There are several contributing reasons for this. Leadership performance is improved because the "majority group (men) improves its own performance in response to minority (female) involvement. Simply put, "nobody wants to look bad in front of a stranger" (Credit Suisse 2012,17). Also, female leaders are consistently more risk-averse, leading to reduced investment volatility and improved portfolio performance. Another contributing factor to improved organizational results is that leadership performance is improved with gender diverse teams, because men and women have different leadership strengths that complement each other. Groups like NASA have found that even space missions go better when the crew consists of both males and females (Credit Suisse 2012).

A final contributing factor to improved success is when organizations reflect their consumer base in order to better understand their customer needs and wants. At a time when women are increasingly viewed as an underutilized resource for the job market, they are also exercising greater influence as consumers. Julie Anne, an interviewee, noted that diversity was a hot topic of conversation at her organization. "Our consumers are largely women," she said. "They are the ones making the purchases for the family, etc., and it's important for our workplace to represent and reflect our consumers." She indicated that the most effective way to gauge the needs of consumers is to have employees who understand your consumers. This may seem obvious, however, Julie Anne recalled that when this conversation took place, only 20 to 30 percent of corporate managers were women. "Well, they should be 50 [percent], shouldn't they?" she insisted. Having management reflect the consumer decision-maker, will give organizations a competitive advantage.

How can the stresses of the workforce shortage be lightened? How can projected economic growth and competetive advantage be sustained? We recommend that organizations "fish where there are fish" — that is, harness educated, capable, and available talent (namely women) and move them, if necessary, to the areas where jobs exist. As this book is being written, more organizations are taking steps to diversify their staff in order to draw the broadest cross-section of qualified employees. Notably, 89 percent of women who voluntarily leave their jobs, for various reasons, want to return to work. However, only 40 percent have secured full-time positions. Significantly, forecasts predict an 80 percent employment rate of all employable women by 2025, in comparison to 71.8 percent in 2009 (World Economic Forum 2011, 6).

Women are an untapped solution. Women comprise over 40 percent of the employable global workforce, yet at the senior management level, women occupy fewer than 20 percent of roles globally. At the executive management level the percentage of women has been frozen at around 16 percent for several years now. Only about 4.2 percent of Fortune 500 or Fortune 1000 companies have women CEOs or presidents (Catalyst 2013).

Gearing up for expatriate women

Given that companies have proven to be slow in moving women into executive roles, an increasing number of countries have elected to introduce binding quotas. Other countries have introduced voluntary quotas, which have proven to be a good incentive as well. Whether or not you agree with quotas, the result of their imposition has been a rapid increase in the number of senior-level positions filled by women. In Norway, for instance, quotas to increase the share of women in leadership positions, were instituted and companies saw a sharp rise in the percentage of women serving on their boards. While women there constituted 7 percent of company boards in 2003, this percentage had risen to 40 percent by January 2008 (Moore 2010). Accessing the highly educated and capable female workforce could create a situation in which talent once again meets needs.

ho is considering an expatriate assignment, your time professional career through international experience d. It may be that you are considering an international aps you have already made the fateful decision to drop your name in the proverbial "international hat." Or, it could be that you've recently been approached about the possibility of taking an international assignment. Reading this book will help you to understand if expatriating is the right career move for you, as it explains the cultural aspects of expatriating, how expatriate women differ from expatriate men, and how expatriate demands differ from domestic demands. It will also assist you in your own efforts to become a successful female expatriate leader.

Circle of women

Before packing your bags and beginning your adventure, we ask you to pause, close your eyes and imagine a bonfire, under the stars, on a warm summer evening. In a circle around the fire sit sixty-two Women in Senior-level Expatriate Roles (WiSER), as well as Sapna and Caroline, the authors. In this circle, they are practicing the time honored tradition of elders (or in this case experts) sharing history, knowledge, and information through their stories and experiences. In *Worldly Women*, you will be among a prestigious group who will pass on their wisdom through the old practice of oral tradition. We invite you to take your place in the circle around the fire. To quote Dante, "From the little spark may burst a mighty flame."

Let us introduce you to the women surrounding you in the circle. The WiSER we interviewed consisted of sixty-two subject matter experts that served as the foundation of all the primary research conducted for the purpose of this book. The WiSER fell into the categories of C-level, executive, or emerging executive. We validated their seniority based on various criteria, including (but not limited to) title, span of control (number of staff and geographical responsibility), salary, and budget managed. They ranged in age from thirty to sixty. The WiSER were single, married, or divorced; with and without children; and worked in either the profit or non-profit organizational sectors—and in a wide variety of functions. Each WiSER had been either engaged in an international assignment in the past or was, at the time of the interview, on an international assignment. The interviewees represented six out of seven continents, with the sole exception of Antarctica. They did not simply manage international teams from their home country, or merely travel for assignments. They have all lived abroad for at least one year and, in many cases, much longer. They constitute the mobile global workforce of today (see appendix B for a more detailed profile of the WiSER).

Although the majority of the WiSER we interviewed attained their roles through the organization, many of them (26 percent) self-initiated their move (see appendix E for more information on self-initiated versus organization-induced expatriation). Interestingly, 34 percent of the WiSER had at least one parent who was an immigrant. This aspect of their family background evidently helped fuel their global mindedness as well as their desire to see the world.

With refreshing candor, they shared information about their formative years, their professional and personal milestones, challenges they were forced to overcome, and the steps they took to manage their career. In addition, they shared stories about their first international move, and described the professional adaptations they made in order to be successful in international work environments. Significantly, the women we interviewed were not merely survey participants. On the contrary, we spoke to them at great length, and they were uniformly enthusiastic about sharing their experiences, both positive and negative. Many of them indicated that these conversations provided an opportunity for them to reflect on their experiences. To the best of our knowledge, these interviews (along with subsequent analysis) constitute the most comprehensive research on women in senior-level expatriate roles to date.

The WiSER we had the privilege of interviewing are a remarkable group of women. There were a total of 150 expatriate assignments held among the 62 WiSER. We would like to share just a few of their career highlights:

- Gabriele was selected as one of the "Top 25 Most Influential Female Engineers in Germany" in 2012.
- Sandra was the most senior woman in Bayer and the first female expatriate in the C-Suite in this organization.
- Anne was the first woman to lead her organization's office in Egypt, in all of the fifty years that CARE had been there.
- Jacqueline set up the first Africa regional recruitment office for World Vision Africa.

- Abby did the IPO for Amazon.com and got a personal call from the CEO of WorldCom to handle its billion-dollar merger with LDDS, the predecessor to MCI.
- Annette was an expatriate in the Arctic Circle.
- Esther is the Global Chair of the Board of Fair Trade International.

We, as the co-authors of this book, have a personal understanding of expatriate life, given that we have lived abroad, worked abroad, and shared the excitement of international life with these women. We can identify with the challenges involved in starting from scratch, building a new network, and relocating one's family. Considering that we share the WiSER's passion for new experiences, their stories resonated with us. In addition, we are enthusiastic about the possibility of helping others to be a successful expatriate leader, and also look forward to assisting those who are making crucial decisions about their path forward.

Get to know author Sapna Welsh

"I grew up as a first-generation Indian American. From my earliest years, my family has meant the world to me; and during my childhood, I enjoyed visiting India every other year. Given that I was separated from my extended family in India (including uncles, aunts, cousins, and grandparents), I wanted to give my own children an opportunity to be close to their grandparents. Curiously, my experience of having relatives who lived on another continent contributed to my decision to live and work in the United States. For years, I showed relatively little interest in international opportunities, and I even neglected to take advantage of study-abroad programs as a university student. Nevertheless, my early exposure to India, along with international vacations I took with my family, led me to develop a global mindset. These formative experiences were reflected in many of my subsequent decisions, including my choice of major when I entered the university. Of all the fields I had to choose from, I selected international business. In addition, I was always enamored with the idea of traveling and understanding other cultures, although I didn't act on that desire until relatively recently. Over the past three years, I've discovered that the beauty of an international assignment lies in the fact that it broadens your mind while also making your world smaller and more intimate. At this point, I would like to share a personal story. Years ago, my husband, Bob, and I were visiting some of my relatives in India, and we spent time at my uncle's house, which was located in a small village. One afternoon, all of the power went out, so my husband and I decided to go for a walk. This was my husband's first trip to India. I should mention that he is of Irish background, and he looked rather exotic with his blond hair and blue eyes. As we walked through the village, we came upon a series of small shops, each of which occupied a space that resembled a garage or carriage house. Most of the shop owners had pulled down their overhead doors at least halfway in order to keep cool until the power returned. Therefore, the village was unusually quiet. Suddenly, a gentleman popped his head out a shop door, and said, in English, though with a strong Indian accent: 'Hello Bob. Would you like a Pepsi?' We were stunned, but it was evident that the man had "recognized" my husband. We still laugh over the incident today. While this village seemed so foreign to us, we were nevertheless welcomed by a complete stranger who offered us a Pepsi."

Get to know author Caroline Kersten

"Although my mother worked when she was first married, she decided to become a full-time mom after I and my sisters arrived. However, she started to work again when my younger sister was eight years old. She earned her licensure to be a small business owner in the Netherlands, and eventually purchased a clothing boutique. She ran this business for twenty-three years and she taught us through her example that, no matter what happens to you in life, it is important to be able to stand on your own two feet. I perceived and admired that same spirit of independence in all of our interviewees. The WiSER have managed to do it all. They have families, and they have careers; and somehow, they find time to travel the world. I, too, like to travel the world, to see different places and to familiarize myself with a country and its culture. However, unlike a typical holiday visitor, who focuses on tourist spots and resides in hotels, I prefer to get beneath the surface of a culture and immerse myself in its depths. Over the years, I have studied and worked abroad, and I have always been drawn to international work. Luckily, I learn languages without too much effort and love being able to speak the language of the country in which I live and work. It is not only an important part of experiencing a new culture but it also makes studying and working abroad so much easier. Indeed, my language skills, along with my love of travel, made it relatively easy for me to quit my job and to leave the Netherlands when I 'followed' my husband to Germany—a move that also required me to give up my financial independence for a certain period of time. Overall, I welcomed our move as an exciting opportunity to broaden my horizons."

If you want to learn more about our professional lives, see appendix G. *Worldly Women* may be inspirational, but it is also filled with practical advice. We will often refer you to our website, LeverageHR.com, where you can find additional tools, links, and articles that can help you achieve success in an international role.

It's a Wrap!

The world is currently facing a global talent shortage, global mobility is on the rise and there is growing awareness that organizations with female leaders perform better. Indeed, governments around the world are encouraging—sometimes requiring—an increased percentage of women in senior level ranks. Therefore, if you're interested in finding a job abroad, you're timing couldn't be better! Not only governments, but employers themselves are coveting international experience. Regardless of how you get there, it's important to remember that an educated, mobile woman couldn't ask for a better time in history to pursue an international position.

We hope you consider joining the modern day female explorers on an exciting journey to an enriching professional and personal life.

Nothing Ventured, Nothing Gained

"It is better by noble boldness to run the risk of being subject to half the evils we anticipate than to remain in cowardly listlessness for fear of what might happen."
~ Herodotus

"When you are doing something, remember that a few years from then, you are always going to turn back and look, and at that point, never ever be in a situation where you say 'What if.'"
~ WiSER Anuradha

Many questions will undoubtedly cross your mind when considering an international assignment, questions such as: "What do I stand to gain, or lose, from this experience?" "Will an international assignment propel my career forward?" "Do I have the combination of qualities needed to succeed in an international role?" "What advice can you give me that will be useful to me while living abroad and working in different cultures?" We will answer these questions and more as the WiSER share how they leveraged and managed careers abroad.

The WiSER overwhelmingly indicated that they believe that expatriate opportunities help individuals grow, both personally and professionally. This may be due to the fact that they increased their network and developed competencies and skills in a way that could not be accomplished through domestic assignments and due to the fact that they felt it enriched their personal life as well. Whether you are single or married, with or without children, young or experienced professional, we believe that their stories will inspire you to consider international opportunities. Significantly, the majority of the WiSER we interviewed were married and/or had children. Those with children suggested their international assignment provided their family with a valuable experience that could not have been achieved any other way. Does this sound too good to be true? Although the WiSER shared with us some of the challenges they faced, they ultimately agreed that the benefits outweighed any negatives.

The Society for Human Resources Management (SHRM) conducted a similar survey and asked assignees, "How far was your international assignment helpful for your personal and professional growth?" (SHRM 2004) More than 90 percent of the respondents indicated their assignment had been very helpful for their professional growth, especially in terms of global awareness, cultural workplace savvy, leadership skills and career development. In addition, assignees indicated that leadership skills and managerial skills could be developed more efficiently during long-term expatriate assignments, as opposed to shorter assignments. As far as personal growth was concerned, more than 95 percent of respondents rated global assignments as very helpful, especially in increasing or creating cultural awareness, strengthening the ability to adapt and increasing flexibility. There is much to be gained from an expatriate assignment.

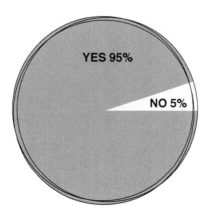

Was career enhanced by international assignment?

Professional rewards

The next generation of leaders will be required to possess a global mindset because they will be managing an increasingly diverse workforce. The characteristics required for global leadership are learned, and they can be developed rapidly in international roles. Yet, to reiterate, women fill only about 17-20 percent of expatriate roles. So we can't help but ask, "Where in the world are the women?"

During expatriate assignments, the WiSER acquired and/or enhanced skills, knowledge and competencies that were valued upon return, and their experience made them more valuable to their own organization, while also attracting the interest of other organizations. In short, it enhanced their careers. Let's take a look at the most frequently mentioned career enhancers.

1. Accelerated learning and development

An overseas assignment can offer an accelerated learning experience that you can't secure any other way. The current pervasive philosophy around learning and leadership development is the 70-20-10 model developed by Lombardo and Eichinger in 2000. The model demonstrates that 70 percent of learning is provided through the use of challenging assignments and on-the-job experience. Another 20 percent occurs through developing relationships, networks, and feedback. Leaving only 10 percent of learning attributed to the classroom or formal training methods (NWLink 2012). An expatriate assignment is an ideal opportunity to develop leaders because it offers many challenging work experiences, constant training on the job and an opportunity to build relationships and expand networks around the world. This is what the new leadership profile is all about.

The fact is, you will be absorbing a lot of information very quickly. "It's not about the promotion," WiSER Andrea said. "It's about being able to learn something new, to understand something different than what you did before." She indicated that gaining a broad range of experience was the true value of working abroad. WiSER Andrea added that, if she had remained in her native Brazil, she would have needed to work at many different companies to accumulate the variety of experiences she gained through one international assignment. "This [fact] that you deal with different people in their own environment...that's very rich," she said. "It's different than if you always stay in your own country." WiSER Hermie agreed. "It's a great learning opportunity, both personally and professionally," she said. "It's a quantum leap in learning. What you would learn over many years, you learn in a very short concentrated span of time." Meanwhile, WiSER Julie Anne revealed that she had unique experiences in Latin America she couldn't have gained through a domestic assignment. "In Latin America the organization is smaller, and it's a growing operation, and [that] is when there's a lot of what we call white space or opportunities that haven't been tapped yet," she explained. "So, even as a middle management person you're making decisions that would ordinarily... be made by people two levels higher than you. The learning is so much richer in that kind of environment where there's a lot of freedom and flexibility to make decisions and make an immediate impact on your business."

2. *Competitive advantage*

For many of the WiSER, the competitive advantage of an overseas assignment was obvious. Acquiring extra skills and competencies during an international assignment is not only beneficial within your current organization, it also positions you as an appealing candidate for other organizations. This is confirmed by a study where expatriates were asked what the career impact was of their international assignment: 40 percent said that they were promoted faster than their peers, 36 percent indicated that it was easier to obtain new positions in the organization and 16 percent indicated they changed employer more often, thanks to their improved competitive position (Brookfield 2012, 16). WiSER Anne noted that, within two years of her return to the USA, she was headhunted for the job of president and CEO of a global non-profit organization. She recalled: "They were looking for someone who actually had a lot of hands-on experience overseas – and I had almost twenty years of it – and someone who would help run a very large organization, and I had done that with my chief of staff job for a year and a half."

3. *Better network, more influence*

A large network does not make you a great leader, but it is well known that great leaders have a large network. You may have heard of the "six degrees of separation," which is based on Milgram's "small world experiment." He conducted the experiment in order to determine how many people were needed to deliver a package to a final recipient living on the other side of America. It took only four days, and two intermediaries, to get the package delivered — hence, the "small world." An international assignment can help you create a similar "small world" and give your network and your sphere of influence an enormous boost. "I think it helped to build my reputation, my credibility, my business networks, my sphere of influence in a way that I couldn't have achieved in the time," explained WiSER Elsa I. "In other words, it accelerated all of that. It's just been so invaluable, I think, for me as a professional in the business world."

4. *Leadership skills*

Working in an international assignment puts your leadership skills to the test in many ways. The popular theories around situational leadership, as developed by leadership gurus Paul Hersey and Ken Blanchard, state that there is no single best stye of leadership. Rather, successful leaders are able to adapt their style to the task, person or situation at hand. When operating in a foreign environment situational leadership takes on a whole new dimension. "I believe that an international assignment can accelerate my career because not everybody has had that experience," said WiSER Allyson. "It has taught me valuable skills especially on the communication front, how to motivate and lead different types of individuals and [it] helped my network tremendously."

5. *Open mindedness, self reflection*

Working and living abroad, you will encounter different ways of thinking, communicating, collaborating, leading, and accomplishing small to large goals, just to name a few. This forces you to reflect on your own ways of doing and being. "I believe an international assignment can accelerate or enrich your career because it makes you a better person," WiSER Stacy indicated. "I think it will do wonders to enhance your career. It will make you more open and more aware of your own assumptions and how at times they may be false."

Personal rewards

Beyond the career enhancement, is an international assignment worth it? The WiSER answered with a strong affirmative! Career enhancement is only one of the benefits of an international assignment. "Absolutely, international experience benefited my career," said WiSER Nina. "But the most benefit was for my personality. I became a much more self confident, fulfilled person." There is a long list of exciting and encouraging benefits associated with expatriating.

6. *A much richer life*

Spending anywhere from one to several years abroad provides impetus and opportunity to see parts of the world you may have not considered, visit new places, meet new people, experience new cultural traditions and in the process enrich your life. "I definitely took advantage of living far away," shared WiSER Anne. "I didn't actually spend a lot of my money or time coming back to the States, particularly early on. My husband and I, and even my kids, we traveled all over the place. [Me] and my kids, we've been to many countries around the world, and that's just a much richer life. My kids still like that. They are very much international citizens, and will take any opportunity. I think it's been a much richer life." WiSER Erica agreed. "I learned that I can live anywhere in the world," she revealed. "I learned that people across the world are very helpful and receptive, and caring, and that it depends on how you approach them, how they approach you back. I just think what has happened to me now is I realize that the world is a really small place but a really interesting place. I have learned a lot and I really have loved the journey."

7. *A different view on the world and appreciation for your own country*

An old proverb says, "Absence makes the heart grow fonder," and this is very true when you live abroad. When you are living in a different country — with different norms, values, and ways of doing things — you start appreciating many of the things you associate with your native country. What you once took for granted, you can now place in a broader context, because you have gained the experience of other cultures. This proves to be elevating, given that it not only influences the way you look at the world, but also the way you look at your own country and culture. "Go for it," said WiSER Carrie. "It definitely shaped our lives. We know people now. We know cultures now. We know a lot of things we never would have known before — and your view of the world, it does change and it also helps you truly appreciate what you have at home." She added that she has learned to recognize many of the assets of her native country. "Canada is a fantastic country," she said. "I always thought it was and I do even more so now." WiSER Pauline agreed: "The international, expatriate experience is a fantastic one, simply because it just completely changes your lens on the world."

8. Better cooperation and problem solving

Intimately experiencing new cultures will lead to a greater understanding and appreciation for different viewpoints and approaches resulting in improved methods of collaboration and issue resolution. "An international assignment is absolutely worthwhile," said WiSER Nina. "It will lead to better cooperation and problem solving that you cannot solve in just one nation. It will lead to a different kind of society because people who are internationally skilled... and have been exposed to an experience in another country, have this certain openness that I think is needed. We have this vision of the global citizen...maybe somebody who can, without forgetting about his own background, nationality, or ethnic identity...still be open. I would go as far as saying that this may lead to a more peaceful world."

9. Closer bonds as a family

Starting a new life—one that takes you far away from friends and extended family—forces you to fall back on each other much more than you would at home. After all, your family is all you have, especially in the beginning, and a new environment invites "discovery" trips. This can give family relations an enormous boost. "It gave me the chance to do things with my family," WiSER Abby revealed. "It's not only the fact that we made these cool trips to Angkor Wat, or Chiang Mai, or Sri Lanka, but because we've done so much travel together...we spend time together, learning stuff, and that's just been so rich—it's really made us so close." WiSER Stacy had a similar experience with her family. "I think the biggest surprises were the little ones, because they were [the] ones we didn't think about," she recalled. "The one thing it did for us, though, is we bonded as a family. The first six months that we were in India was a really big bonding time for us." She explained that she and her husband moved overseas with three children, and after being cautioned against driving in India, they hired a driver who took Sundays off. "So Sundays, we virtually did not go out of the house because we were in this service apartment that was down this dirt road and nothing was around it," she recalled. "So, we just stayed home on Sundays, and it was a really cool time for our family."

10. Enriching experience for children

If you have children, you will definitely want to know how an overseas assignment could affect them. How will they deal with leaving their home, their friends, their family, etc.? Although children are said to be resilient, moving abroad does have an enormous impact on them. They will lose, and miss, their entire social network—and an environment where they always felt safe. Moving to another country may also mean that they have to learn to express themselves in a language other than their mother tongue, which means at least a few months of communication challenges. You may elect to enroll your children in a local school, which brings its own benefits and challenges, including varying educational standards, non-multiculturalism, and different teaching methods. On the other hand, you may enroll them in an international school primarily consisting of expatriates, which also brings its own benefits and challenges, such as managing home, host and expatriate culture. There are volumes written on third culture kids (TCKs).

Regardless of your choice, the good news is that many WiSER claimed that giving their children international experiences developed them. WiSER Diane noted that her children gained much from living overseas. "I encourage women who are often reluctant because they think, 'Well, my kids are in school and they need to be here, in their own country, with their grandmother around the corner,'" she said. "I often share with women that I wish I had taken an international role when my son was young, because kids could go to international schools—just see the world around it. Academically they are often stronger because they go to baccalaureate stream." She added, "So...don't hold your decision back because of what you think you are depriving your children of, balance it by looking at what you will be giving them."

Uprooting children is not easy, of course, but at the same time, the whole family can experience growth and opportunity. Notably, 45 percent of the WiSER first went abroad when they were children or teenagers. If we extrapolate this statistic, we could go so far as to suggest that providing young people with international exposure increases their proclivity to explore further. Given that we live in an increasingly global environment, this is a true gift for your children. "I'm an only child and both of my parents were—or are—university graduates," said WiSER Sezin. "That was pretty uncommon in Turkey at the time that I was growing up, and still. In that sense, I've always lived in an environment where I was told that I have to go to the university, and it was not an option, so I think that's really transformed me." She added that her family's decision to immigrate to Canada had an even bigger impact on her life. "When I was in Canada, it really made a mark in my life, because that's when I learned English," she said. "It's not just that, it's the exposure to a foreign culture and different life. It really formed the rest of my life."

11. Closer relation with relatives

You would think that distance from friends and family would weaken, even destroy, relationships. This isn't necessarily the case, as WiSER Andrea discovered. "The positive thing is that some of the relationships actually grew stronger, with my parents, with my sisters, because we don't have daily issues," she said. "So, whenever we are together, it's actually much more fun than if I am seeing them every day and having to deal with every day issues." Moreover, with the abundance of possibilities for communicating at great distance—email, Skype, social networks, etc.—it has become relatively easy to maintain and nurture contacts at home.

12. Personal contentment

Bearing in mind that 77 percent of the WiSER had some desire to live abroad and actively worked on realizing this dream, it is no surprise that they agreed an international assignment can bring great personal contentment. "Personally, it gave me the opportunity to meet some needs and motivations that I had—that have really made me feel…much more content," said WiSER Diane. "And as a person I feel more satisfied with my life. I feel that it was the place where I was meant to be, and honestly, I find life more interesting and more satisfying."

Potential risks

Moving abroad means giving up, or missing out, on things that are going on at home. As Andre Gide, a Nobel prize winner, wisely said: "(Wo)Man cannot discover new oceans unless (s)he has the courage to lose sight of the shore." You will most definitely "lose sight of the shore," especially if you have to live overseas for an extended period of time. No description of an international assignment would be complete without discussing some of the drawbacks. What follows are some of the prevalent drawbacks that the WiSER shared in the course of our conversations.

1. *Losing a sense of home*

When you live abroad for many years, the concept of "home" becomes more difficult to define. Where is your home? Is it Egypt, where you lived for five years—or France, where you spent the last four years? Perhaps your real home is Singapore, a place that holds many fond memories. The longer you are gone, the more difficult it will be to determine exactly where you belong. Even if you have lived in your home country for most of your life, you are likely to feel less "at home" there after an extended period abroad. This is even truer for children, who move at a much younger age and, therefore, spend a relatively large part of their lives abroad.

After living abroad for many years, WiSER Martha realized that her children had a limited relationship with their home country as well as their extended family. "Suddenly, the kids were getting older—they are fifteen and twelve now—and I woke up one day and realized that they really didn't have any ties to their relatives or to the USA," she noted. "And I thought, I really want them to feel like the States is also their home. They are very much at home in South Africa now after having been here for 7.5 years, because we moved from Mozambique to South Africa." She added that her experience of living abroad has led her to recognize the importance of having "roots." Meanwhile, WiSER Argentina recommends cultivating strong friendships in your host country, while also maintaining ties with friends and family at home. "At some point you will retire or return. You need friends to go to or a place to call home."

2. *Adapted family planning*

Like it or not, as a female expatriate the decision to have children is not as easy as it would be at home, as Andrea explained. "You have to make some choices," she said. "In the beginning, we asked ourselves, 'Should we have another kid?' But, then again, living in Europe with all that was happening, we decided not to, because it would be too difficult." She added: "There are some sacrifices that you make. However, if it was too big a sacrifice, I would have moved back to Brazil and had the second child." For the young expatriate, building a serious relationship and having children may have to wait. "Taking an international assignment, if you're young like I am, you're going to be a few years delayed in some of life's... milestones, potentially," WiSER Meredith told us. "I have a lot of friends that are now having their first children and I am going to be a couple of years from now having my first child. So I think that there is... a little bit of a pause that you might have to take depending on whatever situation that you're in. But if you're okay with that, then that's fine."

Although family planning may be challenging, having children is hardly a disqualifier to become a successful WiSER, as our research shows. Indeed, 63 percent of our sixty-two WiSER had children. So, you don't have to abandon your desire to start and raise a family while maintaining a successful international career. This perceived hold-up by some women considering these positions may be largely unfounded based on the evidence.

3. *Relationships can suffer*

Among the WiSER, 82 percent were either married or had a serious partner. Only 12 percent of the WiSER were divorced, which is lower than many national divorce rate statistics. Even so, having an executive position, domestic or international, can negatively impact relationships, as some women discover. In a study, twenty two out of fifty female expatriate managers indicated that "additional strains [were] placed on personal relationships where the male partner became an accompanying spouse." Likewise, they indicated that "their quality of life suffered where the couple decided to have a commuter marriage" (Linehan and Scullion 2001, 395).

WiSER Fiona experienced herself that the (personal) life of an executive woman is challenging: "I was in a meeting with probably twelve senior women out of some 400 scientists," she recalled. "There were twelve of us and only two of that twelve were in a functioning relationship and that's the toll that it takes on women."

4. *Dual career issues*

When you accept a job abroad, your partner will probably have to change jobs too, or he may need to put his career on hold. In some cases, it is difficult to secure a work permit in a host country, but family reasons can also come into play. Managing dual careers is one of the biggest inhibitors for employees considering international assignments, and in many cases, women are reluctant to express their interest in being considered as expatriate candidates because of this issue. Considering the criticality of managing dual careers and the impact of expatriating on a dual career household, it is very important to discuss the consequences with your partner when you are the "leading lady," and he is compelled to make career modifications for you. "Kids are very mobile," said WiSER Flavia. "That's not a big problem in moving them around, but husbands or partners are difficult because a job is so much—almost the total sense of self for a man." WiSER Flavia advised that women seeking international assignments should take steps to ensure that their relationships will not be adversely affected. "They have to be aware that, if they really want the career, it may be difficult…to have a stable partnership," she said.

It is dawning on many international organizations that facilitating dual-career options will increase their international talent pool and contribute to the willingness of their employees to consider career options requiring international mobility. Currently, however, most organizations do not have a dual-career policy. Therefore, dual career couples and families who relocate for an overseas assignment often experience tensions. Sudden changes in professional life such as the transition to stop working and become a full-time husband, or stay-at-home father are difficult at best. This is further compounded because trailing-spouse environments are still dominated by women.

After the initial settling in period, your partner may wish to find work in the host country, if that is allowed. This can be difficult, but it is not necessarily impossible. In our survey, 58 percent of the partners worked in the host country, despite the fact that most organizations do not facilitate dual careers. Therefore, the partner had to rely on his own capabilities, and perhaps his spouse's network, to find work. In cases where the partners worked as well, they usually held a job with greater flexibility, and they were often self-employed, which seemed to be the easiest way to accommodate family life.

It's a wrap!

New beginnings always present new opportunities accompanied with new challenges. As we began, "nothing ventured, nothing gained". Despite the difficulties and setbacks the WiSER faced, they were determined to complete their assignments and fulfill their obligations. Significantly, in a business world that remains male-dominated, it is important for women to "stick it out," even when things don't go exactly as expected. From the outset, you should know that you are signing up for something very different from your previous experiences. If you keep the benefits of an international experience in mind — while preparing yourself with tips and tools (such as those offered in this book), while eliciting the assistance of global mobility coaches — you are unlikely to regret your decision.

It is important to remember that most of the WiSER who shared their experiences with us admitted that some of their assignments presented daunting challenges. In retrospect, however, they indicated that often the most difficult of assignments turned out to be some of the best experiences of their lives as expatriates. "I remember…it was difficult at the beginning," acknowledged WiSER Flavia. "One day, I was driving home — or being driven home — and I was saying, 'Okay, I have been here six months; this is a three-year duty station, so six months is a sixth of the duration I should be here." At that point, however, she stopped herself. "I said, 'Wait a minute,'" she recalled. "'If that's the way you think, you are not going to make it. So, stop griping, roll up your sleeves, and make the best you can do out of it." Equipped with a new determination, she soon found her assignment "fascinating" and succeeded in accomplishing her goals. WiSER Julie Anne had a similar experience when she arrived for an assignment in Peru. "When you get to Lima, Peru, it's kind of [a] coastal desert," she explained. "There's not one green thing anywhere. It's like the opposite of Holland, where I had been before, and I was like: 'Oh, my God! What have I gotten myself into?'" While she initially found Lima to be an extremely unattractive city, she came to appreciate the people and the culture. This realization did not come immediately, however. "My mom came with me to help me look for a house," she recalled. "And I remember sitting there crying, and saying, 'Oh, my God! I've been sent to the worst place on earth. What am I going to do?'" She did not feel that she was in a position to turn down the assignment, because she believed her company would never give her another opportunity. Julie Anne's mother responded with encouragement, indicating she would eventually enjoy living in Peru. "It turned out to be…the best experience I've had," she said.

An international assignment is bound to include complexities, but as we said, "'you cannot discover new oceans unless you have the courage to lose sight of the shore." That said, the benefits outweigh the drawbacks by twelve to four. The WiSER we interviewed indicated that the experience was worth every hardship, and they described their overseas experience as a period that deeply enriched their lives. "Yes, I would do it again," said WiSER Allyson, with a touch of humor. "It's like childbirth. You put the bad out of your mind, and you only remember all the good of it." WiSER Tuulia agreed. "In retrospect, the challenges and difficulties were a nuisance," she said. "It wasn't the end of the world…. I think people have more regrets about the things they don't do than the ones they do."

The Culture Club

"I don't want my house to be walled in on all sides and my windows to be stuffed. I want the cultures of all the lands to be blown about my house as freely as possible, but I refuse to be blown off my feet by any."
~ Mahatma Ghandi

"I didn't go in thinking I was going to change anybody; I just went in knowing that I was going to be changed."
~ WiSER Jacqueline

Have you ever driven in a country where the laws of the land forced you to drive on the opposite side of the road? Well, during my recent trip to the UK, I (Caroline) rented a Mini Cooper, put the top down, got ready to cruise, and found — much to my discomfort — that driving on the opposite side of the road wasn't as easy as I thought it would be. Before long, I even felt compelled to put the top back up again. Before going further, I should mention that I am a good driver, and I am quite confident in my driving ability and skill. Still, I was surprised to learn that so many aspects of driving were different on the other side of the "Chunnel" (the channel tunnel that connects Continental Europe to the UK). The car's steering wheel and gear shift were on the opposite side within the car. People drove on the "wrong" side of the road. Slow vehicles lingered in what I always considered the "fast" lane, and roundabouts kept me running in circles. Before long, I began to doubt that I could drive at all. This experience came to mind when we were trying to think of a good analogy for the differences between an international job and an international assignment. Perhaps you've worked across borders with a multi-national team or managed global work teams from your home country, both which still require you to deal with cultural differences. However, expatriating — or shall we say, "driving on the opposite side of the road" — has its unique challenges. As the Economist Intelligence Unit (2010, 3) noted, three in five expatriates were challenged by the fact that "their corporate headquarters did not understand the nature of their local business environment," while one in two identified "cultural or national conflicts between staff" as their greatest difficulty. "It's completely different," said WiSER Andrea. "You deal with different people in their own environment…[and] there are different ways to think, different ways to react and to prepare solutions to a problem." She added that her overseas assignment was a "rich" experience that could not have been replicated by simply working with a multicultural team.

Navigating cultural differences

Moving abroad brings with it many changes, including tactical changes. Tactical changes in your daily life could involve (but aren't necessarily limited to) language, manners, food, communication style, public transportation, grocery shopping, schools, and access to technology. As WiSER Julie observed: "One of the best parts about living somewhere is actually, doing some of the mundane things, you know, like grocery shopping and dry cleaning and things like that to really get a sense of how a place works and how a culture works and to meet new people, that's really… what it's all about." Some of the things that we take for granted in our native country, however, may be less accessible in the host country, and when we have to take extra time to manage the tasks of everyday life, it requires a great deal of energy. Sometimes, the experience can leave us drained. Since moving to Germany, for instance, I've found that every time I have a problem with my "handy" or internet, my best bet is to jump on my bike and visit the local T-Mobile store. This way, I have a greater chance of making myself understood, given that I can use hand gestures to supplement my rather limited German. A simple phone call would have sufficed at home. When you start adding up those instances in which additional energy is required to deal with daily tasks, you start to get a feel for the kinds of pressures involved in an expatriate assignment. Now, factor in the tactical changes in your work environment. Among other things, you will have to deal with the following: different consensus-building styles, different teamwork styles, different decision-making processes, different leadership styles, unionized or non-unionized work environments, and a different legal and compliance framework. All of these will be infused with elements of local culture, which are less visible but nevertheless influence the ways in which people behave and react.

What is culture, exactly, and why is it so important? L. Robert Kohls, former director of training for the US Information Agency and an expert in the field of internationalism, describes culture as "an integrated system of learned behavior patterns that are characteristic of the members of any given society." For Kohls, the term culture encompasses "the total way of life of particular groups of people," including everything that group "thinks, says, does and makes." This culture is "learned and transmitted from generation to generation" (Kohls 1996, 23). In many ways, culture is like an iceberg, given that some parts are visible to the naked eye, while others are hidden below the surface. That understanding the latter can be tricky, is something that WiSER Julie Anne experienced herself: "I got there and there were all sorts of unwritten cultural rules that were totally foreign to me." She admitted that it took her some time to discover those rules. "I had several examples of specific business times where it's like, 'hello, … how can I not figure that out?' But it took me probably a year or more into that assignment before I started to realize, 'oh, that's what's happening'. Then it became much more easy for me." The hidden, or "concealed," part of the culture is less accessible, but it is very important to understand. After all, it was the concealed portion of an iceberg that sunk the Titanic, and the concealed portion of a culture can "sink" you on your expatriate assignment.

One cultural complexity you are bound to encounter relates to gender relationships. This may be due to the fact that women in leadership positions are a rarity and therefore people do not know how to react to you. Other reasons may relate to education, religion and standard of living. A culture doesn't change overnight, and even in those countries where women occupy more and more senior-level roles, gender issues remain prevalent. So, you better come to terms with the fact that in some cultures, your gender may be an issue. "You can't get upset by…cultural issues," WiSER Anne stresses. "I remember, early on, if I shook the hand of a Muslim man, he would sometimes refuse to shake my hand, or he would cover his hand with a cloth to shake my hand, because women were impure. None of that ever bothered me. I never took it as insulting." She treated these responses as a reflection of the individual's world view, and while she didn't agree with his perspective, she didn't take these responses personally.

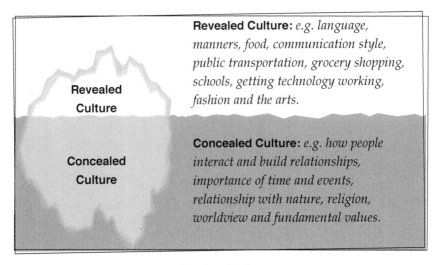

The cultural iceberg

Consider the following situations, which demonstrate how "revealed" and "concealed" culture can affect a given situation. The subtleties are interesting and they contribute to a complex tapestry that can be both challenging and enriching.

Situation #1 : Playboy magazine

Hans is from the Netherlands, and works with a major global employer. He recently attended a global meeting in New York City, and while there, he and Jim, a colleague from the USA, got to know one another and built a positive working relationship. During the rapport-building process, Hans and Jim engaged in a casual conversation, and Jim shared the fact that he considered Cindy Crawford to be extremely beautiful. Jim also told Hans that she was his favorite supermodel. A few months later, Cindy Crawford appeared in Playboy magazine. Hans promptly picked up a copy of the magazine and, when he saw Jim at the next global meeting in the Netherlands, he presented the magazine as a fun gift. Well, it turned out that an American female colleague, who was in the room when Hans discretely handed over the magazine, happened to notice it and became very angry. She indicated that presenting a Playboy magazine to another man in her presence was offensive. Hans was perplexed. What would you do as the female colleague? Why was Hans confused? Was Hans right or wrong in his decision to give the magazine to his colleague? Visit our website for the conclusion.

Situation #2 : Paint in the Amazon

Carlotta secured a position with the United Nations immediately after earning her university degree. She was proud, and excited, to join one of the biggest NGOs in the world, whose mission was to "save the world" one action at a time. Shortly after she joined the UN, she was given a chance to join a team in Brazil. As it turned out, her first major assignment proved exceptionally challenging. Given that Carlotta was young and ambitious (and intent on a successful global career), she accepted the assignment without hesitation. She learned that there were three huge barrels of aluminum paint standing in a small village in the Amazon, and if the UN did not intervene, the villagers were going to dump the aluminum paint in the Amazon River, thereby endangering the local wildlife. The aluminum paint had been left in the village when the company that used it, lacked the resources to dispose of it properly. In the end, they abandoned the barrels in the village. Carlotta went to the village and assessed the situation, but she soon discovered she couldn't communicate with the villagers because they spoke in a tribal dialect. She recognized, however, that one young man was willing to help her, as he had some capacity to understand her and her purpose. The next morning, the young man came out, dressed in a Western suit and helped her organize a discussion around ways to remove the aluminum paint without dumping it in the river. He also helped to explain the ramifications of dumping the paint. She was grateful for his gesture, given that she felt the young man had helped her to meet her goals. Yet, the next morning, the young man was nowhere to be found. Can you guess what happened to him? How was the mission accomplished? Visit our website for the conclusion.

As you can see, culture is a determining factor in the development of norms and values among the nationals of a host country; and therefore, it plays a tremendous role in how people behave. Likewise, you are also the product of a particular culture, and your cultural background determines not only your own behavior, but also how you look at (and judge) other cultures. We examine the world through our own cultural lens, and the greater the differences, the harder the adaptation (or settling process) is likely to be.

Cultural dimensions

Before you consider how you can work effectively in an international arena, you must understand your own cultural values and your own work style. The more you understand yourself, the better you can learn how to work in other cultures, and you will decrease your ramp-up time to high performance when expatriating. Speaking of cultural values, can you quickly identify some of the underlying values of your home country? One easy way to accomplish this is to come up with a list of common proverbs that are shared in your culture. These proverbs are a simple reflection of what is valued or promoted. A good example is, "God helps those who help themselves," a popular proverb in the USA that celebrates initiative. A common Dutch expression (translated into English) is, "adding water to the wine," which underscores a national tendency toward consensus building.

As we grow up among people who share the same norms and values, we depend on people to behave in certain ways in certain circumstances. As soon as we find ourselves among people who do not respond as we expect them to, we become uncertain, annoyed, and frustrated. Even though we know that people with different cultural backgrounds behave differently, it is often difficult to accept these differences when we encounter them (Storti 2007).

As Fons Trompenaars, a leading authority on the topic of cultural diversity in business, notes, "Every culture distinguishes itself from others by the specific solutions it chooses to certain problems" (1997, 8). These solutions are made on the basis of relationships with people as well as attitudes toward time and the environment. On occasion, our values and beliefs will conflict, and sometimes they will converge with the cultures we visit. The fact is, cultural differences are often a source of "confusion, misunderstanding, and misinterpretation" (Storti 2007). If you have a clear understanding of these cultural differences, you stand a greater chance of working effectively with others in an international venue (Trompenaars 1997).

We can distinguish five dimensions in which cultures differ in the way people interact and how they build relationships (adapted from Trompenaars 1997).

1. *The degree to which people do things by the book*

Does a rule always apply or are there exceptions to the rule due to special circumstances or relationships? Rigid application of the rules can sometimes give undesired results. Some cultures take that for granted, knowing that the application of those rules create equality and certainty for all. In other cultures it is acceptable to deviate from the rules to take special circumstances into consideration.

2. *The degree of individualism*

Do individuals see themselves as individuals or primarily as part of a group? Does the individual's interest come first, or is there a greater emphasis on the interests of the group? Many societies are deeply informed by collectivist values, a characteristic that WiSER Marjet encountered when working at a Japanese organization. "In Japan, they consult forever before they make a decision," she said. "That's part of the way they work, and breathe and think." Although individual leadership is not altogether absent, there is a greater emphasis on consensus building. "They don't believe so much in leaders," WiSER Marjet explained. "You are part of the whole system (everyone is part of the whole system), and at the end of the day, of course, there is one top guy, but for him just to express his opinion is…not the way it works."

3. *The degree to which people express emotions in interactions*

Do they stay neutral and objective, or do they show their feelings of anger, frustration, happiness and so forth? This difference proved a challenge for WiSER Marjet when she moved to Japan. She had a difficult time controlling the degree of emotion she expressed in a culture where emotional displays are culturally unacceptable. "I have a lot of expression in my face, a lot of non-verbal expression," she said. "That's something that's frowned upon in Japan. You should keep your thoughts to yourself, but I find it difficult to change that."

4. *The degree of importance placed on personal relationships for business purposes*

Do you do business because you want the product/service, or because you enjoy dealing with the person who's selling it? Is doing business rational, transactional, 'strictly business' or is building personal relationships as much part of it or maybe even a condition to do business and to work together? In some cultures, there is very little overlap between one's professional and personal life, as WiSER Lillian discovered when on an assignment in Germany. "Our work life and our personal life, with extremely few exceptions…don't mix," she said. "What we do at work is work; what we do at home is home, and there have only been just a couple of areas where that line has been crossed or blurred." WiSER Lillian indicated that she and her German colleagues often knew very little about one another. "When I came to Germany, I was actually quite surprised because I had two colleagues, who shared an office — and they had shared an office for over ten years — and I asked one colleague, 'Does that person have children?'. The co-worker had no idea, she recalled. "In Germany, there is more distance between work and personal [life], as compared to Italy or in Greece." She noted that, in Greece, her colleagues often invited her to dinner and introduced her to their wives. When comparing the level of friendliness in Greece and Germany, she said, "[In Greece] it's not just a handshake, but it includes [a] hug and the kisses…whereas in Germany, it's much more straightforward, with a handshake — same in England."

Meanwhile, WiSER Elsa I. discovered that there was a strong emphasis on personal relationships in Latin cultures. "I'd say that relationship is a big part of how work gets done there, and I probably underestimated how to leverage that," she said in the interview. She added that, if she had known what she currently knows, she would have approached her job very differently, and it would have helped her synchronize with the new organization much more quickly.

5. *The factors that are taken into account when judging someone's success*

Are you considered to be successful and do you earn respect because of what you know and what you did (achievements), or because of who you know and who you are (status)?

WiSER Alexis encountered unfamiliar attitudes toward authority when she accepted an assignment in the Czech Republic. "In Czech, I've had to adapt my style... dramatically," she revealed. "I'm used to coming from an environment where I have to earn respect as the boss." This was not the case, however, when she assumed a position as CEO of an organization in Central Europe. "I'm automatically given enormous respect," she said. "They automatically think that I would know everything about what direction we should take, what decisions we should take, and they expected me to have a certain level of studiousness about me." In the end, these expectations led her to modify her management style. "My natural style is, I do laugh a lot. I... make a lot of jokes." she observed. "I'm not a directional manager by nature, but I had to become more directional." WiSER Alexis found that she needed to curb her sense of humor, because her employees expected their manager to be serious-minded.

Similarly, WiSER Anna found that traditional attitudes toward authority in Southeast Asia sometimes made it difficult for her to get honest feedback from her employees. "We tend to have a big Indian workforce and a big Filipino workforce, and they are extremely respectful to you," she said. "So, they are not going to tell you that you are wrong, or they're not going to tell you that's the best idea." The tendency of many workers to nod in agreement made it difficult to gauge their real attitudes. "People are not going to tell you automatically," she said. "You need to kind of figure it out yourself as well." However, the situation was very different in the UK, where employees challenged their managers on a regular basis. "I think in the UK, one of the things I learned quite quickly is...stand your ground, but make sure you know what you're talking about," she said. "People respect you, if you know what you're talking about." WiSER Carrie discovered how status is attributed to age when she was working in South Korea. "The society is set up [with]...strict rules or norms...that you need to follow," she recalled. "For example, [with] a senior or junior man, the junior guy has to use a different language with this senior person." She noted that, in many situations, people are tacitly aware of who is the oldest, and this person will generally be treated with deference.

In addition to the five dimensions that describe how people interact with one another, there are two other cultural differentiators that focus on how people interact with their environment.

6. *The importance of time*

In some cultures, everything is driven by time, while in others, the event is of primary importance. WiSER Jacqueline noticed the differences during an assignment in Africa. "In Africa, there is [an] event culture, and I came from a time culture." She remembered when she and her husband had invited a group of people from 4 to 6. "[T]here is going to be a group that is going to leave at 6... but then there [will be] a group that's going to show up around 4.35 and they will stay until 9 o'clock. The... getting together... was so much more important than the time." While this required some adjustment, she found that she had to insist upon some degree of punctuality in the workplace. "I couldn't adjust to it too much in the workplace, so it was sometimes challenging with my staff to say, 'We need to be on time' — or that type of thing," she said. "But I found in my own personal life [that] I made lots of adjustments." If you extrapolate the idea of time culture further, it defines a culture's sense of living in the past, present or future. For example, Ireland is mired in folklore and their sense of present is strongly linked to their past identity. In the US people are very future focused. It is a relatively young nation, propelling itself forward.

7. *The relationship with nature*

Due to the somewhat abstract nature of this dimension, we will simply mention that it is the relationship people assign to their environment. Some cultures live in harmony with nature, others control it, and others respect it at varying degrees. Further extrapolated and applied to business terms, this dimension influences whether people in a culture are more or less fatalistic or whether they feel they own their destiny.

Many cultural awareness courses and books written on the topic of expatriation focus on helping people who are entering new cultures to manage the "revealed" cultural aspects so that people can get on with daily life. Learning to look for external cues to see if we are doing the right thing is pivotal to managing revealed culture. Cultural experts have created various tools to assess and understand face value cultural differences. If you are interested in links to some of these tools, please visit our website. As mentioned, there are "concealed" cultural aspects that are more difficult to casually observe but are critical to understand.

You can further improve your adjustment to a new country by touching the tip of "concealed" culture by:

- learning behaviors of other successful people in the new culture,
- finding things that are commonly accepted in both countries (ex. sports, having dinner out with others…),
- finding things you shouldn't do in the host culture because they elicit ridicule or disrespect.

Interaction with others	Beliefs and Behavior	
Degree to which you Do Things by the Book	Black & White: Rules are Always applicable	Gray: Special circumstances and relationships may require exception to the rule
Degree of Individualism	Part of a group	'Me, myself and I'
Degree of Expressing Emotion in Interactions	Non-expressive	Expressive
Degree of Importance of personal Relationships for Business Purposes	Strictly business	Business is personal
Factors that are taken into account when Judging Someone's Success	Achievement	Status
Relationship with environment	Beliefs and Behavior	
The importance of Time	Time	Event
The relationship with Nature	Fatalistic	Own your destiny

Cultural dimensions - Adapted from Fons Trompenaars' cultural dimensions

Cultural differences and work style

The more you understand how your own cultural heritage influences the way you work, and the better you can combine that understanding with the ways other cultures work, the more effective you will be when expatriating. There are very popular worldwide tools to help people understand how they work with others. DiSC is one of them. It is a four quadrant behavioral model based on the work of the late William Moulton

Marston Ph.D. (1893 - 1947), a Harvard-educated consulting psychologist, who was widely published in academic journals. Interestingly, Marston is also remembered for creating the lie detector machine and developing the "Wonder Woman" character. He identified four categories of human behavioral styles, types or temperament, now known as,

- "D" for Dominance, Drive, Direct
- "I" for Influence
- "S" for Steadiness, Stability
- "C" for Compliant, Conscientious, Cautious

We have adapted this tool to initiate discussions on how to effectively work and interact with work teams in different regions of the world. Let's explore how we interact and manage our relationships with others, based on different DiSC personalities. Let's take an example relating to the factors that are taken into account when judging someone's success: achievement vs status.

Example: You are an American expatriate reporting to a senior operations manager in India. The team has gone above and beyond to meet the deadline. All of you have worked many extra hours and your manager wants to reward all of you. Your manager proposes giving everyone two complimentary holidays and solicits your opinion on the reward. Based on your DiSC profile, your responses to this situation in your home country (USA) may be as follows:

DiSC profile	Response
Dominant	You inform your manager that the team has many unused vacation days already and let the manager know you don't like the idea.
Influencer	You don't tell your manager that you don't like his/her idea. But rather, sell him/her on a reward that you think is better.
Steadiness	You tell your manager that a reward is a great idea. You suggest that the team has many unused vacation days b/c of overtime and ask if your manager would like you to come up with some alternative rewards.
Conscientiousness	You share a report on unused vacation days of the team and point out that an alternative reward would be better.

How do you think these responses would be received by your Indian manager and colleagues? Is there a response that would work better in India? If you would like to learn more about your work styles, and how you interact with others compounded with the complexities of international relocation, visit our website.

To adapt or not to adapt? That is the question

When we go abroad, we often assume that there is no tolerance for diverse approaches of thought and execution. We tend to believe that we should simply accept the way things are done there. However, when we feel that we simply have to "fit in" as expatriates, we experience what is called "cognitive dissonance" between our internal values and the demands of an unfamiliar culture. This can create great internal conflict and contribute to a lack of personal fulfillment. Great internal conflict can lead to poor performance and/or weak levels of employee engagement. Research has shown that reducing cognitive dissonance in expatriates can limit one's fear of uncomfortable interactions and promote an easier adjustment, which in turn, reduces stress and the chance of an early departure (Maertz, Hassan, and Magnusson 2008). But as an expatriate you don't have to let go of all your own cultural norms, values and habits. As we will explain below, it is even 'dangerous' to do so. As mentioned before, you will have to avoid behavior that leads to ridicule or disrespect in the host culture. Beyond that, there are different degrees of adaptation which offer different ways to deal with new habits. In other words, you adapt by what you select to adopt.

To adapt or not to adapt? That is the question. You may choose to adopt some, many, or no new habits from the host country. Each choice is accompanied with pros and cons. Our model for cultural adaptation is based on research by psychologists Maertz, Hassan, and Magnusson (2009).

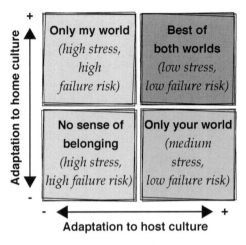

Model for cultural adaptation

1. *'No sense of belonging'*

Worst-case scenario. You no longer have a connection with your home country culture and values, but you've also failed to adapt to the host country. You don't feel you belong anywhere anymore.

The result is high stress levels and a high risk of assignment failure.

2. *'Only my world'*

You do not adopt new cultural habits because you simply fail to understand them, or you don't want to adopt them, or you believe they conflict with your personal values. You remain an outsider, living in a country where you don't feel comfortable.

The result is high stress levels and a high risk of assignment failure.

3. *'Only your world'*

You adapt too well to the host country culture, and in doing so, you abandon your own values, and what you stand for. You risk 'losing touch' with yourself if you become somebody else, if you become a "clone" of the locals. As WiSER Jacqueline cautioned: "Don't try to become somebody (or something) else, but learn from the culture and be willing to make some adaptations. You are never going to be a Kenyan [if you are not], but you can learn and grow and adapt to another cultural context.... I have seen too many extremes. I have seen lots of people who just go there and kind of throw off...their own cultural heritage, and it just seems such a mistake."

The result is medium stress level, and a low risk of assignment failure.

4. 'Best of both worlds'

This is the quadrant where you have achieved a balance between your host and home cultures. The new behaviors you adopt are considered up front, so you can stand behind your decision and feel comfortable about it. You adopt behaviors because you either like them, or you can live with them or justify them. You may also choose to reject host country behaviors that stand in opposition to your values.

The result is low stress level, and a low risk of assignment failure.

a. *Adopt host country behavior because you like it*

The fact that people from different cultures behave differently does not always have to be negative. Indeed, you may find yourself appreciating many things that the locals do, and even adopt that behavior yourself. For example, you may come from a culture where a woman shaking hands with a male is considered inappropriate. Over time, you may decide that you no longer assign the same value to that tradition, and you begin to embrace the new culture's norm of men and women shaking hands. As WiSER Jolanda observed: "I really want to also be living in a different culture, and effectively being challenged in living in another culture, and enjoying the challenge and being, sometimes amazed and wondering... why they're doing this. Also, [there are] these moments where I feel like this is fun.... Why don't we do those kinds of things at home? We could learn from this."

b. *Adopt host country behavior because you can live with it*

There may be cases where you do not agree with the local behavior, or it is something you would not initiate yourself, but at the same time you justify adopting that behavior for any number of reasons:

- *you can link the behavior to a new positive value*

    For example, in your home culture, men and women might shake hands only when they are intimate with one another. Over time, you come to realize that, in the host country's culture, shaking hands is simply a sign of friendship. You can then link the practice of shaking hands to a new anchor, which does not reflect poorly on your own culture or that of the host country.

- *you can attribute the behavior to a higher cause*
  As an expatriate you may feel that you have to compromise some of your values temporarily as the price you pay to "fit in" and succeed in your assignment.
- *you recognize that although your behavior is in conflict with your home country values, you can absolve yourself*
  In extreme cases, an expatriate may refer to different behavior abroad as being reflective of their "expatriate self" rather than their "real self". They may exhibit an "expatriate self" behavior and often accompany it with a personal promise not to do it again when they are their "real self" again. For example, your religion may forbid you from drinking alcohol. However, a large part of the networking in your host country is done after hours, in bars and restaurants, and you are expected to drink beer, wine or cocktails. You decide to drink the alcohol, saying to yourself, "This is the way it is on this assignment, but when I return home, I won't do this anymore."

c. *Reject host country behavior*

The most difficult category of behavior to deal with is any behavior that violates your own fundamental norms and values. Let's stay with the example of men and women shaking hands. If you come from a culture in which women and men shaking hands is considered inappropriate, you may choose to avoid this practice, despite the fact that it is commonplace in your host culture. In this case, you may choose to stick to your own values. As WiSER Emily said: "When something really doesn't feel right, it doesn't matter. You shouldn't have to accept it just because you are in an international environment. If it feels like supervisors are overstepping the lines of protocol between men and women it doesn't matter that you are sitting in another country. You should be able to sort of step back and say, 'That's unacceptable to me.'" Before you make a judgment call, however, it is imperative to understand the reason behind this behavior.

The challenge will be to strike the right balance between which behaviors you choose to adopt or decline in order to adapt to a new culture and perform your work effectively in that culture. If you make too many concessions to the host culture, you may risk losing your own identity, and you will feel lost and alienated. If you don't adapt at all, however, you will also feel lost and alienated. As WiSER Martha put it: "When you live in multiple cultures, there are always pros and cons of every culture. So, you have the opportunity to embrace what's wonderful about that culture. You can reject what you don't like."

We enjoy being the mirror for those who are considering international assignments, repatriating, or transitioning from one country assignment to another. In order to make decisions that you feel comfortable with in your professional career, a mirror is absolutely critical. It helps you see yourself in a clear light. Ideally, this light should help you get to where you want to go.

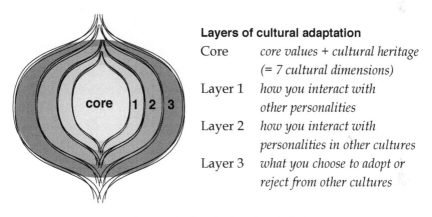

Layers of cultural adaptation

Core	*core values + cultural heritage (= 7 cultural dimensions)*
Layer 1	*how you interact with other personalities*
Layer 2	*how you interact with personalities in other cultures*
Layer 3	*what you choose to adopt or reject from other cultures*

Layers of cultural adaptation (onion)

When you consider yourself in a different cultural setting, it may be helpful to visualize how you will adapt as layers of an onion. This is not intended to bring tears to your eyes, but rather intended to simplify the cultural adaptation process. When we look at the core of the onion, it consists of who you are, formed by your values and cultural heritage. Your cultural heritage is defined by the seven cultural dimensions. At the first layer surrounding the core, you work to understand how you interact with different personalities. At the second layer, you gain a broader understanding of how you interact with people from different cultures. At the third layer, you consider the core, layer one and layer two and decide what host country behaviors you will adopt or reject.

Tips to adapt to a different culture

If you want to be effective in an international assignment, you will want to strike a balance between what cultural behaviors you choose to embrace from both your host and home cultures. We have developed eight approaches based on the experiences of the WiSER, that will help you adapt quickly and smoothen the process of integrating into the new culture. "I was very conscious of the fact that I had to learn the culture, tune in and learn and observe," recalled WiSER Hermie. "I was very conscious of that in my first couple of years because I was keen to be successful in my new environment."

1. *Be respectful*

Showing respect for a host country's nationals, along with your host country colleagues, is not only an important aspect of adapting to a different culture, it is also the basis of being successful in your expatriate assignment. "The single most important element to establish a relationship with your hosts is to respect them," advised WiSER Flavia. "If they sense that you respect who they are and what they stand for, then you can do anything. I was extremely candid with my counterparts on matters that I thought needed to be addressed...." She noted that she spoke frankly to employees about issues including inadequate skills, lack of commitment, and even corruption. "Yes, occasionally, you do get into a little bit of a tiff with some," she added. "But if you do it from the perspective that I really love this country, I really want to see it do well, that allows you to become a credible interlocutor who can—and is—legitimized to carry difficult messages." That said, WiSER Flavia advised expatriates against coming into a situation with an attitude of cultural superiority. "They will just bear with you for as long as you have to be there, and just hope that the next time they'll be lucky and have someone else," she explained. "I think, going into any new situation with the curiosity to learn what they have to teach you—and not just with the pretension that you have things to teach them—is very important."

2. *Understand "right" and "wrong" is relative*

We all are brought up to learn that certain practices are the right thing to do, while others are just "not done." However, when you move to another country, especially one with very different cultural norms and values from your own, you will quickly learn that the concept of right and wrong, more accurately what is acceptable, is culturally defined. Indeed, what you always thought to be "wrong", may be "right" in the host country. For WiSER Diane this was a big eye-opener. She shared that her parents raised her to have a very concrete notion of right and wrong, but this view was challenged when she lived and worked abroad. "It dawned on me that that's actually not the case, because criminality, for example, is a moving target," she explained. "Whereas in Australia, where I was studying, it's illegal to have more than one wife, in Senegal, in West Africa, it's encouraged." Although "right and wrong" may be defined differently, it is still good to own a point of view. As Rohit Bhargava (2012) recommends, it is important to have your own opinion, rather than just agreeing with others, in order to make yourself relevant in any given situation.

3. *Understand there are many ways to do things*

Being open to cultural differences also involves realizing and accepting that things can be done differently, without suggesting that they are being done in the wrong way. There are many "right" ways of doing anything in life. There is not one solution; there are multiple solutions and each culture offers different ones. Remember, when you are always "right", somebody else is always "wrong".

4. *Be humble*

While being humble is not always easy, it is nevertheless important in many situations. Jim Collins (2001), author of Good to Great, analyzed many successful leaders and discovered that "humility was one of the core elements of their achievement." Being humble comes easier to some cultures than others. In Asian cultures, humility is a highly valued quality, and it is therefore less of an issue than for Americans and Europeans, who, on the contrary, do not rank high in the area of humility. It is important to remember that, when you go to another country, you don't know everything, and your knowledge is not necessarily greater than that of the people who live there. Be prepared to know half of what you think you know.

As bright as may be, and as much as you have learned about your business, your industry, and your organization, you are going to have to relearn some of those lessons with a different set of eyes, given that cultural differences are very real. "Definitely don't judge in your first year," WiSER Britta advised. "Don't think you understand your environment. Just take it in, and don't judge." At times, it may seem as though the people you encounter are less intelligent, because their way of doing things strikes you as illogical. If you actually examine their reasons for doing things, however, you may find that they are actually quite clever. It is viable that you can learn a lot if you take a closer look at what's being done, and why.

5. *Listen, observe and ask a lot of questions*

Good leadership is not about arriving on the scene with all the answers, or taking a one-size-fits-all approach to solutions. Instead, it involves harnessing the skills, talents, and ideas of new teams and organizations. This element of good leadership is more important than ever in an international environment. Listening, observing, and asking questions are among the quickest ways to harness the knowledge of others, and to gain an understanding of your new political environment. When you take this approach, you are showing that you're interested in learning about the unfamiliar customs, norms, and values of your host country. Moreover, you are demonstrating a strong interest in your team. This is how leaders find followers. Being a "good listener" in an international setting can also improve efficiency. Rather than trying to figure everything out yourself, asking good questions and listening to answers and feedback will minimize mistakes and hasten your understanding of many processes in a new land. Overall, your expatriate life will become much easier if you dare to raise your hand when you have a question. "I wasn't afraid to ask questions," WiSER Magi recalled. "There was this particular person that my husband worked with (whom we got along with very well), and I said: 'You know what? I am having a hard time with this.'" She went on to discuss with him some of her challenges and asked for his feedback on the appropriate response. "And I would be open to talking to [him] about things like that because he knew his people," she explained. "He knew the culture, he knew the industry, and he knew what would be okay or not okay for me to say…. It just helps that you are able to ask the questions, because if [you] don't ask, you are never going to know."

Magi shared her uncertainties with an outside confidant. However, you can find plenty of people to approach within your organization as well. WiSER Abby recalled that she talked to "everyone" in her organization. She asked them about issues related to leadership, the culture, and the motivation to work in the organization. "I've heard a lot from people that made me think, 'Oh, that's interesting,'" she said. "Then, once, I was alerted to it, I started observing. Once you sit and observe dynamics between people, you start picking up on behaviors and you think, okay, that's really interesting."

Last but not least, you can also draw on the experience of expatriates who have been around longer than you have. In many cases, they can be a valuable source of information. When you get the same kinds of responses from various people who have been successful in that particular venue, it seems likely that you're getting some valuable feedback. Conversations with other expatriates can guide you on how to react to or deal with certain situations.

6. *It is you who will have to adapt*

You have to adapt to the world, because the world is not going to adapt to you. You will need to be observant and flexible, and to find a way that works for both parties, not just for yourself. At the same time, you want to hold on to your core beliefs and values. "You need to be able to change colors without losing yourself, and that's the trick I think," said WiSER Marjet. "If you lose yourself and become too much of a Japanese or too much of a Czech, you lose the strength that…got you to that place and got you to that position in the first place. So, I think you have to find a balance there. That's actually adapting, but not changing."

The WiSER described cases where they adapted to local cultural norms for the benefit of their professional and personal lives. "I think from the work perspective, the working environment in Singapore then was very different from what India was," recalled WiSER Supriya. "In India, it was still very hierarchical. It was still a very male dominated thing. When I went to Singapore, I realized that…I had to mold myself to be more like the professional women in Singapore." In WiSER Emily's case, she found a need to adapt to local customs regarding attire. "I have made mistakes about clothing in places and that's not something I like," she acknowledged. "In Eastern Europe, it was [a] pretty sexist atmosphere, so I started dressing more conservatively." During an assignment in the Middle East, she had an embarrassing experience, when she wore a summer dress that turned out to be too short, by local standards. "Now, when I travel to the Middle East, I pretty much only wear pants," she noted. "I try to make sure that I prevent things that are going to make the fact that I am woman be an issue."

7. *Learn the language*

Language tells you a great deal about the culture of a country. Think about analogies, expressions and jokes. People appreciate it enormously when you attempt to speak the language, even if you are limited to a few words or polite expressions. Notably, language fluency and cross cultural training positively impacts adjustment in the host country during the first nine months, which are some of the most challenging months (Wanberg, Zhu, Harrison, and Diehn 2011). Speaking the language will contribute directly to your professional and personal success in an expatriate assignment. Therefore, all WiSER agreed that learning to speak the host country's language is very important, not only for you, but also for your family.

Yet, it is not always easy to learn the local language. Russian, Arabic, and Chinese, for example, are very difficult to learn for people who are used to the Latin alphabet. Grammar or spelling rules can turn out to be a real challenge, or it may simply be that learning another language is not your strongest competency. What do you do then? How does that impact your working environment? WiSER Marjet, who works in Japan, shared some of her professional experiences. "I have a permanent translator who is my shadow," she revealed. "Everywhere I go, he goes, and that's the way it works." She admitted, however, that this situation is hardly ideal. "It's frustrating because you can never have a one-on-one with someone. You can never brainstorm. It's very difficult with the translator, and, of course, the limitation of the translator is also the limitation of the conversation." She noted that it becomes very difficult to discuss more complex topics such as the company's strategy, given that conversations usually remain at a basic level.

8. Mind the cultural context

Pay attention to what is going on around you. When you put something into a broader cultural context and take notice of how people are feeling at a given moment, they're more likely to respond. Last winter, we had friends from France visiting, and it's important to mention that I (Sapna) don't speak a word of French. One day, in the late afternoon, we were visiting a Christmas market, and the daughter asked her mother something in French. I replied, "It's 5 p.m., and we have about one hour left before we go home." They both looked at me in disbelief, saying, "Did you learn French since you moved to Germany?" I realized that the mere fact of having lived in a country where I am not fluent in the language has required me to become very aware of the "cultural context." At this point, I am so aware that I understand people, even if I don't know exactly what they're saying. WiSER, Diane, shared an example from her own experience. "In Asia, you are not likely to know that you've stepped wrongly," she said. "I mean, there [are] no clear signals. Now, you do that in West Africa, and they'll tell you. In Asia, you absolutely have to invest the time.' Simply put, the tangible way to recognize cultural context is to consider timing, clues, body language, facial expressions (or lack thereof), intonation, and personal interaction.

9. Be patient

When we are young we are taught that patience is a virtue. This is especially true when expatriating to less developed countries. The physical environment in which you will operate is entirely different from what you are used to. Transportation, communication, and daily life are less fluent and take more time than usual. Due to the less 'high tech'/ sophisticated facilities, you will learn that timelines to achieve your goals will be(come) longer than you planned for. This is what WiSER Martha experienced when she was working in Mozambique, Africa: "Just the environment itself, the challenges you know..., there is flooding every year and the poverty itself.... There are just a number of challenges that make doing anything, in a developing context, more difficult. So I think you certainly become more patient in terms of the time table that it takes to achieve change."

It's a wrap!

Cultural differences are the underlying reasons for different behaviors including how people interact and build relationships. Some of the differences will be obvious, but many cultural norms and values will be concealed and difficult to recognize. When adapting to a new culture, find the right balance between adapting new behaviors and staying true to yourself. Understanding the way you work with others, combined with understanding how other cultures work, equals success.

Recipe for Success

"Because I am a woman, I must make unusual efforts to succeed. If I fail, no one will say, she doesn't have what it takes. They will say, women don't have what it takes."
~ Clare Boothe Luce

"You better be pretty passionate, not only about what you do, but about the idea of going abroad, whether that'd be the country itself or just the whole concept of it. It's not something to go into lightly, but I would highly encourage people to consider it."
~ WiSER Kelli

Imagine for a moment that you've been asked to take an international assignment in Barcelona, Spain. Let's suppose this assignment will give you an amazing opportunity to lead a large, high profile multi-national project for which many others were considered but only you were selected. How does that feel? Do words like "exciting," "energizing," and "challenging" leap to mind? Does it conjure up phrases like "feather in your cap" or "professional turning point"? Or, are you filled with hesitation because you are not sure that you can be successful in an international role? We want you to recognize that success on this kind of assignment can be your reality. If you are about to begin — or are currently involved in — an international assignment and want to reach your optimal performance, it can be achieved by understanding and mastering global leadership competencies. Competencies are a combination of knowledge, skills and job engagement, demonstrated through observable and measurable behavior. Global leadership competencies are commonly categorized as leading the organization, leading self and leading others, and result in excellent global leadership.

To clarify this point, let's take the term "competency" out of the classroom and into the real world. What does it mean? What does it look like? How can we conceptualize it? Last evening, as we were preparing a dinner for clients, it occurred to us that the ability to cook is indeed a competency - now there's some food for thought. Our culinary skills came into play when we created a menu, researched recipes, and purchased and prepared the ingredients. Our knowledge was based on preparing some of these same recipes beforehand; therefore, we knew when to add an extra pinch of salt, an extra dash of pepper, an extra teaspoon of oil, or whatever was required to produce a great meal. We also noticed that we displayed different behaviors in the kitchen. While Caroline liked to work with loud music playing and tidied up as she went along, Sapna preferred a quieter kitchen and kept all her ingredients out on the counter until she was finished. With some imagination, envision the meticulous Japanese hibachi chef versus the dough tossing Italian chef. Which one do you envision as loud or quiet, tidy or creative? Do you think that a loud, creative kitchen would be readily accepted in Japan?

It is safe to say that some cultural behavior modification may be required, depending on the country in which one is cooking. As with any competency, our ability to cook was then evaluated through various measures, including feedback from our guests, the length of time involved in preparation, the cost of the ingredients, and the amount of leftovers. But then again, in different countries, different values are assigned to each measure. For example, in the Middle East leaving a certain amount of food on your plate is well accepted, whereas in the Netherlands the host might very well conclude that you didn't really like the food because some was left uneaten. As demonstrated, competencies can be found in everyday activities ranging from cooking to leading.

Do you have what it takes?

Globalization is here, and organizations are in need of leaders who are equipped with competencies that will help them succeed in an international environment. There is a growing awareness of the need to better prepare future leaders for global roles. Fortunately, global leadership competencies can be coached and developed. There are many reasons to understand and master global leadership competencies when working internationally or expatriating with the most imperative reasons being:

- decreased ramp-up time,
- smoother work transition, and
- the need to achieve the same high level of performance in a new country.

At this time, there are easily over a hundred competency models for various industries, roles, professions, levels, etc. There are even gender based competency models. Most models are developed from standard competency lists. Yet, in an international setting, with different countries and cultures involved, global leadership competencies differ from general leadership competencies. The process of selecting and preparing future global leaders begins with determining, at a strategic level, what competencies are required. Although expatriate assignments typically range between three to five times the cost of a comparable local employee, many organizations are lagging in their talent mindset and still do not have a clear view, or a clear policy regarding the competencies that they expect to see in their future global leaders. It is generally understood that global leadership differs significantly from domestic leadership. Although some leadership characteristics are universal, a global leader distinctively "understands—or can find out—how the execution of certain universal practices translates from one culture to another. They understand who they are, how they work with others, and how other cultures prefer to work with them" (Tessman and Wellins 2008).

Extensive research has been done on the competencies that leaders must have to excel in their jobs. A few best in class leadership competency models, which are applicable to both male and female domestic leaders, include PDI and Center for Creative Leadership. As mentioned, the global leader differs from the domestic leader. Well-known global leadership competency models include, the Global Mindset by the Thunderbird School of Global Management, DDI's Global Leader DNA or the ten key global leadership behaviors as defined by Gundling, Hogan and Cvitkovich. These are also applicable to both men and women. When considering global leadership competency models, you must bear in mind that they have been developed with a sample set consisting primarily of men, because, at this point, the majority of expatriates are men. We did not set out to develop another set of global leadership competencies. Rather, we investigated whether global leadership competencies differed if based on a sample set of expatriate women. Our research began with a hypothesis that there are shared global leadership competencies that are more pronounced and important to women in senior-level expatriate roles.

Our groundbreaking research has uncovered that there are four competencies that are shared among WiSER!

- **Self-awareness** – Knowing your strengths and weaknesses, likes and dislikes—which are all based on your values—and using this knowledge to make critical decisions.
- **Conscious Imbalance** – Tipping the scales towards what gives you energy and fulfillment with the realization that the scales will need to be rebalanced on a regular basis.
- **Operating Outside your Comfort Zone** – Embracing challenges coming from new experiences by tolerating ambiguity and remaining calm.
- **Active Career Management** - Knowing what you want from your career and actively working on achieving it.

We will take you on in-depth exploration of these competencies in chapters 6 through 9.

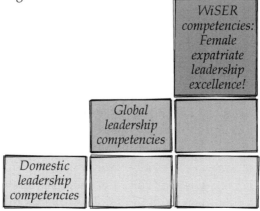

Building blocks to female expatriate leadership excellence

Global leadership competencies

Worldly Women is focused on the female expatriate. Therefore we will omit a review of domestic leadership competencies and begin a foundational explanation of global leadership competencies based on What is Global Leadership: Ten Key Behaviors that Define Great Global Leaders, by Gundling, Hogan, Cvitkovich (2011). This model best supports our goal of creating a hands-on book.

1. Cultural self-awareness
2. Inviting the unknown
3. Results through relationships
4. Frame-shifting
5. Expanding ownership
6. Developing future leaders
7. Adapting and adding value
8. Core values and flexibility
9. Influencing across boundaries
10. Third-way solutions

1. Cultural self-awareness

Key aspects include: "Seeing differences. Recognizing that leadership practices are shaped by the environment around us, and that there are different — and perhaps equally or even more viable ways — of getting things done in other locations" (p. 38-44).

Our mindset, and therefore the way we behave, is formed by our own experiences in a specific cultural setting. When you are a leader in a different environment, you will have to be aware of your own cultural heritage, of what has made you the leader you are today (see also chapter 3). You will not only have to realize but also understand how much the people whom you are leading have different ways of looking at things. They may value situations differently, or they may have other ways of getting things done. "It is extremely important to see the other side," explained WiSER Anuradha. "Never take a decision unless you understand why the other side does the things the way they do." For WiSER Anuradha, strategies are largely situational. "There is not one solution but multiple solutions," she said. "Each culture brings that different solution, and that's very important to see."

2. *Inviting the unknown*

Key aspects include: "Invite the unexpected; be open to new information and experiences. Notice things that you typically don't expect to see. Learn the language" (p. 45-53).

Open mindedness is a quality that was often stressed by WiSER as critical to their success. Many people think that what they did in the place where they previously lived is the right or "normal" thing to do. This is not necessarily true, however. They simply haven't experienced different things, or solutions, before. To be successful in an overseas assignment, you must enjoy learning about other cultures, and ways of doing things. You need a sense of inquiry, of being excited by new things. "If you are going to be an expat, you really have to be genuinely excited by the places that you are going to," WiSER Fiona said. "If you're not excited, and you're not enthusiastic about it, it can be really, really challenging." This means that you must get out there, be open to new insights, reconsider your own ways of doing things, and be willing to change your behavior accordingly. "I think... you really need to be quite open-minded and see... [it] as an adventure, as a process...seeing everything with a smile on your face, because it is different," advised WiSER Gillian. "That's why you went in the first place... You just have to understand that it is different, understand why and work out where you can learn from that.'" She indicated that success in an expatriate assignment requires flexibility and open mindedness.

3. *Results through relationships*

Key aspects include: "Put relationships before tasks. Forge connections, cross functional and regional lines. Find a cultural guide" (p. 54-62).

It is often said that it's lonely at the top. If you are the "boss," you are pressured to come up with the ideas, to solve all the problems, and to make things happen. This is challenging enough in your home country, let alone in a new environment. You don't know your way around, and you may not speak the language. In addition, you have to learn new ways of working and behaving. Everything is new, and therefore, you are very dependent on others. Under these circumstances, building relationships is crucial to your success. Within the organization, you can build strong relationships with people whom you can go to for advice and assistance.

It is also essential to create a social network outside of the organization that is not focused exclusively on business relations. Bear in mind that there are nuances and variances involved in interacting and building relationships in different cultures—an issue explored in chapter 3.

4. *Frame-shifting*

Key aspects include: "Shift your perspectives and leadership methods to better fit different circumstances. Take on new frames of reference and modify your approach to various environments: communication style, leadership style, pace and timing, and leadership strategy" (p. 62-74).

Being flexible, willing, and able to adapt to a new environment is central, as the WiSER agreed. There is no single way to be, or to do things, and you need to be able to respect different approaches and adapt your behavior accordingly. "We live in a world full of all sorts of shades of differences," WiSER Diane said in the interview. "It is important to be able to move in and step into a different space and not...bring in your own assumptions and impose your own frameworks on different environments." Remember, you have to adapt to a world that's completely different from the one that you are used to. The world is not going to adapt to you.

This becomes especially apparent after two or more international relocations. You can find yourself having to adapt to various cultural behaviors, many of which stand in direct contrast to one another. WiSER Marjet, who is Dutch, moved to the Czech Republic and then to Japan. Given that the Netherlands has a consensus-based culture, she found herself having to adapt to a radically different environment. "In the Czech Republic...they want to have orders," she said. "They prefer having clear instructions, they want to have very strict job profiles, and that's what works there." When she was assigned to Japan, however, she encountered a culture that placed an even greater emphasis on consensus than her native Netherlands. "Compared to Japan, the Netherlands are nothing on consensus," she said. "In Japan, they consult forever before they make a decision. It's almost as if everything has to happen on its own; it's like organic."

WiSER Gillian stressed the importance of making an effort to understand why things are done differently. "One of my big [learning experiences] when I got to the Netherlands [was], I couldn't understand the four-day working week; people were always in the park and not at work," she said. "And I very quickly made an assumption that, 'Oh, people in Holland are lazy.'" She later concluded that this conclusion was "narrow-minded." As she examined Dutch society more closely, she found much to admire. "Here is an economy that has very low unemployment, has a very good social system in place, has [a] work life balance I've never seen before," she recalled. "But it's not the Dutch who have it wrong—it's me." In time, she found herself embracing many of the values and practices she initially scorned.

5. *Expanding ownership*

Key aspects include: "Create a sense of engagement in a shared process and accountability for setting and achieving targets with both global and local significance" (p. 79-90).

When considering how to achieve their goals, many leaders make the mistake of initially focusing on the task—that is, what has to be done. At that point, they determine the steps that need to be taken, followed by how they are going to proceed. Again, they focus exclusively on the task. The fact is, one of the most effective ways to achieve your targets is to focus on the people you will need to make it happen. In short, you need to create "buy-in." Helping the people on the team understand both the global and local significance of their efforts, will help you engage them. Make your people responsible, and accountable, for certain targets and involve them in the process of identifying those targets. "I always wanted to bring out the best in people and use the best in people," WiSER Martha told us. "I think that helps to draw teams together, and as a leader that's a very important asset. So not coming in with this attitude that 'I've got the answers, I have got everything that it takes.'" On the contrary, she added, "It's actually 'I need you, and the skills and the perspectives that you bring help to create a team that can deliver.'" WiSER Diane has a similar opinion. "You have to recognize that it's people who are going to achieve that," she said. "As I always say to people, between you and the outcome that you are trying to achieve... is a person. So you need to focus on the person that's in front of you."

6. *Developing future leaders*

Key aspects include: "Enable capable people from anywhere in a global organization to step into leadership roles over time; that is, develop local talent. Be approachable and commit to employee development" (p. 90-94).

Every leader has started at the bottom of the career ladder. Some ambitious workers rise to leadership positions, but many do not. So, how do you get to be a leader? Many roads lead to Rome, and there is not one simple answer to this question. However, this much is certain: It has much to do with (and is most often a combination of) talent, ambition, opportunity, and supportiveness. Indeed, it is absolutely crucial to be a supportive leader. You can have all the talented employees you want, but if you do not know how to utilize them, they won't grow. Leaders must understand how to best employ the talents of their people. In addition, they must allow them to take risks and make mistakes; and, instead of punishing them when mistakes occur, they should help them to learn from their mistakes. Schoemaker (2011), a Wharton PhD in decision science, states that 99 percent of successes derive from failures and that it is counterproductive to view mistakes as a negative thing. None of us, after all, is perfect. He goes as far as to recommend that global organizations plan and promote mistakes in order to improve learning and move on to the next level. It all starts with trusting employees enough to give them learning opportunities that will boost their confidence in their own skills.

Trust + Risk-taking + Evaluation = (Tremendous) Growth

WiSER Diane benefited from such a leader. "His focus was on bringing knowledge to the organization and enabling others to unpack and to apply that," she recalled. "His whole style was about enabling. More than anything he was willing to…discuss and challenge, and he created space and opportunity for me to take risks." For WiSER Diane, the establishment of trust is a foundational piece in building effective leadership. "If you report to somebody, or you work with somebody who offers that foundational piece of trust, and then on top of that they create opportunity for you to take risk, the growth and the benefits of that can be absolutely tremendous," she told us. "I've had bosses like that, and they've been really quite exceptional and quite significant in terms of my own growth."

Now that she is a leader herself, she gives her people the same amount of trust and operating space: "I had feedback from my staff...it was quite a unique experience for them working for me, because I absolutely focused on how I could really develop them into spaces that they probably never thought of going before. Many of them said to me that it was the first time that they had ever had somebody going for that amount of trust in their ability to do or to demonstrate or to perform in an area where they hadn't demonstrated success [yet]."

7. *Adapting and adding value*

Key aspects include: "Balance adaptation to local practices with finding the best places to assert a different perspective or to act as a constructive change agent. Balance between adjusting and contributing" (p. 99-101).

Being sensitive to cultural differences and adapting to the local environment and ways of working does not mean that you cannot do anything different. You may have been hired to implement certain changes, or it may be the case that, after a while, you decide that certain changes are necessary to improve processes, culture, teamwork, strategy, communication, or something else—in other words, constructive changes that add value. Even in those cases where people working in the local organization resist these changes, it is sometimes necessary to stand your ground, if you believe you are correct.

Defending your ground can be especially difficult if you start out with little or no support. When she arrived in Spain, WiSER Andrea developed a whole new plan on how to run the business. "There were many people that were against it, and I had to fight a lot," she said. "And it was very, very difficult to overcome some of these challenges." Adding to this challenge was the fact that she was leading a new company, in which she had no relationships. "When I said I wanted to do this, lots of people would tell me, no, you cannot do that; and I had to fight that," she recalled. "I had to change many things; many people were unhappy." Confident that her plan was "the right thing to do," she forged ahead. "I am very happy now, because I see that the business [is] growing, and it's giving very good results," she said. "And the business model that we chose, even though many people were against it in the beginning, is keeping the company together now in times of crisis. It cost me a lot, but it was a very true achievement."

Notably, constructive changes such as these can be achieved at very different levels. For instance, WiSER Ulrike changed the decision-making process when she was working for her organization in Finland, because she thought it took too long to get results. "Whenever I wanted to do something, I had to collect them all around the table and discuss things," she explained. "So I adapted to it, and I really took the time to sit down with them to discuss things." Employees were pleased with this process, but it soon became apparent that change was incremental, and she was looking for more substantial results. "After a while, when I saw that the outcome was not so big, then I insisted that we do it a bit more according to my style," she said. "So, I am sitting down with them a lot, yes. But they now know that if I ask for something, then I mean it, and I follow up on that one. That was difficult for them to understand; they were not used to it. Now we are at a point where we can get the results out quite a bit faster."

8. *Core values and flexibility*

Key aspects include: "Defend your (critical few) core values, e.g. fairness, integrity, respect, honesty, and be flexible with nearly everything else" (p. 102-107).

Core values are your foundation. They are what make you, at a very deep level. They determine how you behave and act, and how you respond to the world around you. Examples of core values include reliability, loyalty, honesty, positivity, respect, and compassion. You fall back on these values whenever you are in a difficult situation, when you have to judge right from wrong. They are the beacons you need so badly when everything around you is new and different; and they are also the values that you do not want to compromise. Indeed, doing so would undermine your sense of authenticity, your own self-esteem. When a potentially compromising situation arises, you need to know when and where to draw the line. The competency, self-awareness, revealed through our research has some overlap with this value, with the major variable being that self-awareness is broader than values and flexibility alone (see chapter 6 on self-awareness).

WiSER Elsa L. explained to us that she was once in a situation where she felt she had to defend one of her own core values. "There was only one time that I put my job on the table, so to speak," she recalled. "Basically the board was going to make a decision, and the decision that it looked like they might make was, in my view, not an ethical decision." She informed the board that she would go along with any decision they made, given that they served as the organization's decision-making body, but she added an important qualification. "My job is to carry out what the board asks me to do," she said. "But you need to know that this will be my last year... because, ethically, I cannot do my job. I cannot accept this, and I am not going to put myself in that kind of situation. You don't have to accept my ethics, but you have to understand that I also don't need to accept what I consider to be a lack of ethics." Similarly, WiSER Maxine was forced to make some ethical decisions after being given a huge task and opportunity. "The whole idea was that, when the wall came down, when the communists had moved on, what you had was lots of people in government positions who had absolutely no management expertise, no expertise in manning organizations, because it was all about the process in those days," she explained. "I took out teams of management trainers, teams of play therapists, teams of social workers, teams of educationalists to train up in the governments to create training institutions." The five-year program was sponsored by the EU, and after a year-and-a-half, WiSER Maxine took the controversial decision to close it down, given that it was set up in a way that struck her as unethical. "For example, we were paying our local staff in dollars, [which was] completely unethical," she said. "That, for me, was not okay. I have very strong values, set—as you would imagine—from a religious upbringing. I'm willing to flex that as long as it's not the badness of the individuals. When it gets to that point, it's not okay. So I closed it." Meanwhile, WiSER Faith, too, had an experience she described as an ethical dilemma, one that led her to leave an organization whose culture she was unable to change to her satisfaction. She recalled that many people associated with the organization promised clients things that they had no ability, or intention, to provide. "I thought, after being in the region for so many years, that I was going to be doing more damage to the brand—me—if I stayed there," she explained. "Because a lot of clients started to get disappointed in what we were offering, and I couldn't make every change that needed to be done, I left."

These are extreme situations that can arise in domestic settings as in international settings. Hopefully, you will not encounter such situations very often. When your core values are not at risk, however, it is possible to show greater flexibility and adapt to the local situation.

9. Influencing across boundaries

Key aspects include: "Drive collaboration across organizational boundaries in order to craft real solutions" (p. 113-118).

As a leader you deal with many different parties both external and internal to the organization. An effective leader brings people with different talents from various departments together to create solutions and achieve results. On an international assignment, by default you represent your home country, you will also represent your organization in the host country, and you may have to work with local authorities and government leaders to accomplish various tasks. Interaction with local leaders and government officials may be more frequent and possibly more important when you work for non-governmental organizations in developing countries. WiSER Jacqueline, for instance, spent a good deal of time dealing with political leaders during an assignment to Nairobi, Kenya. "I had to meet a network of leaders," she recalled. "I had specific countries that I was responsible for, and I had to spend my first six months just setting up the contacts.'" WiSER Anne, who worked in Somalia, described a similar experience. "We were funded by the US government, but I worked with the Somalian government," she said. "Working with the Somalian government was hard. They weren't very professional. Work and social life was very intertwined. There was a small community, so you knew everybody and everybody knew you. I would go to a lot of social events and a lot of business. We were constantly networking."

10. Third way solutions

Key aspects include: "Find other ways than usual to create shared solutions. Be transparent about assumptions and expectations; be consistent in your actions. Act as a bridge between headquarters and other locations. Create viable solutions; focus on the process of getting there" (p.118-126).

We have already noted that, in a different environment, it may not be advisable or even possible to do things the way you used to. Regardless of this, you may want or need to change how things are done currently. So, if you can't leverage your method, and don't want to leverage their method, you have to develop an altogether new way to get the job done. A so called, "third way solution". Be creative; get your people involved and aim for solutions that are supported by many. WiSER Anuradha was part of such a creative process, and offered this experience: "It was a group of people motivated to work on something. We came up with the creative ideas we wanted to do, and then we decided how we would go about doing it. [Then] we went about doing it. That's how we worked. We did some really creative things, and I'm proud to say I was part of those creative things. A creative thing doesn't happen because of one person, but I was part of those creative ideas."

In summary, it is first necessary to excel in your current role in order to be considered for an international role. Second, research has shown that leadership skills are the most important skills assessed when organizations assess candidates for international assignments (Brookfield 2012, 16). Third, in your effort to be a successful global leader, possessing, developing or refining some key global leadership competencies will greatly benefit you. If you lack any of these competencies, you can devote time to develop them, or you can consider ways in which you can leverage alternate strengths and competencies you possess. Crucially, success in an international role can only be achieved through authenticity, and emphasizing global leadership competencies should not be confused with not being yourself. As WiSER Ayesha explained: "I am just who I am. I am a woman. I am a professional. I am myself. I don't draw my benchmark against other people, be them male or female. I wouldn't compromise on being a woman.... Just be yourself, and you know what, half the battle is won."

Developing competencies

Many global leadership skills can be acquired or enhanced with relative ease. In other words, you can learn some of the "tricks" of global leadership. Competencies, however, are much more difficult to master, because you are not just attempting to learn skills and knowledge but also trying to change a behavior that has been exhibited for many years. Many managers report an inability to incent higher performance behavior, for example, attributing it to the adage "you can't teach an old dog new tricks." We would like to think that bright, ambitious women pursuing an international career are interested and willing to adapt behaviors to situations and needs. You cannot and should not change who you are, but you can be flexible. After years of experience in coaching professionals on developing competencies, we know that it can be done. It is true that entrenched behavior will be more difficult to change than behavior that you demonstrate only on occasion. However, do not despair: "Neuroscience has discovered that the human brain is highly plastic. Neural connections can be reformed, new behaviors can be learned, and even the most entrenched behaviors can be modified at any age" (Rock 2009, 5).

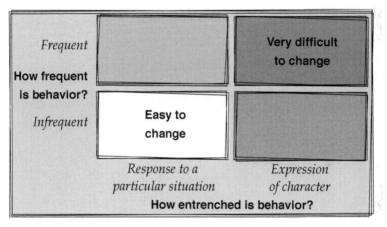

Changeability of behavior
Source: HBR Essentials: Coaching & Mentoring. Adapted from James Waldrop

Our hypothesis that there would be a few shared competencies among successful expatriate women, tested as valid. Prior to accumulating new skills, knowledge or behaviors, we suggest you assess yourself against a standard set of global leadership competencies, as well as WiSER competencies. Next, focus on enhancing a modest number of competencies that will be most beneficial to you on your expatriate assignment. What is the secret to developing competencies? As per expert, David Rock, mindful attention or self-discovery is the first step (see chapter 6 on self-awareness). It is here that your competency development begins.

There are four stages to mastering WiSER competencies. These stages are a progression, leading to mastering a behavior which will lead to success for any female expatriate. Some competencies will be easier to master, or at least develop, than others because of where your own personal strengths lie. In the following chart, examples are provided to help you visualize the different levels of mastering a competency.

Phase 4 **Unaware - Competent** You do the right thing without even having to think about it	Example – WiSER Gabriel: "The Board decided to send me to Mexico to be the CEO and build up their business for Mexico and Central America. I needed to build up big revenue in the first year. You have a complete different situation, you have different culture, you have different people, you have different goals. And I was used to change every time, adapt very fast, and bring results. So I was two years in Mexico, and we had already in the first year thirty million turnover."
Phase 3 **Aware - Competent** You are very focused on doing the right thing and you are succeeding	Example – WiSER Hanan relocated from Australia to Dubai. After six or seven months, she started wearing the local clothing called Abaya. She did that because it seemed more respectful because she was working for a local company that employed many locals. This simple action helped her blend in and she felt more comfortable b/c she was not soliciting unwanted stares. Her co-workers found it to be thoughtful and professional.
Phase 2 **Aware - Incompetent** You are very focused on doing the right thing but still make mistakes	Example – WiSER Abby relocated from America to Singapore and is invited to participate in the annual Holiday "Lucky Draw", which is a raffle. Abby wins the draw, which is a $400 iPod. At first, she was excited then quickly felt guilty b/c she was a firm partner and felt that it would have been better if someone else won. However, she didn't want to offend anyone, so she kept the gift. One week later, somebody told her that partners are supposed to give the gifts back. Oh, if only somebody had told Abby ahead of time.
Phase 1 **Unaware - Incompetent** You make mistakes but you are not aware that you do	Example - For your international assignment, you relocate to Malaysia, which is heavily Islamic. For the annual holiday gift, without further consideration, you present your staff with a basket filled with fruit, pork sausage and wine.

Phases to master a competency
Adapted from Conscious competence model, Gordon Training International

The female factor

Beyond competencies, this would not be a book about women in senior-level expatriate roles if we did not mention additional characteristics women demonstrate more frequently than men. There has been quite a bit of discussion about whether or not women possess a greater share of some specific leadership qualities when compared to their male counterparts. One study, conducted by Caliper and Aurora in 2005, sheds light on this question. This study found that, in general, female leaders possess four characteristics that distinguish them from male leaders and serve to be very useful in an expatriate environment (Caliper 2005).

1. *Women leaders are more persuasive than their male colleagues*

In a different country with different cultural values and different ways of working, you will need to do a lot of persuading to achieve your goals. Women are often times stereotyped as having the "gift of gab." In a global position, this is an invaluable gift.

2. *When feeling the sting of rejection, women leaders learn from adversity and carry on with an "I'll show you" attitude*

When you arrive in a foreign country, you are compelled to face many differences, and people are not always welcoming. You are likely to face challenging situations, opposing opinions, and dismissive behavior. Women benefit greatly from the fact that they are resilient in the face of rejection. Indeed, WiSER Kamini found this to be true when she accepted a self-initiated assignment in India. "The company was going to close down," she told us. "Whatever I [did] would be my success or my failure, and I would be doing it alone. To go over there, set up the whole thing, that sounded really like what I wanted to do. I thought about it for a while... I flew back to Delhi, and the then director, in fact, said, 'You won't survive a day here.' I said, 'Why,' and he said, 'Because it's not glamorous. It's footwear.' I didn't know why, that statement really got me. I said I am going to prove to him, and I am going to prove to myself... that what he said was rubbish."

3. *Women leaders demonstrate an inclusive, team-building leadership style of problem solving and decision making*

When you move abroad, you will have to make sure that you have a team that you can build on. This is true for every leader and even more so abroad. You have to rely more on the local people around you to learn everything there is to know. Having a talent for binding people to you and including them, thus creating buy-in, has proven to be very helpful when working abroad.

Women expatriates tend to be better listeners than their male counterparts. They believe that focusing on listening skills and cooperating and emphasizing harmony will facilitate their interaction with local people as well as help develop better relationships with them (Tung 2005). WiSER Anne related the following: "After being in Egypt maybe a month, or two months,... I remember... a senior man walked into me and said 'you know Anne, we didn't know what it would be like having a woman as a boss, but we decided we liked it.' I think it was because, in my experience, women are just better communicators. We are different kind[s] of leaders and managers, and I think they warm to that; they like that. Again, the person I took over from... stayed on his own; he didn't communicate well; he kind of played a lot of political games. I was just more of a fair and open manager, and they liked that as soon as they figured that out."

4. *Women leaders are more likely to ignore rules and take risks*

As Ray Bradbury said: "Living at risk is jumping off a cliff and building wings on your way down." Women are known to take risks in order to fulfill a meaningful goal, achieve a purpose, or help others. When risks are taken for such purposes, they are easier to support and sustain. Women do not take risks simply to demonstrate their bravery; they do it with a strong sense of purpose.

Beyond the Caliper and Aurora study described above, which identifies four distinguishing female leadership characteristics, further research sheds light on leadership strengths that women demonstrate in the context of expatriate assignments.

5. *Handling stress*

Balancing needs in a relationship with the host country's nationals and headquarters is often a challenge in international assignments. Another source of stress is managing conflicts that arise from multicultural teams, and reconciling differences in goals and ways of working. Women expatriates appear to cope more effectively with these particular sources of stress than their male counterparts do (Tung 2005).

6. Building and maintaining relationships

In a situation that demands the cultivation of relationships, your gender could prove to be an advantage. "I would say not to change who you are," WiSER Magi said. "And I would say, as a woman, maybe try to use [that] as an advantage to getting some things done, because you can establish relationships faster than men can." "An expatriate needs to adapt to [the different] processes and structures in new environment. Adjustment happens as a result of communication behaviors...day-to-day interactions as well as the establishment of relationships"(Haslberger 2007, 4). In daily communication men and women are equally competent; however, women have been found to be significantly better in establishing and maintaining relationships. This can be explained by the fact that day-to-day interactions depend to a larger extent on external variables; whereas, adjustment to relationships depends largely on personal characteristics, such as empathy and social skills. Women's generally acknowledged superior social skills — such as relationship-building, building consensus, and being sensitive to non-verbal signs — help them to learn faster and to be more confident in their knowledge about how to establish and maintain relationships in the host culture. Moreover, these are characteristics that are valued in many other, especially non-Western, cultures, which gives female expatriates in these countries an advantage over their male colleagues (Haslberger 2007). "What I would do was really get into the workers' lives," WiSER Kamini explained. "I would talk to the women about the challenges and opportunities they faced and anything else they would like to discuss. I would then work on their issues…with the management."

7. Being accustomed to being a minority

Women expatriates are significantly better at coping with isolation. This could be explained by the fact that women, while climbing the career ladder, are accustomed to being part of a minority in leadership positions, and therefore, they are used to being excluded from existing networks. This ensures that they have prior experience performing well in situations and environments where they are regarded as outsiders (Tung 2005).

Being a minority also means that women are surrounded by men and, therefore, "they are used to operate in a system in which the preponderance of power is held by people unlike themselves — that is by men — with the result that many businesswomen have learned to attain their goals through influence, collaboration, and sensitivity to the point of view of others" (Hallowell and Grove 1997).

Look before you leap

To succeed in another country, possessing global leadership competencies and WiSER competencies is not enough. You will want to determine whether or not you have characteristics that predispose you to enjoy — and excel in — an international assignment. To help you get an initial idea if an international assignment is for you, we encourage you to visit our website to complete the "Look before you Leap" questionnaire. Here is advice that WiSER, who have already taken the leap, recommend you consider before accepting an expatriate assignment:

1. Think it through

WiSER Elsa L. cautions people considering an international assignment to think deeply about the implications of moving to a wholly new environment. "If you are coming from a small...community, and you suddenly find yourself in Sao Paolo, with 16 million people, you have to think about the fact that you are going [somewhere]...very different from what you've known," she said. Think it through from all angles, such as professional implications, family considerations and personal motivations.

2. It is not all glitter and glamor

The fact is, international assignments may involve settings many people would not consider especially inviting. As WiSER Elsa L. says: "Sometimes it can sound very glamorous.... People immediately think of Paris, London, Barcelona, Madrid — in other words they don't always think of [places] like Asuncion-Paraguay, or Mumbai or Ouagadougou-Burkina Faso." You may find yourself in a setting surrounded by high levels of poverty. "[Given the] nature of international development, or international NGOs, you are going to be working in not particularly glamorous places," said WiSER Diane, who worked for various NGOs in Asia. "You are going to work in countries — maybe — that are in conflict — or you are going to be working in places where there is extreme poverty." She added that workers assigned to international NGOs should be prepared to travel frequently, and often at a moment's notice. "So, the sort of person who is attracted to that, by personality, is unlikely to be someone who wants a clean break from the suburbs, or catches the same bus to work every day, and has gone through a very clear pathway after [she] finished school," WiSER Diane added.

In other cases, you may find that an international location, while not unpleasant, is very different from the place you left behind. "It was a very big contrast from the last twenty years working in Australia, [where] I was working for a media company, similar to the BBC," recalled WiSER Hanan, whose first expatriate assignment took her to Dubai. "My new position was with a start-up company, which meant that we actually worked in port-a-cabins for quite some time in the middle of the desert." She found herself coping with incredible heat, and a landscape featuring endless dunes, asking herself: "How could I go from a luxurious, upmarket... office environment with lovely restaurants and cafes...to the middle of the desert?" On top of everything else, she made a round-trip of 180 kilometers a day, when going to and from work. She decided she must love a challenge.

Adapting to a new environment requires tolerance, and perhaps even a sense of humor. WiSER Fiona, who worked in London, was charged with helping Canadian diplomats adapt to their new posts in the UK, and she became aware of qualities shared by those who excelled at their jobs — and those who failed. "A number of young Canadian diplomats...just couldn't adjust to living in London," she recalled. "And I'm just going: 'Get a grip people. This is London. It's civilized.'" She quietly wondered how these diplomats would adjust to an international venue that involved a different language and radically different values. "They had no tolerance for anything that wasn't from Canada," she said. "Their sense of humor became less and less...because they were getting frustrated — so they just couldn't just stop and laugh...at some of the things they saw." WiSER Fiona concluded that, if one wants to succeed on an international assignment, you need to "be curious and have a sense of humor."

3. *Find an assignment that is a good cultural fit for you and your family*

Studies indicate that companies are increasing the number of expatriate assignments to growth markets, such as China and Africa (Ernst & Young 2012). Such opportunities, however, can come with significant risks. While accepting a "hardship" assignment may propel your career forward, it could also be hard on your personal life. Therefore, it is essential to do your homework in order to truly understand the market and other relevant variables, including safety, living conditions, schools, proximity to daily activities, and so forth. Thoroughly researching a potential assignment location will prepare you for the challenges and in some cases dispel a negative impression that may be based on hearsay or stereotypes. Significantly, many nations in Africa—along with major expatriate hubs such as Dubai in the Middle East and Singapore in the East—tend to offer excellent expatriate experiences, but they may be perceived differently by those who haven't conducted proper research.

Another key is to know yourself and (if applicable) your family, which will enable you to find a suitable international opportunity (Smith 2006). If a venue doesn't seem to be a "good fit," don't hesitate to turn down an international assignment, advised WiSER Maria, who chose not to expatriate to Moscow. "I declined the offer to go to Moscow as life conditions are very tough, and my partner didn't see a fit for him, from a personal and professional point of view. Our look and see trip to Moscow did not go well,... Also, the role that was offered to me was a lateral move, so it did not pay off the hardship conditions we would endure in Moscow. An international assignment has a big impact on one's life and the family, and the assignment therefore has to be a true development opportunity or promotion."

4. *Find a female friendly employer*

If you are considering an employer who provides international opportunities, it is also important to determine whether they are female friendly. WiSER Nathalie K. noted that she works for just such an organization. "I've been very lucky in that sense, that throughout my career, I've had great line managers who always wanted to see me grow and develop—always open to listen, always looking for new opportunities," she said. "So the moment I said, 'Can I go to Spain?' they listened." She added that her managers not only offered encouragement, but also asked searching questions that led her to think deeply about her decisions. In her female-friendly firm, she encountered a corporate culture where managers encouraged employees to identify their goals and then helped them to achieve these goals.

5. Make sure it is your personal choice, not just a career move

Despite the obvious career advantages of accepting an international assignment, you want to make an authentic decision. "There are people who sometimes, may be forced to go, just because it's a box you have to check if you want to advance in a company," explained WiSER Magi. "'Did you work abroad—yes or no?' If you don't check [it], I guess you are not going to go forward." For WiSER Magi, however, the decision about whether or not to work and live overseas should ultimately be a personal choice. There is too much at stake and the impact on everybody involved is so big that we do not recommend anyone take on an international assignment if, deep down, it is not what you want. In chapter 6 we explain how important self-awareness is in making these important personal choices.

6. Make sure your family supports you

During our interview, WiSER Joanne stressed the importance of thinking through every aspect of a potential move, especially if you have a family that will come with you. "You need to think whether or not this is a good move for your family because it does change and impact everyone in the family," she said. "This isn't just about your position or your move." Without familial support, your chances of succeeding will be undermined. "If your family is absolutely against moving with you, don't." WiSER Martine said.

In the absence of children, make sure your partner is fully on board with a move, given that a partner's dissatisfaction could endanger an international assignment. "I have seen, a few cases, [where] people had to move back after about six months, because their spouse could not manage the change." said WiSER Martine, who also advised against pressuring a partner to move with you, for personal and professional reasons. If an assignment ends prematurely due to domestic disharmony, this will not only turn out to be a professional setback, but it may also harm the relationship.

7. Even if it has not been your lifelong plan, working abroad can be for you

Even if you have never seriously considered working abroad, you should examine the possibility—if it is an option that interests you at all. Remember: We rarely regret what we have tried, but we may well regret what we haven't tried. "Quite honestly, it never crossed my mind to do an international assignment," acknowledged WiSER Laura. She explained that she grew up in a traditional American family that had never traveled beyond the borders of the USA, with the exception of brief excursions into Canada. Even her choice of university reflected a strong attachment to the familiar. "I went to the University of Illinois because that was only two to three hours away and it was a safe choice," WiSER Laura explained. "I got a business degree and started to work at a local company because that's what you did." Although her company had international operations, she initially showed no interest in working abroad. "Then, within a year, I was in Vienna, and I spent the rest of my professional career overseas."

8. It is okay to have doubts

Despite their success in international roles, the WiSER revealed that they were occasionally plagued by doubts about their decision to accept an expatriate assignment. "I think that I was a bit surprised by them the first couple of times, because when you're passionate about something, you are only thinking of the great things," admitted WiSER Kelli. "When those doubts and fears kind of sneak up on you, just before you are [about] to jump off a cliff, it's a little bit shocking." She indicated that professional women on their first expatriate assignment shouldn't be surprised if they experience second thoughts, or even feelings of fear. "This doesn't mean that you should give into those doubts", she added. "You just have to work through those things and…have everything in place to take this next step."

These are what you might refer as the "preconditions" for embarking upon an international assignment.

It's a wrap!

Now you have the recipe for success. Combine pre-conditions with a handful of global leadership competencies, and a dash of WiSER competencies and you have the ingredients to be a successful female expatriate. Don't worry if you don't have all the ingredients, they can be developed. In addition to competencies, women possess a portfolio of characteristics that prove to be quite beneficial in the international arena. The foundational information and research in this chapter demonstrates that women do have what it takes to be successful leaders in senior-level expatriate roles. The WiSER we interviewed are amazing women who fulfill challenging roles across the globe. We cannot but admire their commitment, their professionalism, and their achievements. Let's have a closer look at the shared behavior of the WiSER.

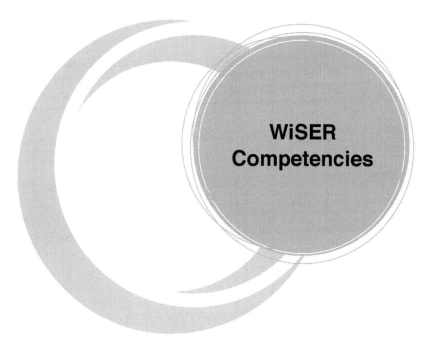

Section II

Bells and Whistles

"There are those who travel and those who are going somewhere. They are different and yet they are the same."
~ Mark Caine from The Breakthrough Institute

"International assignments exacerbate and dial up a lot of the tensions that exist in any working woman's life because you are out of your comfort zone."
~ WiSER Pauline

Whistles warn you of upcoming barriers that can prevent you from getting an expatriate assignment. Whereas, bells refer to the bell curve which illustrates complicating factors that only female leaders face in an international assignment. These factors can influence your success in such roles. Bells and whistles may bear some resemblance to one another but ultimately they serve to warn you of potential hazards that lie ahead. When you review all the bells and whistles, you get a comprehensive picture of the challenges faced by a female expatriate leader.

Warning whistles - Barriers to women moving abroad

In a comment that should encourage women seeking executive roles in a male-dominated business world, Ayn Rand famously stated, "The question isn't who's going to let me; it's who is going to stop me." In Rand's day, opportunities for women were extremely limited, and although women are currently well represented in middle-management positions, they hold a relatively small percentage of senior executive positions (Peters and Kabicoff 1998, 2010). While women attempt to break the "glass ceiling," which has limited their ability to move into top-level management positions, they are also faced with a phenomenon known as the "glass border", the tendency of many organizations to discount women as strong candidates for international assignments.

While this book offers a good deal of encouragement and advice, we would not be doing our job if we failed to mention the potential barriers that stand in the way of a meaningful international career. While it would be nice to believe that no such thing as a "glass border" exists, the fact remains that "men are promoted on potential, women on performance" (Catalyst 2000). Therefore, a greater number of men are likely to be considered for international assignments, even if they have not previously held one. On the other hand, when corporate managers consider women for an expatriate assignment, they routinely limit the pool to those candidates who have already performed well with an international client or global work team. It is worth noting that WiSER Julie Anne expressed her interest in an assignment seven full years before her employer actually offered one. This trend functions as a vicious circle for women, given that those without international experience are often overlooked for international assignments.

Stereotyping leads to many of the barriers women encounter. Although most of us have the best of intentions, our filters influence our thinking. To further compound this, the law of attraction demonstrates that "like attracts like". Therefore, we are inclined to hire people that are like ourselves. A frequently cited example of this is from the 1970s and 1980s, when orchestras in the US began to hold blind auditions to conceal the identity of the candidate from the selection committee. The presence of female musicians in the top five symphony orchestras in the US increased greatly with 50 percent of the increase attributed to the blind auditions (Goldin and Rouse 1997). In an environment where the majority of the talent decisions are still made by male managers, it is apparent that this will contribute to barriers women face to secure an expatriate position.

The WiSER have encountered various barriers, and they share strategies to overcome them. Prior to overcoming barriers, we must discern factual barriers from fictional barriers. This may seem easy at first. However, deciding whether something is true or false, can be tricky. Prior to tackling the heavy subject of which barriers truly contribute to the "glass border", let's get warmed up by doing a short quiz. Read each statement below and answer "true" or "false" (for answers see our website).

- You can recover data from a failing hard drive by placing it in the freezer for a few hours and then reinstalling it in the computer.
- "She just can't be chained to a life where nothing's gained and nothing's lost, at such a cost" was performed by the Rolling Stones.
- Too many visits to the tanning salon can damage your internal organs.
- In space, it is impossible to cry.
- 'Copyrightable' is the longest word in the English language that can be written without repeating a letter.
- An Ostrich's eye is bigger than its brain.
- Thomas Edison, who invented the light bulb, was afraid of the dark.
- There is an airport named after Pablo Picasso.
- Cardiovascular exercise burns more calories than strength training.

Now that you have practiced your quiz skills, let's consider which of the following barriers to women's pursuit of international assignments are true or false.

1. *True or false: Women must work harder and perform better than men.*

True: Women have to prove themselves more than men do to be noticed, to get credited for their achievements. WiSER Esther described how she approaches the problem of being compared to males. "It's always different when you are a woman," she said. "The challenge for you as a leader… is to demonstrate that it does not make a big difference." She added, "It's not that you are going to behave like a man. I have never behaved like a male leader, but at the same time, the challenge was to show that women are just as efficient as men in carrying out their task."

Data relative to both the glass ceiling and glass border demonstrate that in most countries of the world, women still face biases and prejudices that men do not have to face. This is a lesson WiSER Julie Anne learned early in her career. "In the first years of my career, I thought that, if I worked hard and was better than my peers…I would be successful and rewarded with additional responsibilities," she stated. "I learned over time that those traits are only the price of entry…but that it's not enough to achieve what you want." This lesson became more obvious as she rose to the level of middle management and found it increasingly challenging to move higher.

Even when women prove themselves, men get expatriated more often and earlier in their careers. When considering employees for an expatriate assignment, organizations will only consider women in senior management roles, whereas they don't hesitate to send junior male managers abroad. On top of that, the standards for those women in terms of education and technical qualifications are higher than for their male counterparts (Altman and Shortland 2008).

2. *True or false: Women are not interested in international assignments.*

False: Research dating as far back as the Eighties has shown that men and women are equally interested in international assignments, and that there was no difference between single and married people (Catalyst 2000). Indeed, 77 percent of the women we interviewed expressed a desire to live abroad and steered their career in that direction. While women from the US, for example, comprise only a modest percentage of expatriate roles, "they make up nearly 50 percent of the middle management pool from which employers choose most candidates for international assignments. Management assumed that men would be interested in expatriate assignments, [whereas] women had to ask management to be considered for an international job" (Tyler 2001).

Meanwhile, 26 percent of WiSER self-initiated their international careers in order to expedite their opportunity to work abroad. Research shows that women self-initiate expatriation approximately 30 percent more frequently than men (Vance, McNulty and Chauderlot 2011). This trend tells us that women are interested in international assignments and are willing to take considerable risks and "go it alone" in order to secure these assignments. Moreover, they are unwilling to wait for employers to recognize their interest. See appendix E for more information on self-initiated and company induced expatriation.

3. *True or false: Women don't want to go on international assignments because they think it is difficult to combine an expatriate job with a family.*

True: It is true that women believe this to be a barrier. With increasing global relocation, mobility issues are mainly attributed to family considerations, including dual careers. Reasons such as the partner having to give up his job, the loss of a second income and the financial consequences of discontinuity in pension, make dual career couples hesitant to relocate. Women tend to worry about how their partner and/or children will cope with the change, whether or not they will be happy and whether or not they will be able to combine their expatriate job with family obligations and expectations, Because of this, women think it is difficult to combine an expatriate job with raising a family. However, just because women believe this is a barrier doesn't mean that it actually has to be one. As WiSER Esther said, "The...difference is that women have to take into consideration their personal situation much more than men." She indicated that a healthy awareness of your family's wants and needs is the best way to ensure that your family will not become a barrier. Many WiSER recommended securing the family's approval for a move beforehand. The pressure of an international move can be further eased by taking steps to ensure the presence of a supportive network, academically strong schools for your children, and (if possible) a job for your partner. Many WiSER, however, downplay potential problems and actively promote the benefits a family is likely to derive from an overseas assignment. "It's just been so invaluable for me as a professional in the business world, and invaluable for my kids and how they view the world and how they tackle problems," said WiSER Elsa I. Similarly, WiSER Lori indicated that her family thrived during her first expatriate assignment in Hong Kong: "My children went to an International School, they loved it. Certainly for my daughter who was in middle school at the time, it really shaped her outlook on life…. It was a great assignment."

4. *True or false: There is a lack of organizational support for women.*

True: At this point, human resources management policies do not fit the needs of women expatriates, given that they are designed primarily for men. Organizational support in terms of career counseling and career planning are less tailored to women. Most career pathing models are linear, resulting in sourcing candidates around their early 30's for management as well as international opportunities. Coincidentally, this is when many women are taking time off for family reasons. Consequently, many women lack the kind of organizational support they need to push their careers forward (Shortland and Altman 2011). A viable solution is to simply seek talent at various intervals and various levels in the organization. The WiSER recommend overcoming this barrier by calling attention to your unique needs and taking into consideration the demands involved in the role.

5. *True or false: Women lack senior-level female role models.*

True: Few women hold senior-level roles, and even fewer hold senior-level international roles. Although it may be challenging to identify female role models, it is nevertheless important, because these role models can ease your doubts about accepting an international assignment. Indeed, role models can actually inspire you. They are living proof that women can meet the challenges involved in an international assignment. They can also provide much-needed support in difficult times. In addition, role models can smooth your path to a successful overseas career. WiSER Julie Anne experienced this during her first international assignment in Peru. "They happened to have had the only female general manager in Latin America [who] was running the Peru operation," she recalled and noted that the woman's success in this role significantly increased her own chances of securing a leadership position. In the absence of role models, we recommend that you seek a role model through a professional network. In addition, you can look for role models on the boards of (non-profit) organizations in which you have an interest, or even among the WiSER. Remember that we are "Linked In" to many WiSER, so, please, join our network at LeverageHR.com.

6. *True or false: Women lack professional networks within their organizations.*

True: While women have always been recognized as natural relationship builders, their networks in professional arenas are generally not as strong as those maintained by men. There are many reasons for this phenomenon, but we will focus on just a couple of them. First of all, women often have more after-work responsibilities, and these tend to limit their opportunities to network beyond the office. Secondly, many professions still harbor "old-boy networks," which systematically exclude women. Whatever the reasons for this scenario, it is important to remember that professional networks are invaluable, given that they serve as informal channels that enable you to learn what is going on in an organization. You become aware of opportunities, including the availability of international opportunities.

7. True or False: Women fail more often than men on international assignments.

False: Research has shown that there is no significant difference in the rate of success between male and female expatriates, even when the country of assignment is taken into consideration. While women in leadership positions encounter barriers in their host country, they also are forced to overcome barriers in their home countries. Nevertheless, they managed to succeed (Tung 2005). The WiSER have demonstrated that women are just as qualified as men in various roles across the world.

8. True or false: Women create their own barriers.

True: Some common barriers that women create are: 1) being less professionally assertive, 2) not asking for what they need, 3) not supporting the broad professional choices of other women, and 4) not promoting their achievements.

Women are known to be less professionally assertive. The fact is, if you want something, you have to ask for it. Learn to speak up, and make your aspirations known. Don't be too modest about your achievements, or about your potential. "I've heard many women beating themselves down, although they are doing a great…job managing both professional and personal lives," said WiSER Marieke. She noted that many professional women set unrealistically high standards, which can lead them to underestimate their own levels of competence.

Given that women tend to be more modest in their assessment of their professional worth, they are more likely to assume that an organization will not accommodate them when they request additional support to make an international assignment work. This is a challenge that WiSER Pauline addressed directly. She indicated that the best advice she ever received was to ask for help when she needed it. "Just ask for whatever it is you want," she said. "I think sometimes we put [up] our own barriers. Right now, I've asked to stay in Brussels at least until my older son is through school, and they've said, 'yes,' which is great."

It is also true that women frequently fail to support the professional choices of other women, thus sabotaging the professional development of women, in general. It seems likely that many of you have been involved in a conversation where women judge the professional career choices made by other woman. Perhaps your choices have been judged, at one time or another. This kind of "sniping" can reinforce negative perceptions of women that tend to be prevalent in male-dominated organizations—and it can sharply reduce the chances of women being selected for coveted international assignments.

In addition, as WiSER Maxine notes, women don't call enough attention to their own achievements. While it would be nice to think that your accomplishments would be recognized by your superiors without you having to call attention to them, this is not the way it works. "You have to do a great job, look at yourself, and ask to be rewarded," she explained.

9. *True or false: Women won't be accepted in the host country.*

False: This is an excuse that is typically used by male managers, although it has little basis in fact. The truth is, even women assigned to traditionally patriarchal regions have managed to succeed. "What I will say is I am currently working in the Middle East, and I have never worked out here before," WiSER Annette observed. "I was a little bit concerned about it, and I have to say it's the most refreshing place to work." She indicated that people with whom she worked were pleasant and cooperative. In the face of longstanding, and mostly negative, perceptions of the Middle East, she found that many men in the region were surprisingly receptive to female expatriates. Overall, gender does not have a significant bearing on how expatriates perform in their jobs, and the idea that host-country males will not accept women is patently false.

Interestingly, many WiSER indicated that nationality was more frequently an issue of contention than gender was. "I don't think that being a woman was a disadvantage," said WiSER Elsa I., who worked in Latin America. "I think in fairness, [the] bigger disadvantage was the American thing."

Based on research by Adler, one of the first researchers in the field of expatriate women, "women more often experience greater difficulty commanding respect from their home country peers than from colleagues abroad, even where the cultural differences between home and host country were large" (Shortland & Altman 2011). While a host culture may regard women as naturally subordinate, local males do not necessarily put foreign women in the same category as local women. First of all, they see the expatriate woman as a senior-level professional who is deserving of respect. Secondly, they see her as a representative of her culture and/ or nation. It is only then that they regard her as a woman. In many cases, they simply don't know how to classify a foreign woman who holds a position of authority. "Women expats weren't put in the same category as their own wives, their daughters, or sisters or whatever," said WiSER Anne, who lived and worked in Somalia. "We were kind of [in] a separate category." This perception was shared by WiSER Alexis, who lived and worked in Central Europe. "I am a great novelty in Prague because I'm the CEO, I'm a woman, and I'm an Australian—and maybe because I'm a foreigner they let me get away with more than they would if I was a local," she said.

The unique position that female expatriates enjoy in a host country can even work to their advantage, as WiSER Carrie discovered during an assignment in South Korea. "There are so few Korean women holding those...roles...that....they didn't really know what to expect," she said. "If I had been a Korean man, there [would have been] tons of rules, societal rules that they would know they have to follow.... But because I was a foreigner, and because I was a woman, I just told them, 'Well, the good thing is that there are no rules, and we'll just make them up as we go.'"

This does not suggest that women working overseas are unlikely to encounter difficulties and restrictions, however. Different cultural codes may require women to modify their behavior, or to find different ways of working. For instance, WiSER Hanan was invited to lunch by her manager in Dubai, and was surprised when she entered the staff canteen. "For me, it was the first time that I saw a canteen where there was a female area only," she recalled. "So, we sat in the area that was just for females and, then, there was an area for mixed or for men, but mainly the females sat alone." Hanan realized that impromptu meetings over a cup of coffee with her manager would be difficult, and that she had to find other ways to interact with him. The key to success is to try and prevent situations that are likely to make your gender an issue.

10. True or false: Women are not suitable because of safety issues.

False: Any expatriate, a man or a woman, should be aware of safety issues. Granted, women may incur an increased risk of sexual harassment, but that does not mean they cannot handle these kinds of situations. If you learn about the behavior codes of the host country before you go, and you are proactive in making your limits clear in such a way that your male counterparts are not embarrassed, you are likely to be successful and avoid problems (Reed and Cook 2008).

Assuming you have overcome barriers to secure an expatriate assignment, your next consideration may involve identifying complicating factors you may face in your expatriate role.

The bell curve - It is different for female expatriate leaders

Do you know who was the first to reach the summit of Mount Everest? If you answered Edmund Hillary, you are partially correct. The first ascent was actually completed in 1953 by both Edmund Hillary and Tenzing Norgay. Edmund Hillary is commonly recognized whereas Tenzing Norgay is obscure. "Who was he", you may ask? He was the Sherpa who accompanied Hillary. Sherpas have been recognized for their strength and climbing capabilities since the time European mountaineers first arrived and employed their services as guides and porters (Handwerk 2002). Norgay carried the climbing supplies, served as the navigator, set up camps, and had the natural ability of the Sherpa people. Hillary was unfamiliar with this terrain, had formally prepared by climbing various mountains in different countries around the world, and had to rely on the guidance of another. We can assume that either of these men would describe their climb to the top as extremely difficult and rewarding. This story highlights two people who accomplished the same feat while facing different challenges. In other words they are the same yet different.

Why it is different

The fact that we've discovered the presence of four competencies among a large number of WiSER does not suggest that expatriate male leaders or domestic female leaders would fail to possess or demonstrate them. These competencies are important to them as well. However, the WiSER global leadership competencies are different for female expatriates. Let us explain why this is the case.

Among the women we interviewed, we discerned tremendous differences, but also found some striking similarities. You might ask, "How can you compare these women from such different cultures and backgrounds to each other, let alone compare them to female domestic leaders, or their male expatriate counterparts?" The data we consolidated demonstrates that there is indeed a variance among WiSER – in other words, they are spread across a bell curve relative to each competency. The bell curve for WiSER competencies is simply different than the bell curve for domestic female leaders or the bell curve for expatriate male leaders. Let us illustrate our point by asking you a simple question. "Do you work hard?" Your answer may be "yes" or "no" – it is not all that important. The real question is, "How do you know?" You probably know because you've compared yourself to other people: colleagues, friends and acquaintances. However, each culture has its own criteria for what constitutes "hard work." In Germany, for instance working 50 hours a week is considered working hard; whereas in Japan the standards increase considerably and you have to work 80 hours a week to be considered a hard worker. In fact, there is even a Japanese term, "karoshi", that roughly translates to "work yourself to death".

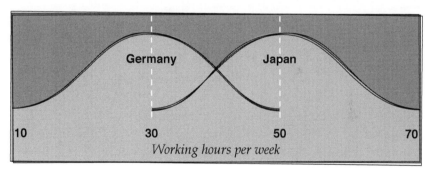

Bell curve average working hours per week for Germany and Japan
(Note: the hours used are not based on statistical data)

The workers in Germany are scattered across one bell curve whereas the Japanese are scattered across a separate, parallel bell curve. Although both bell curves plot the answer to the "do you work hard?" question, it would be statistically inaccurate to plot them all on a single bell curve. In the same way, when comparing WiSER competencies, we have essentially separate, parallel bell curves, or norms when comparing expatriate women to expatriate men and domestic women.

Expatriate female leader vs expatriate male leader

As mentioned before, expatriate leaders, whether they be male or female, need to master global leadership competencies in addition to their domestic leadership skills. We have uncovered that WiSER share an additional four competencies that helped them excel in their expatriate assignment. You may wonder if their male counterparts do not possess or need to demonstrate these competencies. In German the answer would be 'jein' (a combination of yes and no). Yes, male expatriates do need to actively manage their career and they do need to be self-aware. They will face balancing and rebalancing their priorities and they also will need to be able to operate outside of their comfort zone. However, for men the circumstances are simply different than for women. Female expatriates are still pioneering in these roles whereas male expatriates are the "standard". For this reason, the four WiSER competencies lay on a different bell curve for female expatriates than they do for male expatriates.

Expatriate female leader vs domestic female leader

Domestic female leaders face the glass ceiling in their efforts to move up, the "unseen, yet unbreachable barrier that keeps ... women from rising to the upper rungs of the corporate ladder, regardless of their qualifications or achievements" (Federal Glass Ceiling Commission 1995, 4). In their efforts to move "out", female expatriate leaders face an additional barrier, the "glass border", that prevents women from securing expatriate assignments. Because an expatriate environment exacerbates domestic challenges tenfold, global female leaders face special challenges that magnify the importance of the four WiSER competencies.

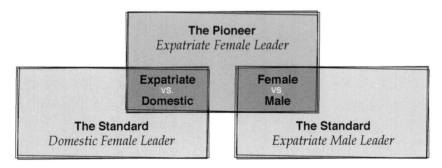

The bells and whistles

How it is different

History serves as a starting point for the future. Let's start at the beginning. Mahatma Ghandi tells us, "A man is but the product of his thoughts; what he thinks, he becomes." We can assume that the great spiritual and political leader was talking about human beings, in general — and his point is well taken. Without doubt, our perspective plays a major role in determining our place in the world; and therefore, it's important to know ourselves and to understand what we think we should become. In the business world, volumes have been published on the subject of creative visualization — a term that refers to a process of envisioning what you want, where you want to be, who you want to be, what you want to do, and how you want to be remembered. The process begins with visualization and ends with action. Based on the historical role of women, more men than women visualize themselves in executive and expatriate roles.

Times are changing and as a result, women are able to visualize more opportunities than ever before. This wasn't always true. Just a few decades ago, women — even those living in developed nations — were expected to be at home, taking care of the family. Regardless of expectations, there have been women who visualized something different for themselves, throughout history. Think for example of Elizabeth Blackwell, the first female doctor in the US (1849), and Blanche Stuart Scott, the first woman to pilot an airplane (1910). Imagine what the world would look like if they hadn't taken steps to make their vision a reality. Today, we are convinced that greater than 17-20 percent of professional women (the percentage of current female expatriates) are interested in expatriate roles. Imagine what the world would look like if they all took action to make their vision of an international career a reality.

As a woman, it is your responsibility to know yourself, visualize what you want to do and who you want to be, and to do it! WiSER Joanne offered these simple words of encouragement: "Nothing is impossible, ...you need to reach for what your dreams are."

We encourage you to take a moment, no more than five minutes, to practice creative visualization.

The bucket list
1. Create a bucket list filled with things you may be good at, enjoy doing, are just interested in or have dreamed about. These can be things you have already done or still aspire to do.
2. Cross out everything you have already done.
3. Circle everything you like to do but don't love to do.
4. Put a square around everything you really want to do. That is your bucket list.
5. Now that you have a bucket list (the squares), prioritize the list to actually do some of the things on this list that give you energy.
6. Take action to realize your plans.

Following is a list of reasons why the bell curve is different for female expatriate leaders. Bear in mind that some of these reasons are more or less relevant depending on the host country.

1. *Where society sees women*

We want you to picture the following situation. You have just been introduced to your new boss. It is a very demanding position that requires more than sixty hours of work per week and plenty of travel. You want to learn more about your boss. What bits of information would you like to know? Are you inclined to learn more about your boss's qualifications and credentials? Or, do you want to know more about how your boss manages work with personal life? Is the answer different depending on whether your boss is a man or a woman? Based on an example that is currently being played out in the media, it would appear that gender makes a big difference in the answer many people would give. In the well-publicized case of Marissa Mayer, CEO of Yahoo, scores of people questioned why she would accept such a high-level position at a time when she's expecting a baby, and many other questioned whether she would be able to balance her professional and personal responsibilities. This example reflects the ways in which societal expectations differ for senior-level men and women. When is the last time that you heard of a male executive being promoted to the C-suite with a pursuant media outcry because he and his wife were expecting a baby?

Traditional societal expectations, which vary across nations and cultures, enhance the challenges expatriate women face. Although progress has been made, the traditional view regarding a man's and a woman's role in the family and at work remains deeply entrenched: men work, and women take care of the home and the children. Statistics show, that more men work full-time in the traditional model than women do. Although these statistics vary by nation, "women are nearly twice as likely as men to work part time. In 2010, 26.6 percent of women worked part time compared to just 13.4 percent of men" (DOL 2011, 1). Both women and men have a range of career choices, which may include working full-time or part-time, consulting, or staying at home. Nevertheless, we do not see an abundance of either female executives or stay-at-home dads.

In most cultures, it is generally accepted that women with children can work. However, people don't know how to react when a woman is the primary breadwinner of a family, while her husband is the stay-at-home dad. Luckily, WiSER are changing societal expectations, one step at a time. WiSER Alicia described the ways in which such social and cultural expectations affected the dynamic of her and her husband's roles within her own family. "My husband... was expected to be the breadwinner of the family," she said. "[For the] wife, it was okay to have a job, but not a high career job. So, it was a lot of social pressure to be just the opposite of that situation...both from his parents and from my parents... So, not only did we have that...[within] ourselves...but it was our families' social, cultural expectations that we had to shift also." WiSER Sezin, shared with us the traditional expectations concerning women in her country. "I'm from the modern Turkey," she said. "But still, traditionally, we do expect...women to do so much more in a household.... My mom was always angry with me that I wouldn't be cooking for my daughter the type of food that she would be cooking me....that I would prefer to have somebody else make it for her."

Significantly, criticisms that you don't fit into the traditional role model of a stay-at-home mother may not emanate entirely from the local community. You may also face criticism from members of the expatriate community. In most cases, the expatriate community is dominated by female trailing spouses. The majority of them are educated women, and many have had professional lives. In the same way that former smokers are harsher on smokers than people who have never smoked in their lives, women who have "sacrificed" their own careers to become trailing spouses will be more likely to judge you negatively if they think you've placed your career "first." They may envy you because you have a fulfilling job, and they may judge you for not spending more time with your family. You will feel as though you have to justify your choices time and time again.

Societal expectations get even trickier when expatriating. In addition to meeting domestic societal expectations, expatriate female leaders face societal expectations of the host country and the expatriate community. If you enter your assignment with your eyes wide open, you're more likely to be comfortable with your decision. Think of yourself as the modern-day Marie Curie or Kiran Bedi, someone who is overturning stereotypes as you move forward in your career. Don't get defensive, and keep in mind that we all make our own choices in life — and that those choices are personal. We don't need to justify them to anybody but ourselves. Over time, you are bound to come across many like-minded individuals.

2. *Everything and then some*

Gender diversity in the realm of top management is limited due to two primary reasons. The first is what is called the "double-burden" syndrome, where women are responsible for work and the majority of the home responsibilities. The second barrier is the "anytime, anywhere" performance model, which calls for top managers to make themselves available with great agility (McKinsey 2010, 6). The interrelationship between these two barriers - "double burden" syndrome meets "anytime, anywhere" performance - is obvious. To further compound this intensity, "employees on international assignments report working an average of 13.4 more hours per week compared to the number of hours they work at the home location (Smith, 2007)."

How do you manage household responsibilities, and work responsibilities which include going anywhere that the organization needs you to go at the drop off a hat? WiSER such as Lillian and Lori indicated that extensive planning was the linchpin that held their lives together, although it involved many sacrifices. Their whole life was built around the family calendar, in which responsibilities were alternated to ensure that there was always one parent in the country with the children. A woman's role in the family (regardless of whether or not they work) is different from a man's role. Studies show that dual-career couples have an unequal distribution of household responsibilities, with more responsibilities being managed by the woman. McKinsey (2007) has found that European women for example, devote twice as much time to household activities than men.

If we compare expatriate men and expatriate women with familial obligations, we find that the expatriate woman takes more initial (and ongoing) responsibility to ensure that the family is settled, happy, and cared for. Therefore, female expatriate leaders are making a professional transition, even as they remain deeply involved in managing the personal transition involved in an international assignment. These differing expectations create a different type of "workload" for women, which is magnified in the expatriate setting.

3. *So many choices, so little time*

Women in general, much more than men, have to make choices in life that have an impact on their professional career, such as:

- decisions about the importance of a career relative to other areas of life;
- whether or when to marry;
- whether or not to have children;
- arrangements for managing housework and childcare;
- managing relationships with partners, relatives and friends;
- managing competing demands from various life roles.

"This research, however, has identified that for female expatriate managers, lifestyle choices are even more difficult than they are for domestic female managers" (Linehan and Scullion 2001, 395).

Not all of the available options offer everything we might be looking for. For instance, working as an executive often brings professional fulfillment, prestige, a healthy salary, and unfortunately, long hours. Working as a stay-at-home parent brings personal fulfillment, quality (or at least quantity) time with family, time to pursue passions, and unfortunately tedious daily recurring household chores. Compromises will have to be made, of course. Therefore, the more choices and compromises we have to make, the more self-aware we need to be. "It helps to know what you want, know what's important for you personally," advised WiSER

Pauline. "The point of choices and decisiveness, I think, is an important one in general. It's a little bit more important for women because we are forced to make more choices than men."

4. *The male trailing spouse*

Women professionals often have a partner who also has a professional career. This makes it more likely that the partner will have to modify his career when the woman is leading in an expatriate assignment. Even though many women of male expatriates do have a professional career before moving, it is more common and socially accepted that a woman will quit her job to follow her partner than the other way around. When the male partner is not able to find a job, or when he is not allowed to work in the host country, this may create tension. It can undermine his sense of self-esteem and self-confidence, and this could place a strain on the relationship. Often there is no network for male trailing spouses, which compounds these pressures. Therefore, it is safe to assume that it will be more challenging for male trailing spouses to plug into a social network and find contentment during an international assignment. WiSER Lori acknowledged that her husband faced this challenge when they relocated for her international assignment. He gave up his position so that they could move and, then, faced boredom in their new home. As she observed, "If you do not have a partner who is equally committed to your career as you are, I don't know how it will work."

The obvious solution would be for organizations to create more dual-career possibilities, so that both partners can pursue their careers. Unfortunately, there are few organizations that offer dual-career solutions for the partner of an expatriate. Organizations are more and more aware of the necessity to set up dual-career policies to encourage employees to take up international assignments. However, regulatory environments pose various stipulations on allowing foreign nationals to work within any given country. So, remedying dual career issues is not simple. Some organizations have started to offer trailing spouse benefits, such as stipends, language classes and education reimbursement. Perhaps, if more women pursued international assignments, organizations would consider these options more often. Visit our website for additional ideas to help smooth the transition for male trailing spouses.

5. *Building new networks in host country*

In an expatriate environment, most women are trailing spouses, and they frequently end up not working. Consequently, the greater part of social life and networking happens during the day — coffee mornings and working out together, for example. Evenings are usually left for family, which places limits on enjoyable social events. As per WiSER Alexis: "…there are certainly not many working expat women, and you can feel very lonely and you have to be very aware of that, and I think be strong enough to push through that."

An important aspect of doing business is joining and leveraging professional networks that will benefit your assignment and help you achieve your goals. How often have you called someone from your network for help, for another contact, or for advice? As a female expatriate, joining professional networks in a foreign country can be difficult, if not impossible. First of all, there is the language barrier. Secondly, many networks remain dominated by male executives, the "old boys' network (PriceWaterhouseCoopers 2007). As per WiSER Alexis, "At the start, particularly, you lose that network of working women that you've stored up over many, many years." She shared that "in a foreign country it takes a long while to build up [your network] because you don't have the school or university friends that you had before. I found the loss of the woman's network the biggest thing to handle at the start." As she warns, often going to places like pubs with male colleagues in certain foreign countries can be misconstrued as something more than it is. Expatriate men can more readily build their professional network among other male expatriate colleagues and "old boys" networks.

6. *Living in a fishbowl*

As one of the few (or maybe even the first) expatriate women in an executive position in your host country, your actions will be closely monitored by many people. This is not necessarily because you are a foreigner, but it is more likely because you are a female foreigner. That is why there are different bell curves in this respect. WiSER Elsa L. noted that she was the first female head of her organization in Paraguay, and therefore, she experienced what it was like to a successful woman in a machismo society. "[It] was like big news," she recalled. "I mean the newspapers came out…to interview me…because people were surprised." She added that, to some extent, she became a victim of her own celebrity. "There was nowhere that I could go that I was not—I mean even the supermarket—that I was not the director general of the [organization]." She stressed that there was a real need for caution and prudence, given that people were observing her every move. "You have to be a little careful of what you say and the opinions you give, because then you find yourself being quoted, sometimes misquoted," she said. The good news is, having such a high visibility also puts you in a position where you can be very influential and achieve many great things.

7. *Leading by example*

As we said, you are likely to stand out—not only in the host country, but also in your organization. Hopefully, many people will want to see you succeed, but some may wish to see you fail as well. That puts a high degree of pressure on you. You are an example: a role model for other women within the organization, in the country, and perhaps even in the world. If you make a mistake—or worse yet, if you fail—the consequences of your misstep will move beyond the organizational effect. When she was in Peru, WiSER Julie Anne had a female colleague who left the country after having been there for only three days. "It was the worst thing ever," she remembered, "It's such an insult to the country...If you are lucky enough to get one of these assignments, you better stick it out, because you ruin it for other women if you're not able to stick it out".

Self-awareness is an essential competency if you are to serve as a role model. Notably, being a role model involves being confident of your own qualities and merits and dispensing with the notion that you might be the "token" female. The fact is, you will have to repeatedly demonstrate that you are the "right" person for the job. WiSER Joanne, who was the first female on the leadership team in her organization, was asked once if she thought she had been chosen to join the team simply because they needed a token female. "You have to deal with that, and the question [that] you may have to ask yourself is, to what degree...some of that is true or not true," she said. "But you can't let that hinder your decision or conversation. You [have] to believe...that the reason...you are there is because of what you have been able to demonstrate and show. No one is going to invest money to take you on an expatriate [assignment] and... put you in such a visible position...on the whim of 'we need a female.'"

Although there is great pressure involved in being a role model, not many of us have such an opportunity. Remember what Clare Booth Luce said, the first American woman appointed to a major ambassadorial post abroad: "If I fail, no one will say, 'She doesn't have what it takes.' They will say, 'Women don't have what it takes.'"

It's a wrap!

Prevalent bells and whistles serve as a caution sign not a stop sign. Women interested in international jobs may face barriers, which in many cases can be overcome. Furthermore, female leaders may face complicating factors when on an expatriate assignment. They simply sit on a different bell curve than either male expatriate leaders or domestic female leaders. Although there are bells and whistles, it is doable and worth it. As WiSER Jolanda says, "It's a very big stimulant to actually travel the world and…actually live in different cultures and different environments, and it shapes you in different ways." As more women enter the expatriate scene, the barriers and the bell curve will change and perhaps even cease to exist.

Self-awareness

"As you become clearer about who you really are, you'll be better able to decide what is best for you - the first time around."
~ Oprah Winfrey

"I remember how naive I was and yet how clearly I saw my future that last year of high school. I see my [younger] self with dangling legs, sitting on a school bench and saying, I don't know what I want to be, but I want to do something that has to do with international culture and administration - which is exactly what I ended up doing."
~ WiSER Britta

"Mirror, mirror on the wall, who's the fairest of them all?" Ah-h-h, this is a classic example of self-awareness — or is it? Sometimes, our sense of who we are isn't necessarily shared by those around us. It's also worth mentioning that humans may not be the only self-aware creatures on earth. Evidence exists, for instance, that bottle-nose dolphins, elephants, and certain apes have the capacity to be self-aware. So, perhaps humans are not as special as we thought, in this respect. However, the question is, are you self-aware? Do you see yourself as others see you? What does it mean to be self-aware? Why is it important?

As someone who grew up in the "flatlands" of Ohio in the USA, I (Sapna) had never skied before. Therefore, after moving to Germany, my family and I couldn't resist at least trying the sport. So, we went on a ski trip in Switzerland, and we had an incredibly good time — although I must admit that I'm still not much of a skier. A few months later, we went camping with some friends, which proved to be yet another "first" for me. Our friends indicated they had no affinity for skiing, which they had tried recently, but they evidently enjoyed camping. After an evening spent in a cold tent, however, I returned home with the strong feeling that I would choose skiing over camping any day of the week. Simply put, there are different strokes for different folks. If I had understood myself better, I might have opted out of the camping trip in advance. I like sleeping in soft beds and staying away from insects—not roughing it and, then, as it happened, packing up a lot of equipment shortly before a heavy rain. Besides, I find it much easier to learn a new skill from a professional, like the ski instructor on our ski trip. When I considered going on the camping trip, I should have acknowledged what I've learned about myself—my strengths and interests—and avoided putting myself in an uncomfortable position.

When starting our research, we estimated that one of the competencies WiSER would most likely possess would be self-awareness—and we were right: 82 percent of the WiSER demonstrated self-awareness. For the purposes of our study, we defined the competency "Self-awareness" as follows:

Self-awareness
Knowing your strengths and weaknesses, likes and dislikes—which are all based on your values—and using this knowledge to make critical decisions.
1. You have a strong understanding of your values, personal strengths, weaknesses, opportunities, and limits.
2. You know in which situations you will thrive and in which you will feel stressed.
3. You trust yourself and follow your intuition.
4. You know how you differ from others and accept these differences.
5. You know how you are perceived by others.
6. You spend your time and the time of others on what is important and quickly zero in on the critical few and put the trivial many aside.
7. You demonstrate the ability to strengthen your own weaknesses through training and development

Our research has shown that the presence of self-awareness was highest among women working in not-for-profit organizations (100 percent), followed by women working in governmental organizations (88 percent), and women in for-profit organizations (83 percent). Also, those women who had self-initiated their expatriation showed more self-awareness than women who were sent abroad by their organization, at 94 percent and 77 percent, respectively. This could be explained by the fact that, when you self-initiate your move abroad, you have already considered all the decisions that must be made regarding the country, the new job, and various aspects involving the move. Therefore, you are more fully aware, in general. In our study, we found that those WiSER who demonstrated a high degree of self-awareness took their careers into their own hands through active career management more often than the WiSER who did not show a high level of self-awareness, at 69 percent and 55 percent, respectively. All of this points to the fact that you are better able to steer your career when you know what you want—and also, what you don't want.

Self-awareness is important, from the smallest decisions to the ones that really matter. In a global role, the complexities involved demand an even greater sense of self-awareness. Usually, when talking about being effective in global roles, we tend to focus on "external" aspects. In other words, we ask ourselves questions like the following: How do you deal with challenges? How do you rally a team to achieve a goal? How do you lead? Before you are able to consider the answer to such questions, you need to know and understand yourself. What are your personal strengths and weaknesses? What are your tolerances? What are your limits? Which situations will make you thrive, and which will give you stress? Do you know how you differ from others, and do you accept these differences? Do you know the effect of these differences when you operate in a different cultural environment? Do you know yourself well enough to trust your instincts?

If you want to be effective in your international assignment, you need to know the answers to the above questions, and many others. For only by truly knowing yourself are you able to make critical decisions well, to adapt your behavior appropriately—or to adapt to changes without losing yourself.

The international gold standard

Before everything else, know your values. In order to truly know yourself, you have to go deep. You have to ask yourself, "What are my values?" In many ways, your values are the essence of who you are as a person. They are your beliefs, your mission, or your philosophy. Whether or not we are consciously aware of our values, every individual has a core set of personal values. Values can range from the commonplace, e.g., the belief in hard work and punctuality, to the more abstract, e.g., a belief in self-reliance, concern for others, and harmony of purpose. When we examine the lives of famous people, we often see how personal values guided them, propelling them to the top of their fields. Individuals that may come to mind include notable figures like Nelson Mandela, Mahatma Ghandi, or Mother Theresa. Other examples include Rosa Parks and Helen Keller, who changed the world by having the confidence to follow their beliefs. It is also possible, however to find such individuals in the course of our daily lives — and the WiSER certainly fit into this category.

Values differ from person to person, and household to household, and many of them are shaped in our formative years. The WiSER shared childhood memories that had a profound impact on the rest of their lives. Values are nurtured based on familial experience. WiSER Julie's parents were immigrants to Canada and her life was filled with moving around for her father's job, a working mother and memories of "growing up in a blueberry farm which was wonderful for we had animals, we had a pony and goats and pigs and chickens and 6 acres of blue berries." She shared that the main principles in her childhood home were "respect for one another, love for one another, looking out for each other, respecting our elders. We weren't a particularly strict household but there was discipline in it, that just provided the kind of structure and kind of kept us on the straight and narrow, but it was a pretty great place to grow up, a great family." When we take stock of our values, take them to heart and weave them into our daily lives, great success will be ours.

We tend to abide by our core values, which serve as a compass in an ever-changing world. Our values are numerous and far-reaching. That said, core values are not always clearly reflected in our choice of work, but they are surely evident in the way we go about our work. They are (or should be) reflected in the practices that we employ every day when engaged in a broad range of activities. They are particularly reflected in leadership, which offers an extraordinary opportunity to affect other people. What we call "values-based leadership" tends to affect people on a much higher level. A values-driven leader's actions will inspire employees through example, motivating them to do positive things, and to focus on what truly matters.

Core Values list		
Achievement	Privacy	Excellence
Leadership	Decisiveness	Self-Respect
Advancement/Promotion	Public Service	Excitement
Loyalty	Democracy	Serenity
Adventure	Persistence	Physical Challenge
Market Position	Self-Motivation	Competition
Challenging Problems	Knowledge	Financial Gain
Meaningful Work	Humour	Personal Development
Change and Variety	Economic Security	Competence
Money	Quality Relationships	Independence
Clear Communication	Effectiveness	Status
Nature	Recognition	Freedom
Close Relationships	Ethical Practice	Supervising Others
Open and Honest	Wisdom	Friendships
Cooperation	Work Under Pressure	Teamwork
Order	Integrity	Growth
Community	Work with Others	Time Freedom
Influencing Others	Involvement	Helping Society
Pleasure	Working Alone	Truth
Creativity	Expertise	Honesty
Power and Authority	Stability	Wealth
Customer Service	Security	

WiSER Sandra revealed that she encountered one of her darkest milestones in her career, when developments in one organization where she worked at the time spurred many questions about the business's future and growth/profit model. "At the end of the day, I think the thing I learned is, if I don't have alignment with the people's values and what the business is trying to accomplish and why it's trying to accomplish it, it's not a great place for me to be," she said. So, once again, it all comes down to self-awareness.

Although our values are so integral to who we are, it is not always easy to point them out and to consider them objectively. Following is a simple, yet practical approach to consider your own values.

Values exercise

1. Review the Core Values List, add other values if you want, and keep in mind the following:
   - What are your favorite values?
   - At the end of your life, how do you want to be thought of?
2. Place a star or check next to the words that resonate with you or the ones you connect with.
3. Narrow the list to ten values.
4. Narrow the list to three. These are your Top 3 Values
5. Prioritize them.
   If you don't prioritize among these 3 values, they can conflict with each other. Let's say that two values on your list are financial independence and honesty. What if someone offers you an opportunity to earn a lot of money in a relatively short period of time? The only hitch…it may be slightly illegal although you probably won't get caught.
   If you have prioritized honesty over financial security you will decline the offer.
   The bottom line…if you don't rank your values you will find yourself making decisions that may not make you happy.

Mirror, mirror on the wall

Self-awareness for effective leadership

As an international leader, self-awareness is paramount because

- self-awareness will help you decide how to adapt or not to adapt in your new environment.
- self-awareness will help you manage other's perception of you. Because of the cultural differences this will be different from how you are typically perceived in a domestic setting.

Self-awareness is integrally tied to emotional intelligence, both of which are critical to effective leadership. As Daniel Goleman (2005) noted, "Self-awareness, the ability to recognize one's own emotions, is the foundation for other emotional competencies such as leadership skills." These qualities are especially important in a global arena.

From self-awareness to success

In the chaos of modern life, however, most people are unaware of their emotions. Statistics show that customer service workers and middle managers both score higher than other workers in the area of emotional intelligence. Surprisingly, C-level executives rank the lowest. Therefore, we can surmise that C-level executives are not strong in self-awareness. The good news is that everyone tends to get emotionally smarter as they grow older. The better news is that women score somewhat higher in overall emotional intelligence than men, particularly when it comes to managing relationships. The best news, however, is that we can all improve our EQ and self awareness through various tools and techniques. "When you're emotionally intelligent, your emotions work for – not against – you, and you are respectful and mindful of other peoples' feelings" (Bradberry and Greaves 2005). Thus EQ results in a great predictor of a person's success.

There are a few steps you can take immediately to improve your EQ and level of self awareness. Like the queen in the fairy tale, "Snow White and the Seven Dwarves", you could use a "mirror" – that is, an assessment tool – to see what you look like. Examine yourself from all angles, and with a 360-degree tool that even accounts for the way others see you. Self-awareness, after all, does not merely encompass how we see ourselves; it also takes into account the way others see us. As WiSER Heidi aptly said: "I think making any move – whether it's from one institution to another or one country to another – makes you reassess how you look at yourself, and how other people look at you." Reassessing yourself is especially important when you are in a country with different cultural values than your own. As L. Robert Kohls (2001) noted, "By lowering our defenses and viewing ourselves through the eyes of people from other cultures—from what is called the cross-cultural perspective—we can get a strikingly fresh view of ourselves" (45). Revealed and concealed culture impacts how people from a different culture perceive you. For example, Americans value confident opinions and questions when collaborating, whereas that same behavior is seen as brash in China. This one example alone demonstrates that the "mirror" is indeed a magic mirror: depending on where your are, you will look different.

Just like the queen in "Snow White," we may be unsettled by the image the mirror reveals, but we must be prepared to accept it. After looking in the mirror, most of us feel a need to fix our hair, change our clothes, or make other modifications. After we make these changes, we might even as ask friends for their feedback. In the same way, once you've identified things you would like to change in terms of your professional image, you may want to solicit feedback on your behaviors and work habits from your manager, colleagues, friends, and family members. After all, practice makes perfect. "Practice accounts for far more than most of us might realize," observed Michael Howe (1998). "Several recent studies have demonstrated that high levels of performance—often higher than experts had previously regarded as possible—can be attained not only by those with innate talents and unique abilities but by perfectly ordinary adults given enough practice. In fact, the producing of an outstanding 'talent' seems to be most directly correlated to the right kind of deliberate practice that involves specifically tailored instruction and training, with feedback and supervision" (Howe 1998). In the same way that you improve your golf swing or upgrade your performance on the piano, improving your professional performance requires that you practice your modified behaviors and work habits over and over, until they become second nature. Feedback is a critical part of the process of consciously modifying your behavior. Please reference the section on developing competencies in chapter 4.

Seeking feedback can also facilitate a change in others' perception of you. For example, let's say your boss believes you are too forceful when it comes to decision making, and you attempt to modify your behavior by asking more questions and taking other steps to be more inclusive and collaborative. Given that your supervisor has a strong perception that you are overly assertive, it is not just important to change your behavior but also to change your boss's perception of your behavior. "When I got promoted, that was kind of a big milestone," said WiSER Allyson. "It was also [a] really good learning experience, because...I got some really good advice when I was promoted." Among the most valuable pieces of advice she received was to be attentive to other people's perceptions of her. "There was some concern about my level of conduct," she recalled. "I didn't think I was doing the things that people said I was doing, because that wasn't my impression of how I was behaving—and I got a really good piece of advice during that time that said it doesn't matter what you think you're acting like. What matters is what other people think that you're acting like." She recognized that the impressions of others played a crucial role in her effectiveness. "You have to kind of look at it from other people's perspective," she added. "It helped me to just take a step back and look at myself,...not only so it can help me progress, but also just as a person." In chapter 5 we discussed that organizations often think that women are not competent to take on an international assignment. By opening this discussion and soliciting feedback on your performance and capabilities as a (future) expatriate, you have an opportunity to influence your manager's mind about certain biases.

In order to leverage self-awareness, in order to maximize performance, you need to focus on strengths you can continue to build on, and focus on your most critical development needs. In addition, you need to focus on the things that hold value for you. As Jocelyn Berard (2012) observed, "Improving self-awareness is analogous to preparing and enriching the soil before planting a garden; the whole purpose is to maximize the chances that everything will grow more effectively. Improving self-awareness will help you grow and thrive in the workplace."

Any point in your career is a good time for self-assessment. Tools like DiSC, Hogan (HDS), Gallup Strengths Finder, and 360-degree feedback are all excellent starting points. These tools function like a mirror, and in addition to that, we can serve as the friend that helps you make sure you're at your best. Apart from coaching, feedback from bosses, colleagues, mentors, and friends is critical to changing targeted behaviors and maintaining peak performance. Part of self-understanding is to gain an insight into your values, qualities, talents, and interests.

From the experiences of the WiSER you can extract great lessons that will assist you on the path to self-discovery. "I did 360 [-degree] feedback frequently," revealed WiSER Laura. "Some people hate that, but I loved it, because [I] learn so much about myself and others and just interactions, like how to deal with people. I think that's one of my key success factors."

Self-awareness for career and personal decisions

Life throws many curveballs our way, and self-awareness will help us decide which ones to catch. Hopefully, you will come across interesting professional and personal opportunities, and you want to be sure that you make the right choices. In order to do so, you have to know what makes you tick — you have to understand where your passion is. Sometimes, it may seem tempting to enter into something just because it looks good on your résumé, because you feel embarrassed to say "no", or for some other reason. And then, you end up in a situation where you feel uncomfortable, unhappy, and you are not at your best. Your career may take a turn that, upon consideration, is not the way you want it to go. Relying on a strong sense of self-awareness will help you make the right decision about expatriating for example. Doing things that are not in your strength zone will drain your energy and leave you exhausted and frustrated. Knowing what you want out of your life, and your career, knowing what you like and dislike, enables you to actively take action to steer your life and career in that direction.

Here are some examples of WiSER who leveraged their self-awareness to make such essential decisions. WiSER Argentina was young, a single mother of two, and in the middle of completing her degree when she decided to accept a position in Burundi. Why? Because she enjoyed adventure, challenge, and found learning new things interesting. Her colleagues at the time commented: "Are you crazy? Those people kill each other. They have ongoing wars between the Hutus and the Tutsis." She took the risk, finished her degree while there, and the risk paid off in accelerating her career. Even when we are aware of our values and make the right decision for ourselves, it does not mean that it will be a bed of roses. In Argentina's case, her husband proved unsupportive of her career, and she eventually moved forward without him.

WiSER Gillian also had a difficult experience. "I was recruited into the global role and the global CEO retired about a month after I started," she recalled. "The guy that took over from him.... We were just not a match at all." Over time, WiSER Gillian became so insecure that she dreaded going to work every morning. "I can remember how I felt," she said. "I [would] wake up in the morning, almost on the verge of tears, and it's not like me.... It was [a] really, really dark moment." After a while she made up her mind and decided to leave. Just by making that decision, she started getting her confidence back. Before leaving, however, she felt a need to regain some of her lost dignity. "I went to my boss," she recalled. "He was a board member, one of six board members. I said to him, 'Look, I don't want to work with you anymore,' and I told him why. ... So, we... departed and, then, the global head of HR asked me not to leave and put me on some projects, and I ended up in another global role about three months later. So I survived what I thought was a bridge burner." Gillian's example demonstrates how important it is to know your limits and adhere to them. It can get you out of the most difficult of situations.

Self-awareness is also essential when making personal decisions. WiSER Supriya's first experience of life as an expatriate came when she followed her husband to Singapore. When she became pregnant, she had to be on "bed rest" for some time and, then, she took about two years off to spend time with her daughter — a decision that brought its share of joys but also made her realize that she really missed working. "When [my daughter] was about two, I put her into a play group and went to work part-time in research," she said. For as many mothers with young children who want to stay at home, there are just as many who want to have a space in their lives that is entirely their own. Oftentimes, work can fulfill this need. However, we have to be self-aware in order to understand what personal choice we really want to make. One of the most prevalent choices a working woman faces is in regard to children. WiSER Kamini left a high powered position for a few years when she had children. WiSER Nathalie G. decided to work part-time, while WiSER Claudia acknowledged: "I'm not married, and I'm not willing to have kids. Because, if I have to choose, I prefer my career — I prefer the excitement that a new challenge gives me. I prefer this liberty, this freedom to take my decisions and to choose the right way." WiSER Fiona made a similar choice. "There was a choice at one point of my life I had to make where I had a career opportunity to go to Vietnam and be a part of a pretty important study, which I knew would help get me publications," she said. "And I had to make a decision would [it] be that or...stay at home and get pregnant. I made the decision to continue with my career."

Regardless of how self-aware you may be, bear in mind that it is wise to avoid letting your ego get the best of you when making decisions. "I had worked at [a financial institution] for ten years, and that truly was a great working experience," said WiSER Alexis. "I'm very proud of many things we did there." In retrospect, however, she recognized that her decision to accept the next job was ego-driven, and the job turned out to be short-lived. "I sort of knew that company would be bought or taken over, but they offered me a lot of money, and I didn't have to do any interviews, and I took that job," she recalled. "It was a stupid career decision, and I...really didn't enjoy any time there." To make matters worse, she had to deal with a scandal the bank became embroiled in, involving a $25 million fraud scheme. Remember to always rely on your international gold standard - your core values - and be acutely ware of them when navigating rocky waters.

The journey to self-awareness - tips

While 82 percent of the WiSER clearly demonstrate the competency of "self awareness," in the course of reviewing their personal experiences, we can also share eight tips to help you in your journey to increased self-understanding.

1. *Tune into what you enjoy, what gives you energy*

The simple calculation of multiplying the average number of 246 working days per year by forty-five working years reveals that we spend about 11,000 days of our lives working, between the ages of twenty-one and sixty-five. That is an enormous amount of time spent engaged in one activity. This begs an important question: What do you like doing? We can only assume that you want to spend this amount of time doing something that you actually enjoy. We knew how we wanted to spend our time over the past two years. We wanted to engage in meaningful work that was organized around our values, talents, and interests. For us, this meant conducting research on women's opportunities in the global workforce; we wanted to help women manage international transitions; we wanted to use our own expatriate experiences to pass on lessons learned; and, we wanted to use our creativity to forge into an area that is relatively unexplored. Understanding who you are—your values, talents, and interests—will help you gravitate toward activities that give you energy. First, however, you need some insight into who you are, how you absorb information, how you process information, how you share information, and how you move to action. Many basic assessment tools can help you gain a perspective on these issues. If you understand where you spend your downtime, or where you recharge, then you can spend these few hours in the right places. What gives you energy in your professional life? This is essential information. After all, taking an expatriate assignment is not like taking a vacation. It is tough, both professionally and personally. So, you have to make sure that the position you select gives you energy. You will also have to manage energy throughout your career. Visit our website for links to online energy assessments, or to further explore what gives you energy.

Significantly, not all of the WiSER we interviewed became aware of their preferred career choice at an early age. That said, most had a strong sense of what they liked, and what they didn't like. WiSER Gabriele indicated she had no idea where she wanted to take her career. While completing her degree in engineering in Germany, she taught evening classes at a private school. Clues to her long-term professional goals, however, were evident in her choice of recreation. During this time, she used every spare cent she had earned to travel, often to places as remote as Southeast Asia. "It was very clear [that] when I was finishing my studies that I wanted to go abroad," she said. "I said, 'If I need to work the whole day, then it must be fun, something that I really like, which is traveling.'" Meanwhile, WiSER Flavia remained steadfastly true to her interest, even though it limited her career. "If I had made different career choices throughout, I would be certainly at a much more senior level within the system," she admitted. "But I would have had to make compromises." She concluded that these compromises would have turned her position into a routine job, as opposed to an activity she found enriching and enjoyable and she refused to let that happen. "If you don't come to it with an enormous passion, it becomes very difficult. I think all my choices have been not geared to where do I make the best career choice, but what sings to me. That is important, because if you like what you do, you do it better."

2. *Trust your inner voice*

Believe it or not, hearing voices in your head can be a good thing. These inner voices often reflect your gut reaction to specific circumstances. They serve as an echo of your values and your sense of self. So, listen to it. That's the advice of WiSER Jacqueline, who knew from an early age that she wanted a career that involved overseas travel. "I was the only child for six years, and my dad used to bring home…these National Geographic magazines and Life magazine—and I used to read them from cover to cover," she recalled. "I remember when I was…twelve years old, I said to my dad that I was going to write for [a] magazine like this, and I was going to live in Africa." She was convinced that she would write, and that she would travel in Africa, but she had no idea what she would do beyond that. As it turned out, WiSER Jacqueline's first international assignment was in Kenya. WiSER Anuradha shared with us that, at a very young age, she knew exactly what she wanted to be. She was attuned to how a very common experience inspired her and recognized it. "When I was 10 years old, I was taken to the observatory in Hyderabad. I looked up and saw… what the universe has to offer…. I saw…[only] six planets…but that event…solidified what I wanted to do in my life. I wanted to become an astronomer." WiSER Faith related a similar experience, which dated back to her childhood. "It's my mom who really drives the world travel…and that year we were going to China, Japan, Hong Kong, and Korea," she remembered. "I thought, 'You know what? I'm going to study a semester of Chinese and be able to at least say, "turn left," "turn right," "how much does this cost?"' And I fell madly in love, not only first with the language, but once we landed in China I was like—I am home."

3. *Know your own limits and dislikes*

In the absence of self-awareness, you may find yourself on a dangerous path that is filled with "energy zappers." One of the WiSER shared a story about a female colleague who worked hard and long, traveled the world, and was constantly training for the next marathon. Much to her embarrassment, she passed out on the shop floor after arriving for a meeting. Similarly, another one of the WiSER, Karin, found her job to be a dangerously exhausting experience. "I was actually working so much that…that I had to find another job," she recalled. "And, I wasn't able to…know or feel within myself when enough was enough. So, I was working seven days a week, ten to twelve hours a day to keep up with the projects." She added that it took her a couple of years to recover from this experience. "So, in a way, you could say that I almost got killed by my own success because I wasn't able to...stop it," she added. Obviously, high-performing men and women also require the self-awareness to recognize when they are exceeding their limits of physical and emotional endurance.

WiSER Alicia was a different case, however. She was aware of the limitations of a dual career marriage with the joint responsibility of raising a child, when she considered a particularly challenging job. She chose to turn down the offer. "So that's the first time I ever had to say 'no' to a job," she noted. "And I was very honest with my manager at the time, saying, 'I know my personality.... I need to be able to do both well.'" WiSER Friederike also suggested that women should be honest with themselves when making the difficult decision to either turn down a job or to leave an existing one. "I have the guts, always, to identify if there is something wrong and, then, to stop and say, ... 'You know, I think I need to open up to something else,'" she explained. "Love what you do." Similarly, WiSER Fiona discussed some of the reasons she refrained from advancing in her career: "I realized that I didn't want to go any higher," she said. "That was an important milestone. It's not that I have stopped working hard, or [that] I have stopped striving to do the best I can do. I could work harder to become a deputy director general; or, let's say, a director in a much larger center...but I don't want to go there, and that was sort of [a] light bulb going on for me. I know where I don't want to be in my career."

4. *Recognize your talents*

Our strengths characterize us as a person. The key to success lies in ascertaining your strengths and building on them while ensuring that your weaknesses don't become roadblocks to your success. We recommend that you run a quick exercise to discover your talents. Visit our website for the discover-your-talents tool.

WiSER Joanne described how she went about leveraging her strengths. "I thought I was going to be a starving artist," she revealed in the interview. "Now, I used to draw because I love to draw, and I am really good at it. I had...[an] industrial technology professor at university, and we had to design a product for his course." Although she was initially intimidated by the assignment, her professor encouraged her to build on her strengths: "He said, 'You love to draw. I watch you draw. You design things all the time. Remove all the roadblocks and just design.' This was a critical experience that prompted me into a manufacturing environment." Similarly, WiSER Lillian, who was drawn to creative writing, found a way to leverage her strength into an exciting international career. "I really liked writing a lot more than speaking in front of people," she said. "I just liked writing...but I wanted to also do something very international—and so, the one thing that [fit it] together was law."

WiSER Magi, who was always interested in how things worked, had a similar experience at the age of twelve. "I was visiting with one of my mother's customers at her business, and she was...just asking me, 'What are you interested in; what do you like doing?'" she recalled. "So I explained to her how I take things apart and understand how they work and things like that." The woman strongly advised her to look into engineering, which eventually led her to a career. Meanwhile, WiSER Claudia discovered a way to capitalize on her capacity to learn quickly. "I absorb knowledge really fast, and this I think is a quality, a competence that helped me to grow...in...a huge company such as the one I work for," she said. "It's the ability to learn things, assimilate the concept, and translate this in the way that makes sense...according to my concept. It's not the company's rule; it's my rules. I believe in what I'm doing. That I believe is the difference — my competitive difference."

5. *Learn from your experiences*

Don't discount the value of any experience, even a negative experience. All experiences can contribute to your self-awareness. WiSER Esther, for instance, described an event that she referred to as a painful learning experience. "I worked for almost five years in Liberia during the war," she recalled. "It was a very difficult time security wise.... I did learn that, as a person, I am very vulnerable. I guess it was something that I needed to learn about myself." During this period, she witnessed things that she would never forget, and had no desire to witness again. Although WiSER Esther's experience was extreme, all international assignments are challenging, and they offer rare opportunities to deepen your understanding of who you are. WiSER Jolanda described the experience as follows: "All of a sudden you are put out of your comfort zone...in multiple ways, and it means you're going to learn a lot about what you like and don't like about yourself."

6. Look to your upbringing and role models to better understand yourself

It is sometimes helpful to examine the past in order to gain a fuller understanding of your present—and future. WiSER Esther described the ways in which her own upbringing shaped her lifelong quest for social justice. "I never met my grandparents, because [they] both died in a concentration camp," she said. "But my father, in particular (even more than my mother), was very strong on the issue of social justice, and perhaps this is why I ended where I ended. He taught me at a very young age that it is important to remember that all human beings are equal, that social justice comes before anything else." She ended up working in social relief organizations. Meanwhile, WiSER Stacy shared an amusing, but insightful, anecdote about becoming an "alternate" kind of cheerleader, with the help of her mother and a friend. "When I was in primary school...I had wanted to try out to be a cheerleader [as] I had done the year before," she explained. "This year, I happened to break my toe while I was doing gymnastics. So I went to the try outs and did everything they needed me to do with this little cast on my foot." Nevertheless, the coach of the cheerleading team rejected her over concerns that her cast would prove an obstacle. "I was frustrated," she remembered. "My mother... didn't think that was fair, because I did everything that they needed me to do in try outs, and I did it well. So, she started a pompom club, and any girl that wanted to [could] be in it. Her thing was [that] there were no try outs, and she took whatever girls wanted to come... Anyway, I think the interesting thing about it is my mother saw something that she thought was wrong, and...without any experience, she took action and she did something about it." She now spearheads many change initiatives within her organization.

In a similar vein, WiSER Kelli told us that her parents' expatriate backgrounds helped to shape her values and interests. "My parents lived—and my father worked—in...Ethiopia...for about four years, just before I was born," she revealed. "They had that kind of expatriate background and, of course, they always told great stories about that when we were kids." She indicated these stories fueled her interest in living abroad. Likewise, WiSER Magi revealed how growing up in a military family influenced her. "I have always been the kind of person who doesn't have a problem just going up to people, meeting them at the coffee breaks or during lunch time or just going and talking to people at their desks," she said. "I am a very big people person, and I think that that goes back to ... growing up in the military." Given that her family often moved, she recognized the importance of making friends quickly. "It just became a part of who I was," she added. "I like being around people; I am very interested in other people's culture and the people."

7. The power of introspection

"Have you reached the top of the ladder and found that maybe it's leaning against the wrong building?" (Fortune Magazine). In some cases, you may find that you need personal time to make decisions about your future. WiSER Ayesha had reached a stage where she was no longer stimulated by her professional career. At some point, she decided that she wanted something that was "far more noble, far more exciting, and far more challenging and pioneering." Recognizing that her current path was no longer viable, she began to consider alternatives. "Can I put other steps into place?" she asked herself. "Or do I just make a clean break now and spend some time deciding what the next step in my life should be?" Ultimately, she decided to take some time off and make some clear decisions about her future. In some cases, a change of scenery can be helpful. WiSER Friederike left for India to do some serious introspection. She knew that she enjoyed working with people and liked networking. "But I also need to know who I am," she added.

8. Engage the help of a coach

A coach can be a professional, or someone in your life that you feel you can trust. WiSER Anne related her experience with a coach. Fearful that she would remain with the same organization for the remainder of her professional life, WiSER Anne found that her coach helped her imagine other possibilities. "I think, really, what helped me make that change was, when I got back to the states, I got a coach," she said. "She helped me go through a lot of kind of imagining new possibilities for…the future—something I [had] never really done. She kept saying, well that could be good, that might happen, so what else could happen?" she recalled. "I think it was just visualizing different things."

If you're interested in understanding yourself better, please visit our website, and take the "Soulful" Assessment.

It's a wrap!

As Lao-Tzu wisely said: "It is wisdom to know others, it is enlightenment to know one's self". Being self-aware involves knowing your strengths and weaknesses, your likes and dislikes, which are all based on your values. It's more than that, however. It also involves using this knowledge to make critical decisions. Prior to accepting an international assignment, knowing yourself will help you making the right decision. For the duration of an expatriate assignment, self-awareness will be your compass as you consider how to adapt, based on your values. And finally, when repatriating or moving on to your next assignment, self-awareness will come into play again. Hence the crucial importance of self-awareness. If only the queen in "Snow White" had possessed a greater sense of self-awareness, and taken the time to understand the reflection in the mirror, the story might have ended differently. Your story, however, has yet to be written.

Conscious Imbalance

"Life is like riding a bicycle. To keep your [im]balance you must keep moving."
~ adapted from Albert Einstein

"I decided to throw the word 'balance' out of my life, ... Balance suggests this sort of stable, level [scale] where one side equals the other. In my philosophy... life is very dynamics and it's always moving, so...things never stay the same. So, I call it managing the dynamics, as opposed to balance."
~ WiSER Abby

Would you do us the favor of standing up, stretching yourself to your full height, putting your arms above your head, lifting and crossing one leg over the other while standing—a popular yoga pose? Hold the pose for thirty seconds. How did it feel? Good? You may even be proud of yourself, and if you're ambitious, you may want to try to hold the pose for a full minute. What would you say if we asked you to hold this pose in perfect "balance" for a full day, or even a week—let alone a lifetime? The pride you felt would most likely be replaced with a sense of feeling overwhelmed. Who would want to do that?

Balance is defined as an even distribution of weight that enables someone, or something, to remain upright and steady. Have you ever tried to maintain perfect balance in your life? If so, how long did you manage to maintain it? What, or who, did you say "no" to in order to maintain it? Did you achieve an authentic balance, in which the scales of your personal and professional lives were perfectly even, or did you find that you spent more time tilting the scales, calling it balance because it felt right to you? You're probably wondering where this is going. Are Caroline and Sapna going to suggest that it's okay to tip the scales—to go against all of the recent literature on the importance of work-life balance, personal balance, professional balance, etc.? Well, yes, we are. However, we're not the only ones offering this advice. Dozens of WiSER have chosen to live their lives this way, and they have found tremendous success and happiness in the process of practicing conscious imbalance. Dan Thurmon (2010), author and motivational speaker on the topic of living off-balance, describes it as living life intentionally off- balance for a specific purpose.

WiSER Britta draws from her personal experience when discussing this phenomenon. "You have to go after what you want, when it is the right time for you," she advised. "People have criticized me for wanting it all— child and family and living abroad and ambitious career." She added that many people have recommended that she scale down her commitments and her aspirations. "I think it is important to accept when you have a demanding job and a child or family, there is no balance—forget it," she said. "Prioritize and outsource things like house cleaning, lawn care, and other low-priority items in order to spend your time on high-priority, high-value things."

In addition to yoga, off balance exercises are the new trend in core strength training. In fact, instability training is a valid way to strengthen your core muscles when just starting to exercise. When you use exercise equipment, such as a yoga ball, it forces you off balance, therefore requiring you to use your core muscles more frequently. This unique twist to strengthen your core keeps things interesting, so go off balance! Especially as you enter your first expatriate experience, conscious imbalance can strengthen you at the core in order to perform optimally in your new leadership role.

A positive definition

Imbalance is often regarded as a negative thing, and we tend to view imbalance as an undesirable condition. The common view is that someone in an imbalanced situation has not chosen his/her lot, and he/she must be unhappy. However, this isn't always the case. Imbalance (or more correctly, the imbalance perceived by others) should be a consciously, deliberately chosen situation in which one feels happy and fulfilled. The imbalance can result from the fact that you spend most of your time working, but it can also be the other way around. You may choose not to work at all, and instead, you spend your time devoted to your family. Back in 1992, I (Sapna) graduated from The George Washington University's International Business Program, prepared to travel the world and enter the realm of global commerce. Not long after my graduation, I joined Deloitte & Touche. I worked extremely long hours, and thought that I was well on my way. When my son was three years old, I was offered a global role with a well-known insurance firm, and this time, I declined the offer. I had no regrets about turning down the position, though I did have a few questions. Several years (and a couple of kids) later, we relocated our family to Germany when my husband received an international assignment. It struck me as ironic that my right-brain, musician, political science-major husband accepted a senior international role, while I handed my budding consulting practice to my partner to take up a new post as international hausfrau. Well, at this point, I had even more questions.

People are searching for deeply satisfying personal and professional lives, not a balance or compromise between the two. Often there are competing priorities, and we need to understand which way we want to tip the scales in order to achieve deeper fulfillment. When Matthew Kelly, author of Off Balance, conducted interviews, he found that responses to his questions about people's most satisfying periods involved descriptions of extreme situations. They were stories about putting in seventy hours per week for a few months in order to deliver a high-profile project on time and under budget. Or, they were stories of sitting on the beach in the Bahamas doing nothing more than sipping on a Pina Colada. They were rarely stories about working on the beach, for instance, which would reflect the proverbial balance.

For the purpose of our research, we defined the competency "Conscious imbalance" as follows:

Conscious Imbalance
Tipping the scales towards what gives you energy and fulfillment with the realization that the scales will need to be rebalanced on a regular basis.
• You set your own priorities regardless of standards or others' opinions. • You create or maintain a conscious imbalance between professional and personal life. • You determine when one must dominate the other. • You get what you want from both priorities.

Half of the WiSER (50 percent) demonstrated these skills. Interestingly, if we examine types of organization, women working for governmental organizations demonstrated this competency far more than the others: 88 percent compared to 49 percent of women in for-profit organizations and 38 percent of women in non-profit organizations. Women from North America demonstrated this competency at a comparatively higher rate (57 percent) than women from Europe (44 percent).

We once listened to a speaker who outlined some of the pitfalls of compromise. Imagine that! After all, from the time we were children, we were taught to share, compromise, and work through things. One thing we need to bear in mind is that, when we compromise, nobody wins — and oddly enough, no one is fully satisfied. So, as a child, when you were asked to share that candy bar, you were probably disappointed that you had to give away a portion of your candy to a friend, cousin, or sibling. Meanwhile, they were probably unhappy that they didn't get the entire candy bar. It sounds crazy, but the fact is, if you'd simply eaten the entire candy bar, at least somebody would have been entirely satisfied — that is, until you were reprimanded by an adult, of course. The same paradigm comes into play when we discuss conscious imbalance: the idea of tipping the scale as a conscious, deliberate choice in order to feel fully satisfied. We are not talking about maintaining a status quo, given that the situation is forever changing.

Balance	Off Balance
Stagnation	Growth and action
Sameness	Change
Protecting what is	Embracing what might be
Imaginary / unrealistic	Real / our natural state of being
Having a little of everything	Having more of what truly matters

Source: Dan Thurmon "Off balance on purpose"

Considering that we were talking to career women, many of our interviewees were inclined to tip the scales in the direction of work, projects and travel. When you talk about men tipping the scales toward work, it is considered normal, and it's certainly regarded as acceptable. However, when a woman does this, it is often questioned. "How could you be happy doing this?" Interestingly, some of the women who discussed with us their efforts to maintain a work-life balance revealed choices that in fact demonstrated conscious imbalance. For example, we spoke to many WiSER who said they had found work-life balance while working long hours and traveling frequently. How do you explain this dichotomy? Perhaps it reflects their desire, as women, to be seen as equally focused on the home and the workplace and to avoid being judged. It is like sharing that candy bar. It is the proper thing to do..... or is it? We believe they achieved a "deliberate intentional off- balance, tied to purpose", and because their — what most of us would consider — imbalance was tied to a purpose (namely being successful in an international assignment), it felt like balance to them.

Notably, many of the WiSER defied the accepted standard, given that they chose to do things that gave them energy in an imbalanced manner. There are various tools available to help you understand what gives you energy. If you are willing to tip the scales towards those things that give you energy, please visit our website and follow the links to online energy assessments or to further explore what gives you energy.

Maintaining imbalance - tips

"There is no secret to balance; you just have to feel the waves." ~ Frank Herbert. Successful surfers must develop a feel for where their body is positioned relative to the flow of the waves. They do this by keeping their eyes on the horizon, looking ahead and never down. They have trained their body's muscle memory to instinctually tense and release muscles at the right times and in just the right increments allowing them to stay on the board. In female expatriate terms: you have to constantly recalibrate and reassess your priorities to remain content. WiSER demonstrate time and time again how they have unbalanced their lives in order to do what gives them energy and happiness. Here are their tips.

1. *Don't let societal expectations determine how you live your life*

One of the most important messages the WiSER imparted was the importance of going after your dreams. Don't give up on your goals because of other people's attitudes toward you, your lifestyle, and your choices. What may work for you does not necessarily conform with other people's values and practices—and vice versa. "I love my work, and I couldn't live without work," WiSER Maria revealed. "Balance is a very personal thing. Probably, when friends of mine would look at my life, they would think I am not at all in balance. Well, I am fine with it. It all depends on what your priorities are, obviously."

The WiSER stressed that there is no need to give up on your dreams after you're married and/or have children. Our women demonstrate that it is possible to have a wonderful international career, along with a partner and a family. It may not always be easy, but if your goal is to move abroad, you should do everything possible to realize your ambitions. In the end, all that matters is that you are happy with your own life, and how you lead it. As WiSER Gabriele shared with us: "When [my daughter] was born, it was a real challenge because I could no longer work late nights regularly. That is when I changed the way I was working. I was managing a project between Indonesia and Germany, which entailed a 7 hour time difference. I occasionally had my daughter playing while I was on the phone. Coworkers would just ask about her. Having a child is an important part of my life, not a separate part of my life... When I returned to work after a six month break everyone forewarned me that it would not be easy. When I returned, I actually felt like I was just putting my hand back into a glove and just fit…it just felt right. Love or passion is such a strong word but being conscious of when something just feels right can be a signal to be aware of."

All the women whose personal scales tipped in the direction of work loved what they were doing. They enjoyed their work so much that they did not view spending less time with family and friends as an unreasonable sacrifice. It was their deliberate choice, and it made them feel happy and fulfilled. It gave them the energy to take it all on.

2. *Validate the needs of your family and employer*

Although you may be open to the idea of doing more of the things you enjoy, chances are that you will also be concerned about tipping the scales in such a way that you risk letting down either your employer or your family. Therefore, it is important to get a clearer understanding of their expectations of you. By this we mean that you have to really know what they expect as opposed to you presuming to know what they expect. A fascinating study cited by Marcus Buckingham may shed light on this subject. The study involved more than one thousand young people in the USA between the grades of three to twelve. The participants were asked this question: "If you were granted one wish that would change the way that your mother's/your father's work affects your life, what would that wish be?" In a parallel study, more than six hundred employed mothers and fathers were asked to guess how their children would respond to this kind of question. Here's what they found: "Most parents (56 percent) guess that their children would wish for more time with them. But 'more time' was not at the top of children's wish list. Only 10 percent of children made that wish about their mothers and 15.5 percent about their fathers. Most children wished that their mothers (34 percent) and their fathers (27.5 percent) would be less stressed and tired" (Buckingham 2009, 228). In other words, kids want parents to be happier, not necessarily to have more time with them. We believe the term that is used is quality time.

3. *Boost your energy*

The more energy you have, the happier you will feel and the better you will be able to deal with the demands in your personal and professional life. You will be better at facing unfamiliar situations, dealing with uncertainties and coping with work pressure. You will be a happier partner and mother, which will have a positive effect on your family as well. As WiSER Faith told us: "I think that when you love what you do, it gets really hard to know what this whole work-life balance is, because it doesn't always feel like work to me. Other people, like my partner, need to remind me. I'll never forget the night, at around 3 o'clock in the morning, he got up to go to the bathroom and he found me. The whole house is dark. I'm sitting in my nightgown, with my face blue, glowing from my Blackberry. He was like, 'What are you doing? Why are you online? Come back to sleep.' I was like, 'Yeah, yeah, yeah.' Clearly that's not healthy, but I loved what I was into.'" For WiSER Martine, the term "work-life balance" is misleading. "It's not about work-life balance; it's about being satisfied in both — or multiple — aspects of your life. It shows. If you are frustrated at home and you are not having a good time, it's going to spill over into your work." And if your work is frustrating, your personal life and relations will suffer as a result of it. Therefore our advice is: do what you love to do and how you love to do it.

4. *Make worthwhile concessions*

The WiSER discussed with us many cases in which they had to give something up in order to meet their goals. They indicated, however, that, in the long run, the sacrifice was worth it. Even if you are a stay-at-home parent with more than one child, you may find a time where you need to devote more time and energy to one child than you do to another. As noted, the whole idea of achieving perfect balance, whatever the situation, is unrealistic. WiSER Supriya offered insights into some of the challenges involved in raising a family, while engaged in work that required a good deal of travel. "Looking back, I don't know how we did it," she recalled. "I remember my daughter had something on school, and I had rushed from work. I just couldn't make it in time, and it was finished, and she was crying that 'mummy didn't come to see me', and I felt lousy. Then I remember her teacher saying: 'Come on, you came. You came all the way. You left your work and came.'" While WiSER Supriya experienced a certain amount of guilt as a result of such episodes, she also recognized that, as a full-time mother, she was often unhappy. "The two years that I stayed and looked after her…I realized that I am not really happy when I don't have something of my own. So when I am not happy, I think it shows."

Meanwhile, WiSER Anuradha found that consciously imbalancing her personal and professional life required her and her husband to live in separate locations. While she lived in India, her husband resided in the USA. "My husband went off because he got a big job offer, and I was not ready to give up this wonderful thing that I...had worked so hard for," she explained. "We lived for three years with our firstborn in two separate households where the child moved—like a separated family. We were not separated. We worked very hard to meet every six weeks for a week. I had a lot of support from my parents." She noted that her parents often served as the caretakers of her child, who traveled back and forth between the two households every six months. "I would say my parents literally took the job of raising my son for me because I was still working fourteen-hour days," she recalled. "Six months he stayed with his father; six months he stayed with his mom.... He spent his first four years traveling back and forth. He had more frequent flyer miles than I." As the boy grew older, however, WiSER Anuradha and her husband concluded that the arrangement was no longer viable, and she made the decision to move closer to her husband. Similarly, WiSER Ulrike, who has a partner, decided on a long-distance relationship for professional reasons. When she received an assignment in Finland, he chose to remain in Germany. "We don't have kids," she explained. "So, in that respect, it was quite easy." They are meeting twice a month.

When making sacrifices, however, it is not always the family who gets the short end of the stick. Many WiSER have given up on a great career opportunity to the benefit of their family. WiSER Veronika chose not to accept a position because of her familial responsibilities. "There was a time when I could get a better and very, very good job in my company being responsible for so many more people," she revealed. "But I just had to say, 'no,' because it really didn't fit into my family life."

Imbalance should be purposeful, and even with a strong sense of purpose, it is not always easy. In the case of WiSER Emily, her life changed significantly after she had children and moved to the USA Both she and her husband travel for work, and she holds a senior-level global role, which is difficult to manage from the USA, given that it is not as centrally located as Europe. Despite living close to family and having plenty of support and assistance, she found the situation challenging. "It's just really hard on all of us," she said. "It's very hard for me, and it's hard for my husband. I am struggling with how to stay in an international job that I love but also be the kind of mom and wife that I want to be. I have missed things that I would have preferred not to miss." Similarly, WiSER Britta had to give up on some of her favorite pastimes. "You... need to prioritize and aim for self-fulfillment, while realizing that you will have to give some things up. Yoga classes, retreats...are not part of my life," she acknowledged. "Do I miss it? Yes. But I am prioritizing."

The overall message is: no-one can have it all. Concessions will have to be made, they will be worthwhile.

5. *Don't try to be Wonder Woman*

Our advice is, don't try to be Wonder Woman—the woman who can do it all. No one can manage to do everything they want to do, as WiSER Flavia came to realize. "I think I've come to terms with that, in the sense that we can't be perfect and there will be some degree of imperfection—both professionally and personally," she said. Therefore, it's important to ask for help. No one can do it all by themselves, nor should anyone be expected to do so. This is why it is so important to build up a social network on international assignments within a short period of time. "Whilst living in South Africa, I hired a full-time nanny and was also backed by my family and friends," said WiSER Erica, who is a single mother. "In Australia my kids were a little older, but I had a housekeeper that helped me with basics, such as cleaning the house, ensuring the laundry was done, ensuring that the kids got fed when they came back from school and then in the evenings I would cook and enjoy time with my boys." She added that her support structure included a strong network of friends, whom she didn't hesitate to contact when she needed assistance.

Most of the WiSER who were married indicated their spouses played a critical role in their professional success, given that they provided constant support, encouragement, and assistance. "It is difficult to balance the two," WiSER Lillian observed, when describing her efforts to maintain professional and personal responsibilities. "It's not a very steady balance because there are moments...where sometimes work gets priority, and there are moments...where the family gets the priority." She noted, with a touch of embarrassment, that the balance often tends to tip in the favor of work, because her husband is extremely supportive of her professional goals. "Definitely, without him being as involved as he is at home, it would be much more difficult than what it is," she said. "But I never wanted the fact that we had children to stop me." Interestingly, WiSER Abby had a similar story to tell. "My husband has always been really, really supportive and comfortable," she revealed. "That meant that sometimes he would do more stuff with the kids' school than me." She added that her husband often spend more time with the children on weekends as well, because her job requires her to travel. WiSER Karin had a similar experience, and especially appreciated her husband's role in caring for their children. "I think that I have been blessed with a very, very nice husband," she said. "I think he took all the hard jobs; and I could kind of take on more of the fun things, such as going to amusement parks…when I was home."

As WiSER Marieke sums it up: "I've heard many women beating themselves down, although they are doing a great, excellent job managing both professional and personal lives. What we have to work on is believing in ourselves."

6. *Let go of the guilt - Balancing is challenging for most people*
Balance is so evasive, and yet, we're inclined to pursue it endlessly. Let's face it — most of us don't even come close to a "perfect balance" in our lives. We all know stay-at-home parents who struggle to achieve some kind of balance, because they have to distribute their time among more than one child, for example. Likewise, we know of women who don't have children, but who divide their time between work and caring for an elderly parent, and they rarely find time to do much of anything for themselves. And, of course, there are plenty of working women who struggle to find quality time for their jobs and their home life. The whole idea of "balance" seems almost Utopian. The fact of the matter is, all of us are constantly making choices that involve tipping the scales in one direction or the other. "You can have work-life balance issues, regardless of what job you're in, because I think a lot of it depends on [the fact that] jobs get bigger and smaller, scope changes," said WiSER Stacy. She revealed that her son experienced problems at school. When talking to the teacher about it, he told her that her son had said he was very angry that she had a new job where she had to travel. "So, as a mother, of course,

you can imagine—it just cut my heart out... As I talked with my son about it, one of the things that I wanted him to understand is that the travel is part of the reason I took the job," she explained. "After all, we wouldn't be seeking out this opportunity in Asia if we, as a family, didn't like to travel. I wanted him to know that I like to do some business travel. When he gets older, I hope he will take jobs that he likes to do and I hope that he knows that job fulfillment is important." She added, "I feel like it's important that he knows that I'm not a victim."

WiSER Flavia described some of the challenges involved in attempting to "balance" professional and personal responsibilities. "I'm very conscious that there is a stress element," she said. "When my daughter was small, I would spend the time in the office doing what I had to do, but feeling atrociously bad, because I knew she was at home sick with temperature." During periods when she stayed home to nurse her sick daughter, however, she was plagued with feelings of guilt involving her responsibilities at work. "So, women are good at that—a tendency to always feel that you fall short," WiSER Flavia added. "I think I've come to terms with that, in the sense that we can't be perfect and there will be some degree of imperfection, both professionally and personally." She noted that her professional work has led her to rethink the unrealistic standards she imposed on herself. "In development, we've been very engaged in promoting governance in countries where we work," she explained. "A few years ago, the UK Department of Development [told us] we shouldn't go for perfection. We should look for good enough governance, and I think we need to look for 'good enough' balance as well."

7. Be honest - it is the best policy

A number of WiSER indicated that the best policy is to be open with employers about your needs and desires to either take on an international assignment, a big project or to "be there" for your family. Requests for time off to address these needs are usually granted without any problems. "I have always said that my family comes first," WiSER Erica noted. "So, whatever I do in life, I have safeguarded this as a priority. To this end, I have always made sure that the kids were taken care of and that I could go to their important matches." Moreover, she has usually enjoyed the support of her supervisors. "I was lucky to have bosses who understood that it was important to me and gave me this necessary leeway," she explained. "I think it is crucial that you communicate clearly with your manager and when they cut you some slack, you need to make sure you get your work done on time and with high quality." She added that if you do so, you will generate trust and credibility, which is vital for managing work and family.

Senior-level expatriate assignments will be demanding. Nevertheless, being honest with your manager may give you extra flexibility in order to tip the scales.

8. *Review and reconsider options regularly*

As we mentioned, the scales of your life will need to be re-calibrated on a regular basis. This means that, over time, you may desire to spend more time with your family — or after devoting a good deal of time to your family, you may wish to start working again. "I made the choice to be a single mom and I adopted my daughter," WiSER Janice revealed. "And when I made that choice, I kind of took a step back in my career for two years, and I took a role...[with a]...good title, and I got paid very well, but...I had no professional growth — but I also adopted my baby girl, so I made that decision." Similarly, WiSER Nathalie G. made some changes in response to the demands of raising a family. "When our first son was born, I had a quiet phase for twenty-four months," she said. This meant little traveling and working part-time. "And then, I took on the global strategic marketing role, and I was traveling again to the US, China, and to India. I'm not traveling, anymore, since two years, but I will start again at the end of this year." Not surprisingly, WiSER Nathalie indicated balancing professional and personal responsibilities requires a great deal of flexibility. In addition, you need to keep your company abreast of your plans so that there are no inconvenient surprises. "You cannot expect them to change their time schedule because you need to pick up the kids from school," she observed. "That will not work. Quite often, I stopped working at four p.m. to pick up the kids, and I started again at eight p.m."

At some point in her career, WiSER Laura tipped her scales completely to the other side to support her husband's professional goals, even though her career was actually much more lucrative. "We made the conscious decision that my husband deserves a chance. He has a master's degree. He has a lot to give to students." While she was confident she could do her job extremely well, she indicated: "We did make the conscious decision to make that switch, which involves a lot of sacrifice as well…but…in a good sort of way."

9. *Take time for yourself*

When life is going at a hundred miles an hour, which it often does when you're engaged in an expatriate assignment, you might forget to look after yourself. Regardless of how you tip the scales, or which priorities you set, it is essential to take time for yourself. Even if you spend eighteen hours a day doing what you love doing, you still need time to relax, reload, and take your mind off things. If you don't manage your life purposefully, you won't have time for yourself. Visit our website for twenty simple ways to take "time outs". "I think that, because of the stress and the time that goes into the job, you have to be aware of it and you have to really plan some time for yourself, some time to reflect, time to relax, because if you don't consciously plan it, you won't have it," advised WiSER Elsa L. "The job will wear you out."

It's a wrap!

We have but one life, and we withdraw time from the same time bank, which provides twenty-four hours a day, spread over 365 days a year. We aren't simply trying to balance, say, a cup of "work" and a cup of "personal life." We're looking at one cup that is brimming with who we are, and we don't want anything valuable to spill out. "Yours will not be a balanced life — as we'll see, balance is both impossible to maintain and unfulfilling on those few occasions when you do strike it," observed Marcus Buckingham (2009). "But if you learn to create and celebrate your strong-moments, yours will be a full life, inclined, tilted, targeted toward your strongest moments" (95).

Never stop thinking about the moments in your life that have brought you great joy and fulfillment. While writing this chapter, we discussed some of these moments in our own lives, whether they were personal or professional, and once again, they were not moments of balance but rather moments of passion. For Sapna, these moments included being the sixth employee to join a dot.com and hiring of about one hundred employees, while introducing all HR policies, tools and procedures to standardize the organization within nine months. Speaking of nine months, other imbalanced moments included the birth of her three children, which occurred while she was working. Caroline remembered very intensive team building sessions with a management team where the managers had lost their trust in the CEO and spending late nights talking, facilitating and working on bringing the parties together again. On the other extreme end of the scale she has very fond memories of the time she and her family took a three week break to travel through the US.

Once you understand what gives you energy, you can make the hard choices that are involved in tipping the scales — and leading a more fulfilling life. As you pass through different phases in life, the scales may be tipped differently, so it's necessary to calibrate them on a regular basis. Adopting a conscious attitude of imbalance means that you are setting priorities according to your own standards

Operating Outside your Comfort Zone

"Security is mostly a superstition. Life is either a daring adventure or nothing."
~ Helen Keller

"Being an expat feeds my sense of adventure and my sense of always wanting to challenge myself, to see how far can I push myself."
~ WiSER Fiona

After a hard day at work, I (Sapna) went home, ran a warm bath, put on my "comfy" pajamas, made myself a cup of tea, and settled in my "comfy" chair to watch one of my favorite television programs. My husband was kind enough to bring me a bowl of macaroni and cheese, my favorite comfort food. Sounds pleasant, doesn't it? As it turned out, this was one of the last evenings I spent in Ohio before my family and I made an international move. A few months later, I was stuck half way across the world in an unfamiliar city, with no lights in our new house, and a single plastic chair to sit on. The food was totally different, and we had no television! If you go abroad, where everything is likely to be new and different, you have to be willing to move beyond your comfort zone. If, however, you prefer known patterns and enjoy predictability, you may have a difficult time. WiSER Lindsay told us that even the smallest differences can make you feel a bit uncomfortable. "Prior to moving, I looked at the list of the team that worked for me," she said. "I [thought to myself]: 'G-E-R-G-E-L-Y Z-A-J-K-A-S? How on earth do I say that?' He likes to be called Greg, which is a lot easier, actually. But it was those kinds of strange things that make you feel really quite uncomfortable and unfamiliar."

Your comfort zone is that area where you can operate without anxiety, and perform steadily and predictably in a risk-free environment (White 2009). When you operate within your comfort zone, your brain shifts into a kind of "automatic pilot" mode, and you perform your tasks without thinking too deeply about what you're actually doing. Like every human, you are a creature of habit. You tend to prefer certainty and predictability. When you step outside of your comfort zone, however, you find that you can no longer rely on your "automatic pilot," which increases your level of uncertainty and anxiety. To handle an unfamiliar situation confidently, you'll need to focus and concentrate, and you may need to use different behaviors in response to new and unfamiliar circumstances. There is nothing wrong with mild uncertainty, since dealing with unfamiliar situations can increase your performance level, while it also provides an opportunity to develop new skills. However, when people are overwhelmed by feelings of uncertainty, they're more inclined to panic and make poor decisions (Rock 2009). That, of course, is not what you want to do. All types of leaders, whether they're operating locally or globally, must be prepared to deal with uncertainty. The level of uncertainty, however, is bound to be especially high for expatriate leaders who have moved to a new country, where everything is new and different. Therefore, being able to operate outside of your comfort zone is very important.

Operating outside your comfort zone

"Elastigirl"

The above description of comfort zone suggests that you usually operate without a perception of risk. That said, operating outside your comfort zone does not necessarily mean that you are a risk-taker. There is an important difference between the two concepts. Risk-taking involves behavior that could be destructive but may also yield some positive outcome. Likewise, operating outside of your comfort zone is notably different from Gundler's global leadership competency, "Inviting the Unknown," which focuses primarily on open-mindedness. Operating outside your comfort zone may include taking risks, and it may simply require you to be open minded. Ultimately, however, it stretches you far beyond your current personal and professional boundaries.

We defined the competency of "Operating Outside your Comfort Zone" as

Operating Outside your Comfort Zone
Embracing challenges coming from new experiences by tolerating ambiguity and remaining calm
• You shift gears quickly and comfortably.
• You learn quickly when facing a new problem.
• You quickly grasp the essence and underlying structures.
• You enjoy the challenge of unfamiliar tasks or situation.
• You show resilience in the face of constraints, frustrations or adversity.
• You work constructively under stress.
• You anticipate and manage effectively when facing unusual difficulties.
• You effectively cope with changes.
• You have low security needs.
• You experiment and will try anything to find solutions.
• You deal constructively with own failures and mistakes.

Notably, 87 percent of the WiSER clearly demonstrated that they were able to operate, or were operating, outside of their comfort zone. All of those working on an international assignment in Africa and Asia were able to operate outside their comfort zone (100 percent), compared to 87 percent of those working in European countries and 75 percent of those working in North America. The percentage was lower (75 percent) among WiSER who had self-initiated their expatriation than among those women who had been sent abroad by their organization (91 percent).

Many expatriates believe that they were brought in as experts. In many cases, however, they were brought in simply because they were talented and adapted to new situations easily. When you operate outside of your comfort zone, you will invariably encounter new situations, dilemmas, and problems—and you will need to be creative in order to develop solutions. That said, there are many tools, tips, and pieces of advice that can help you to see what's coming. It is wise to educate yourself about how business is conducted on a daily basis. We are not referring to commonplace etiquette or how you should conduct your daily life. We are talking about understanding the cultural norms and values that are deeply rooted in a particular country and its culture. We are talking about how two cultures can look similar on the surface yet be so different in how they influence the way that business is conducted and decisions are made, and how people interact with one another. Understanding this won't change you. However, it could affect your approach, your level of acceptance and tolerance, and help you to operate in greater ambiguity. If you understand the basics of a culture, you can deduce the right action to take on the basis of that knowledge. If not, you are bound to follow your routine decision-making process, which may not be effective in another country.

Managing stress

During an expatriate assignment, you must exercise global agility, pushing yourself to "boldly go where no (wo)man has gone before." Difficulties are often exaggerated, and you are required to embrace the challenges that come with each new experience. Moving outside of your comfort zone involves taking risks and being brave. At the same time, you must remain calm and focused. It is easy enough to speak of these things, but how does that work in practice? How can you manage anxiety and stress in order to concentrate and perform well under such different circumstances? How do you avoid panicking? How do you make sure that the increased level of stress does not interfere with your power of judgment? How do you remain logical without letting your feelings get the best of you?

Our response to new situations is visceral. When we find ourselves in unexpected situations, for example when we experience the shock of a new culture, our limbic system is immediately stimulated. This means that our brain is struggling to determine whether this unexpected situation offers potential benefits or poses a significant danger. The more open-minded you are, the greater the chance that you will see the potential benefits of an unexpected offering. If you perceive an unexpected situation as dangerous, your mind moves to a "fight or flight" response, which essentially hijacks your higher reasoning — the capacity for which you were hired (Rock 2009). Severe stress can even morph strengths into liabilities that can derail the best of leaders. Let's illustrate this with a parable.

At a restaurant, a cockroach suddenly flew from somewhere and sat on a woman. She started screaming out of fear. With a panic stricken face and trembling voice, she started jumping, with both her hands desperately trying to get rid of the cockroach. Her reaction was contagious, as everyone else in her group also got panicky. The lady finally managed to push the cockroach away but ...it landed on another lady in the group. Now, it was the turn of the other lady in the group to continue the drama. The waitress rushed forward to their rescue. In the chaos, the cockroach next fell upon the waitress. The waitress stood firm, composed herself and observed the behavior of the cockroach on her shirt. When she was confident enough, she grabbed it with her fingers and threw it out of the restaurant. Was the cockroach responsible for the women's hysterical behavior? If so, then why was the waitress not disturbed? She handled it near to perfection, without any chaos. It was not the cockroach that caused the chaos and the stress. Rather, it was the reaction to the cockroach (the problem). As an expatriate leader, outside of your comfort zone, it is important to remember that there will be many "cockroaches". It is even more important, to stay calm under stress and respond appropriately. The women reacted, whereas the waitress responded. Reactions are instinctive, whereas responses are thought through.

Managing stress is crucial, given that unmanaged stress leads to reacting rather than responding, poor decision making, poor health, and unhappiness. Some common effective methods of managing stress include:

- rationalizing (unreasonable) emotions
- eating and sleeping well
- accepting that some things are outside of your control
- remaining positive
- developing emotional intelligence
- practicing creative visualization
- venting your emotions by talking to someone (such as your partner or a coach, counselor).

Our emotions range across a spectrum. This spectrum goes from positive to negative feelings, with either extremes being unhealthy. Typical emotions include anger, fear, surprise, happiness, sadness, disgust. When you move abroad you may feel negative emotions more frequently because you are outside of your comfort zone and everything is foreign to you. You may feel frustrated because you cannot get your point across due to language complications. You may feel sad because you are lonely. You may feel afraid because you are unfamiliar with local customs and don't know how to interpret them. Feeling negative emotions will give rise to stress.

Here is a tool you can use to help manage stress.

Stress reduction exercise – integrating feelings and logic	
Step One:	Present the Facts
	What are the facts and just the facts?
Step Two:	Feel the Feelings
	What are you feeling beyond the facts?
	Identify feelings seperately:
1.	I feel angry that…
2.	I feel sad that…
3.	I feel afraid that…
4.	I feel guilty that…
5	I feel…
Step Three:	Reason with the Opposites
1.	Why am I feeling the emotions I have?
2.	What are reasonable / unreasonable thoughts?
3.	What would I like to feel?
4.	Challenge unreasonable thoughts and replace them with powerful, positive, rational thoughts.
Step Four:	Brain Re-Wire
	Repeat the powerful, positive, rational thoughts ten times per day for ten days
Step Five:	Identify the Actions
1.	What actions do I need to take in order to be effective with minimal stress?
2.	What support do I need, if any?

Based on Laurel Mellin and University of California School of Medicine,
Creating Effective Organizations

Make it comfortable - tips

The WiSER provided some guidelines that will enable you to move outside of your comfort zone to achieve success in an international role.

1. Be flexible and open-minded

Many of the WiSER emphasized the importance of flexibility. "Be flexible," advised WiSER Martine. "Don't try to continue doing things your way. Adjust to the culture that you are living in, and remember you're a guest.

That is very significant. What you do at home is your decision, but it is very important that you adjust to the world that you are living in when you are outside your own home." She revealed how her own experiences in East Germany, in 1997, influenced her perspective on life. "In general, people are always complaining that we are going through so much change," she said. "When I moved to that area [East Germany]…a few years after the wall came down, that's when I really realized how much change these people had gone through — and were able to cope with it." She noted that her colleagues in the former East Germany had witnessed more change than most people were likely to experience in a lifetime. "That is [a] very memorable experience that I've learned a lot from — also with respect to my own flexibility," she said.

2. *Be resilient*

Mental and physical resilience are essential if you want to be successful in an international role. "The most important thing is resilience," WiSER Annette contended. "You've got to be mentally and physically robust. People working in the international arena are often above market, and with the traveling involved, it is tiring." She added: "It is even more tiring working in an unfamiliar environment [where] you have to be more on your toes. You have to be more prepared to deal with things that you don't know about."

3. *Step up to the plate*

You opt for an international experience, assumably because you want to experience something new. You may be curious to know how you will handle the challenges that inevitably will cross your path. However, when we are overwhelmed with new experiences, the 'fight or flight' response will come into play, often resulting in flight. Recognizing this, WiSER advise you to 'fight'. In other words, step up to the challenges and be tough on yourself. WiSER Annette revealed in the interview that she forced herself to move beyond her comfort zone to explore a new city. "I was in Paris by myself for eight months, and I used to go home quite a bit over the weekends," she said. Recognizing that this was an opportunity to learn more about a major metropolitan center, she began to set aside time to explore the city. "One night a week, I would take the metro to somewhere that I'd never been to before," she recalled. "I would get something to eat in a restaurant, and then I would walk back to my hotel. Paris is really small, and [I decided]...I'm going to see Paris at least while I do this." The alternative, she realized was to spend time in a hotel room watching DVDs. "But what's the point?" she said. "You have to ask yourself, why are you are doing this? I think being able to be...tough on yourself is important."

4. *Be bold as the boy next door*

We had a conversation with a WiSER who shared a story of courage that eventually inspired her to demonstrate professional bravery. Early in her career, she conducted academic research in conjunction with a leader in the banking industry. The research was intended to shed light on some of the reasons why graduates with similar psychological profiles, degrees, and backgrounds find themselves in such a wide variety of positions. The WiSER had a chance to conduct what was considered one of the study's most critical interviews, which involved an influential and successful bank manager. She had carefully reviewed her list of questions in advance and walked into the interview well prepared. However, at the end of the interview, she was deeply disappointed. The interview had yielded nothing groundbreaking, or even that interesting.

As the bank manager slipped into his coat and offered the WiSER her coat, she made one final bid for information. "Off the record, you really haven't told me anything interesting," she said. "Please tell me, what is the secret of your success? I want to know, when was the moment you believed that your career took a leap, and you set yourself apart from the pack?" He laughed and said, "Do you really want to know?" At that point, the manager related an experience he had at a major company dinner early in his career. When he walked in, he recognized that he was the lowest figure on the totem pole. Indeed, his name tent sat on a table that was located at the very back of the banquet room. He happened to spot the chairman of the bank, who had just arrived, and he noticed that the chairman's seat was at a front table, with many senior people on his team. On impulse, the bank manager made the simple yet ever so difficult decision to be brave. He walked up to the chairman, shook his hand, introduced himself, and asked if he could sit next to him. At that moment, the bank manager looked into the chairman's eyes and knew that his career was either made or broken. There was a bit of hesitation, and then the chairman said, "Please take a seat." The bank manager said that, from that moment his career was made. A brave, and risky, decision helped him to become one of the bank's top branch managers. Breaking "glass borders" is not about luck. It is about taking risks and demonstrating courage.

5. *Harness humor*

An old proverb tells us, "Laughter is the best medicine." Indeed, there is much truth to this, as laughter improves heart health, strengthens your immune system, and strengthens your abdomen. According to a study at Vanderbilt University, laughter burns about one calorie per minute; so if you laugh fifteen minutes a day, you can lose four pounds in one year. Take a moment to smile or laugh out loud. Can you feel your spirits being lifted? Those same endorphins can reduce stress and help you to operate outside your comfort zone.

If you want to survive the challenges of an overseas assignment, it is best to avoid taking yourself too seriously. "Take your work seriously but don't take yourself seriously," WiSER Sandra advised. You may find yourself in awkward cultural situations, and laughing at yourself will help get through these experiences. This is what WiSER Julie said: "Above all, maintain a sense of humor because a lot of times, it's the only thing that will get you through." As the humorous expression goes, "Don't sweat the petty things, and don't pet the sweaty things."

6. *Ask your spouse and children for their support*

No goal can be achieved without support. WiSER Lindsay found that the support of her husband was absolutely essential. She got a job for which she had to travel a lot. "Probably, the bigger decision was not about my job change," she said. "It was about the fact that, instead of being nine to five in the office in Liverpool, I [would] be covering the north of England and Scotland, and traveling with a four-month old baby." Given that her work schedule overlapped with that of her husband, the couple realized that one of them would have to stay at home. "So, the bigger risk was how Alan would feel staying at home with the new baby, given that we had no experience with small children," she recalled. WiSER Lindsay indicated that her husband not only agreed to be a stay-at-home parent, but also provided crucial support when she was offered an international assignment in Prague. "I openly admit…that had Alan not been pushing us to do that, I'd had chickened out," she recalled. "At some point, I'd have said, 'No, this is just too difficult, too scary.' It was only because my husband... was kind of...pushing me. That's why we did it."

7. *Build a social network*

Taking immediate steps to build a social network in your new venue will reduce loneliness and many of the discomforts of moving outside of your comfort zone. While you face a plethora of challenges during the adjustment period, mitigating loneliness will help shorten the transition period. Often the possibility to fall back on a social network (friends) will help you reduce stress as well. It will take some time and effort to build a social network and the results will be invaluable. What can you do?

- Attend or participate in events in your host community.
- Get involved in boards, committees, or organizations where you can build relationships with other members of the expatriate community, while at the same time polishing your résumé. Many of the WiSER are involved in groups such as the Girl Scouts, school boards, and non-profit organizations in their international venue.
- Build flexibility into your schedule. WiSER Joanne indicated that she arranged her work schedule so that she would be able to attend important school events.
- Seek to build friendships among your colleagues. Some of the WiSER have shifted business meetings from a restaurant in order to invite their colleagues to dinner at their homes. You and your colleagues will get to know one another on a more personal basis, and this can be the beginning of establishing friendships among your co-workers.
- Schedule activities you enjoy in order to meet like-minded people, whether these are dance classes, trips to the gym, visits to a local beach or swimming pool, or cultural activities. These activities will bring you energy, enjoyment, and maybe even friends.

8. *Build a professional network*

Moving geographies in a domestic setting, let alone in an international setting, and possibly even to a new organization, can reduce the power and helpfulness of your existing professional network. The more significant the move, the greater the loss. In fact, many WiSER indicated that when moving to different organizations and countries, they temporarily lost their ability to perform at the same level because they no longer had the relationships they had cultivated over time, and they had to learn the local business subtleties. Professional networks are key to help you get your job done. When you know who to call and who to collaborate with, it will shrink your to do list more quickly and help you complete deliverables with greater ease. To learn more about strategic networking concepts, please see chapter 9 on active career management. The following hands-on list offers a starting point to begin building your new professional network.

- Join expat meet up groups. These are professional networking groups that exist in many cities and are organized around nationalities, industries or fields of expertise.
- Visit business events and join panel discussions.
- Share your skills and knowledge and become a mentor.
- Find out everything you can about global professional female networks. While men benefit greatly from "old boys' networks," there are a growing number of professional women networking organizations that can benefit you.
- Start a new network, as many women have done. Keep in mind, though, that it is important that your network is not exclusively composed of women. Allow men to be part of your network as well.
- Join a suitable social media network or group.

It's a wrap!

Operating outside your comfort zone involves having the ability to embrace challenges that derive from new experiences by tolerating ambiguity and remaining calm. It may include taking risks, and it may require that you be open minded. Ultimately, however, it involves stretching yourself far beyond your current personal and professional boundaries for the purpose of growth. There are many reasons that an international assignment tends to place additional demands on women to operate outside of their comfort zone. WiSER Joanne revealed that her biggest move was actually her first one, and it was a domestic assignment. She had been with her organization for almost twenty years when she was recruited for a leadership position. "It was a very emotional and personal change in my life, and that of my family'," she recalled. "But in hindsight, it was only nine days. After that move, albeit domestic, the move to Germany was an easy one. Once, you make that big move, the rest of the moves become easy." Your comfort zone grows larger allowing you to manage stress effectively in order to improve work performance, while also maintaining your physical and mental health in an unfamiliar environment.

Active Career Management

"Think not of yourself as the architect of your career but as the sculptor. Expect to have to do a lot of hard hammering and chiseling and scraping and polishing."
~ B.C. Forbes,

"Life is short, life is yours, don't rely on someone else to make your dreams come true."
~ WiSER Faith

Think back on your most recent vacation. When you took that vacation, did you simply jump in your car and start driving, with no hotel bookings, no map, no GPS, no intended destination, and no plan in mind whatsoever? If you've ever done this, you're more adventurous than most people. That said, if you understand the basic parameters of your vacation you will reduce travel time and stress, while getting you to your intended destination more quickly. Taking an expatriate assignment is a similar kind of proposition. On the one hand, you must be willing to throw caution to the wind, to some extent. On the other, advance planning will increase your chances of getting to your destination and hitting the ground running, while also reducing entry shock. In addition, planning will enable you to leverage your international experience in order to move ahead faster. Remember, you cannot throw a dart and call whatever it hits the bullseye.

Now is the ideal time for women to pursue an international career, given that there is a dire need for talented professionals across the globe. If you start with this end in mind, active career management is the map to your destination. Once you define your destination, take the time to ensure that you understand why you selected it. In other words, know where you are going, and why you want to go there. Why do you want to pursue an international assignment? Are you moving in this direction for career advancement, for the challenge of the specific assignment presented, to make more money, to keep up with colleagues who have already taken an international assignment or because your boss has pressured you to go? Or do you want to experience a new place, familiarize yourself with a new language and culture, escape from something, or maybe find purpose in your professional and personal life? (Kohls 2001) This is important to know because you don't want to end up on an international assignment that, despite an ideal geographic location, fails to help you achieve the goals that you have set for yourself. When creating your map, remember that career management is a very significant and specific process that can help to ensure your long-term career success. Indeed, the concepts involved in career management are very similar to those of financial management. In both cases, a disciplined investment can yield a tremendous return (Scivicque 2012).

Take the driver's seat

We defined the competency of "Active career management" as:

Active Career Management
Knowing what you want from your career and working with intention to achieve those goals
• You make things happen for yourself and pursue your professional interests regardless of geography, profession or field. • You are able to influence and shape the decisions of upper management. • You market yourself and don't wait for others to open doors. • You pro-actively manage a network to reach career goals by winning support from others. • You actively learn and develop yourself. • You welcome solicited and unsolicited feedback and modify your behavior in light of it.

Two-thirds (66 percent) of the WiSER we interviewed had actively managed their careers, and they indicated this played an important role in their rise to a senior-level expatriate role. Among those who did not actively manage their careers, the majority recommended that others should. Those WiSER who demonstrated the competency of self-awareness, also demonstrated active career management to a greater extent (69 percent) than those who did not explicitly demonstrate self-awareness (55 percent). The presence of conscious imbalance was greater among women who did not actively manage their careers (62 percent) than among those who did (41 percent). Interestingly, WiSER who had self-initiated their expatriation had been less active in managing their career (57 percent) than women who had been sent abroad by their organization (70 percent). This may be due to the fact that working in an organization requires more active career management to be considered for an international assignment (remember the barriers) than when you take the initiative yourself. An early desire to live abroad did not have an effect on this competency, neither did the type of organization the WiSER worked for.

Strategic networking

Let's revisit the analogy we began with—your vacation. At this point, you have defined your destination (an international assignment) and mapped out your route (what actions will get you there). Now, you need to find some friends to include on your journey. These friends may include your co-pilot, or someone who helps you read the map or refuel. They may include someone who occasionally takes over the driving. In career management terms, these friends comprise your network, which consists of mentors and sponsors—influential people who know you and recognize your value. Talent management decisions, including the selection of expatriates, are usually made with the input of many people, and information is passed through formal as well as informal channels. One of the most common reasons for not achieving any type of goal is that we don't seek support to get there. Therefore, the more supportive people you know the better. The majority of the WiSER (85 percent) cited one or more sponsors and/or mentors.

Two years ago, I (Caroline) decided that I wanted to run a marathon. Having run several half-marathons before, I thought it would be a great challenge to run a full marathon. First, I set my goal by selecting the marathon in which I wanted to run (in this case, the Bonn marathon), marked the date in red on my calendar, and plotted my training schedule. I started an intense training regimen—four times a week—and did very well for the first few weeks. Then, some work commitments surfaced, the weather grew worse, and the training became longer and more intense. Those of you who are runners may recall that the difference between training two hours and two-and-a-half hours seems like far more than thirty minutes. To make a long story short, I did not run in the marathon, and I was deeply disappointed with myself. However, I still wanted achieve my goal, and I realized I had to alter my strategy. I found myself a running mate— someone as determined as I was to achieve this goal. I also started telling more of my friends about the marathon, and they began to provide active support, asking every week how I was progressing. They even promised to come and cheer me on during D-day. As I began spreading the news, others approached me about joining me on different runs, and I realized that my network of supporters was growing substantially. That gave me even more purpose and determination and last year, I finally did it!

WiSER Julie Anne described some of her strategies for creating an effective network. She noted that her success in cultivating two key sponsors and a large network of supporters depended, to a large extent, on conscious planning. She put together an Excel spreadsheet that included the names of everyone in her organization that could potentially help her advance in her career. "It included managers for other functions, managers that I hadn't worked with in years, managers that were around me now, previous managers," she explained. "You name it, I had it on the list." She kept these contacts informed on a regular basis regarding her activities and achievements, thereby giving herself positive and frequent exposure. This not only demonstrated to them her range of skills, but it also ensured that she would be on their minds constantly. This strategy proved effective, where hard work alone had failed. "Part of the reason I almost left the company is that I didn't have a sponsor," she recalled. "There was no one fighting for me. You know, you can be a hard worker and you can deliver excellent work; you can be better than your peers. But if you don't have key decision makers supporting you actively and sponsoring you, it is lucky if you get what you want in your career." She concluded: "I garnered my first supporters in 2000, and they were the ones that were with me until the day I left the organization in 2010...That's what I did, and that's what worked."

In some cases, networking is just a matter of being open and sociable with colleagues as well as former colleagues. WiSER Annette recalled that, during a trip to New York City to visit with friends, she happened to run into a former co-worker at her previous company. "We started chatting, and he invited me to come to a party that he was having that evening" she explained. "I went along to that party, and I was talking to him and another guy there, and they had basically just left [their previous firm] to go and work at [a global media organization], and they were setting up this project team to do all of the big changes associated with early digital music." WiSER Annette noted that this was before the advent of the iPod, and the project team was going to be involved in a whole array of change projects. "And they basically said to me, 'We're looking for change managers to come and join our group. If you fancy it, the job is yours,' and I was like, 'wow!'" She explained that she had always loved music, and therefore, she jumped at the chance to work in the music industry. "It was important to me because it made me realize... that a lot of being successful at what you do is about the relationship and the network, rather than actually what you know," she said. "I think there is a tipping point in your career where you know almost as much as the next person, and [where] people are making a decision about whether they want to work with you based on whether they like your personality or not, whether they know you—rather than a decision based on what you know." As per Rob Cross, UVA professor and expert in social networking, "Your network determines, in part, the size of your paycheck. But it is not just a big network that enables high performance. Instead, what distinguished the highest performers was a set of connections that bridged the organization in important ways." The more diverse your network is the more interwoven and impactful you are throughout the organization (Cross, Cowen, Vertucci, Thomas 2012, 4). If you are interested in assessing your NQ (networking IQ), answer the following questions. These questions will help you better understand the scope and strength of your network. This assessment is adapted from The Connect Effect by Michael Dulworth (2008). The complete assessment, including the questions along with the scoring and rating, can be found on our website.

Networking IQ Assesment
1. How many total people are in your personal, professional, and virtual networks?
2. How strong are your relationships with the people in your network?
3. How diverse is your network?
4. What is the overall quality of your network contacts?
5. To what extent do you actively work on building your network relationships?
6. How often do you actively recruit new members to your network?
7. How often do you help others in your network?
8. To what extent do you leverage the Internet to build and maintain your networks?

Furthermore, it is important to build and maintain your network before you actually need it. It takes a lot of time and energy to build a network. You have to get people to notice you, like you, trust you, value you and believe in you. Only then will they speak up for you when important decisions are made. If you wait to build connections until you need them, it will be too late. "There are more than a dozen people that have had a big impact on my career," revealed WiSER Sandra. "I always talked about being successful in terms of the content of the work you do and the contacts you make and how you work with other people." She added that she has remained in touch with many professional contacts over the past twenty or thirty years. "I have been able to maintain lasting relationship with them," she added, noting that this task, while not easy, is well worth the effort.

The importance of mentors - a sounding board

A mentor typically helps you develop your skills and competencies, acts as a sounding board, and gives you general feedback and career advice. Mentors support you in a more practical sense. They are people with whom you have a more interactive and personal relationship. Thus, they are able to give you insights about yourself, and provide sound career advice.

WiSER Hanan shared her experiences regarding a mentor who helped make a positive difference in her career. "I had a mentor, and he pushed me," she recalled. "He pushed my boundaries. He had confidence in me, and he pushed me...to the next level." Her mentor did not just offer encouragement and advice, she noted, but he also continually challenged her. "He would say, 'Don't come to me with a problem; come with me with the solutions,'" she said. "So, he started to actually set up my mind for business problem solving, and...what general managers were looking for." This helped her to understand that she would need to work hard and be totally committed to achieve her goals. Similarly, WiSER Flavia benefited from mentors throughout her career. However, she cautioned against depending on the advice and support of a single individual. "You cannot necessarily expect to have someone who will carry you along throughout your career, or through a good part of your career because we are so mobile," she warned. "So, you need to...develop not just one mentoring relationship, but a series of relationships so that, depending on the type of advice or support, you can tap different individuals...to ask for advice."

A mentor can also help you put things in perspective. "In every job that I have been in, I have been very fortunate to...have a relationship with someone whose input has value," related WiSER Hermie. "So, it's not like I have had one mentor consistently through my career, but I think at least three people." She noted that, while a couple of them were immediate supervisors, she was nevertheless able to discuss professional dilemmas, and to use them as sounding boards. In some cases, a mentor will actively cultivate a mentee. This was true of WiSER Argentina's mentor. "He would go out of his way to open the space to let me be, let me shine, and put my potential out there like never before," she recalled.

WiSER Fiona described one mentor who proved to be an invaluable sounding board for her. They had met when she was first assigned to Kenya, and they developed an excellent rapport. "She was a French woman who was the head of HR," she recalled. "We became friends, and when I left Kenya, she went to Hong Kong and went from working with an NGO—working with the poor and the hungry in Africa—to being an executive for Louis Vuitton in France." WiSER Fiona kept in touch with her former colleague over the years, and gained a perspective on issues that she wouldn't have gained by talking to someone in her own sector. "She's always been a great sounding board for me because she understands the systems, yet she stands outside of it and works in a totally different field," she explained. "Every once in a while, when she starts going on about the prices of Louis Vuitton handbags and how she can get people to increase sales figures to like billions...I start saying to her...'Well, yes I'm dealing with people that have less than a dollar a day and can't educate their children.'" She added: "It's great that we can do that with each other. I understand the world in a much more balanced way."

Meanwhile, WiSER Karin encountered one of her most effective mentors after joining a Big Five consulting firm. "He is the best salesperson I have ever met in my life, and I respect him a lot and he has become a very, very good friend," she said. "I think it's the similar pattern...he trusted me more than I did. So, he persuaded me to take a role in management consulting and to take the bigger roles abroad." At one point, her mentor encouraged her to give a presentation in Spain, where the 200 guests included influential professionals from some of Europe's largest companies. "He put his trust in me," she recalled. "So, I thought, 'If he says I can do it, I can do it,' and then I just did."

The importance of sponsors - career advancers

Sponsor are often confused with mentors, but the difference is significant. Unlike mentors, sponsors serve as important advocates within the organization and can help you move your career forward. Sponsorship involves the active support of a well-placed individual within the organization who is involved in decision-making and acts to promote or protect the career advancement of an individual. As you advance to senior levels, sponsorship becomes increasingly important, given that you are "fighting" for scarce positions. A sponsor can propel you to the top of a list of candidates, thus immensely increasing your chances of getting your dream job. Sponsors can give you access to powerful networks, something that women have far less access to than men. It is one of the key reasons that women are underrepresented in executive positions. A sponsor can also prepare you for the complexities of new roles or assignments, help you develop skills that support advancement and help you gain visibility (Foust-Cummings, Dinolfo, and Kohler 2011).

In many cases, a sponsor can help you "buck the odds," and WiSER Alicia shared a particularly touching story about a manager who made a crucial difference in her career. "One thing I kept in my career is handwritten notes from what I consider one of my best managers," she said. "He took a big chance on me early on." The manager in question was a tall African American who had worked himself up the managerial ladder. After recognizing WiSER Alicia's talents, he pulled her from a number of co-op assignments and gave her a job that involved real responsibility. "He gave me a very big managerial assignment, very young," she recalled. "I ran a 100-person, all-male machine shop when I was twenty-three. Of all three shifts, I was the only salaried person. Everyone else was hourly, and I had two hourly technical representatives." As the only woman manager, she immediately faced resistance. "I had people, right away, come up to me and say, 'I don't want a woman in the job,'" she said. Her manager, however, who had dealt with racial prejudice in the course of his own career, proved highly supportive. "He used to write me handwritten notes such as 'Hey Alicia, these are the things that you really need to focus on; you can't change the world, focus on these activities, choose your battles,'" she recalled. Although she worked for this manager for less than three years, she has kept all of these letters of encouragement. "When I heard he was retiring, I flew back, went to his retirement party, pulled out my little cards, and read them, and brought him to tears," she said. "But he was one of those pivotal people that took a big shot with me and guided me, when no one else would have taken that risk." WiSER Alicia indicated that her "luck" with managers has inspired her to serve to younger colleagues. "I try to do the same and take chances on people, take risks on people, all while giving them the hard feedback," she said.

WiSER Maria noted that her first expatriate role owed much to the intervention of a sponsor. "You need people in the company that know you and that would support you," she said. "My sponsor knew that Canada had to get a new Director. He knew that I was looking." She added that her sponsor approached those who were recruiting for the position and strongly recommended her for the job. "They weren't aware, actually, that I was looking for a job," she said. "But he told them, and then they immediately jumped on it and came to me." WiSER Maria stressed the importance of cultivating sponsors who are aware of your strengths—and who will promote you within the organization. Likewise, WiSER Janice indicated that she owed an important break in her career to a sponsor's intervention. "When they announced that we were going to become more of a European-based company, I threw my hat in the ring and said, 'I would like to be a part of the new company,' and I had a really good advocate," she revealed. "There was someone at a high level who believed in me, and...that person was a good advocate for me to be in this role."

Significantly, effective sponsors can help you to overcome barriers, to plug into a larger professional network, and to promote you. They can also help you navigate the political environment that is inherent in any large organization.

Women for women

Identifying a good sponsor or mentor is just as important as being a good sponsor or mentor to others, especially in the case of women due to the relatively small percentage of women in (expatriate) leadership roles. Notably, close to 40 percent of WiSER said they had a female mentor. As international female leaders, they shared some of the ways in which they benefited from coaching and mentorship. Many of them also described how, after moving into senior level positions, they attempted to serve as role models for young women, encouraging and supporting them in their efforts to build an international career. "I think other women can really help women and encourage them and to kind of fight so they get heard and they get considered," WiSER Martha stated. "I was really fortunate in that respect, as I had a colleague...that was willing to do that for me. So, maybe, as women, we have a role to play in terms of seeing that potential and really encouraging women to go after those positions and to aspire to those positions." She stated that such support is essential because men are more likely than women to envision themselves in such roles. "So, maybe", she said "we need other women to come alongside and say, 'Hey, you can do it, I believe in you. Go for it.' ... and sort of mentor them through that process."

WiSER Martha revealed that she had some excellent female sponsors who encouraged her to apply for an expatriate assignment, and who supported her even when she was pregnant. "In the application process, I actually found out I was pregnant with our second child," she recalled. "So, I wrote this long email saying that I was going to have to withdraw my application, because their Mozambique program was really big."

She explained that the $25-million program covered five provinces and involved 900 staff members. In addition to being pregnant, WiSER Martha was just thirty-three years old. "So I said, 'Look, there is no way the organization should want me to do this because I just found out that I am pregnant,'" she recalled. "I now remember my sponsor marching into my office and saying: 'No way! You need to put your name back in. Women have babies. Just tell them what sort of support you need. Africa is a great place to raise a family. You can do it.'"

Admittedly not all female leaders are ideal mentors or sponsors. Undeniably, there will always be "queen bees," who would prefer to be the only competent female leader in an organization. Some of us have had run-ins with these kinds of personalities. "I often find that females in higher positions are very competitive," WiSER Karin said. "And I often feel that because of that, they will get a little jealous of me, meaning that it's difficult to have that [trusting] relationship." Such rivalries are unfortunate. Professional female leaders supporting other professional women can only result in more progressive work environments, where women are well represented in leadership and expatriate roles. The WiSER are certainly women who want to see other women succeed. Indeed, some have gone so far as to recommend the benefits of female-to-female mentoring relationships. "I think that with female mentors you can…be more transparent…and not feel as guarded," said WiSER Elsa I. At one point in her career, WiSER Nathalie G. decided to seek out a female mentor who had more children than she did, and she managed to find one. "There was an American lady working in the US, and she has four children, and she is doing fine," she said. "She has made a great career for herself in our organization." She added, "It was very helpful to me to be able to talk with another woman, and I had only one child at that time." This experience was so positive that it has inspired WiSER Nathalie G. to mentor younger female colleagues. "It's funny, because now I'm a mentor," she said. "So, after a point in time, you become the mentor and you do it the other way."

You are invited to build your network by leveraging ours. Through our website you can exchange ideas with us, many WiSER, and others interested in female expatriation.

Hit the bullseye - tips

The WiSER offered some very practical advice about how you can take your career into your own hands.

1. Make sure you have what it takes

The basic prerequisite to be considered for an international assignment is a combination of having the right skills, working hard and performing very well. There are different ways to learn about the technical skills and competencies required for international jobs. The simplest way to do this is to review job descriptions, that is, if they are available. Another approach is to leverage your network to better understand your targeted job, the company, and the country. Yet another way is to take the initiative to request a meeting with the leader whose function you're interested in learning more about, and asking that individual about the requirements of the role. As WiSER Joanne told us: "I remember when I went to the VP of operations, and I asked him: 'I want your job someday.... Can you tell me a little bit about what it takes to do your job? What are the skills that you would need?'" She noted that she learned a great deal from these kinds of frank discussions with leaders. "You need to talk to the person... sit down with them, and have a conversation," she said. "If they are a leader, and they are a proper leader, they'll share everything with you, because succession planning means that they are not going to be in that position for very long. They need to...know when it's time to go, that they have enough people behind them that the business can continue to be successful."

One skill often required for being seriously considered for an international role is the ability to speak a second language. Rather than waiting to get an assignment and then learning the language of the prospective host country, why not take the initiative to learn your favorite language? There are many free websites and community courses that provide learning opportunities in this area, and learning another language could turn out to be enjoyable recreation and a way to meet like-minded people.

WiSER Argentina shared that she grew up in a highly disciplined environment, which she came to appreciate as she set out to develop her career. "My mother came from a tribal group called the Shangaana, in the south of Mozambique," she explained. "The men are warriors, and the women are really the ones who take care of the homes." She noted that, in more recent times, when inter-tribal warfare was no longer a factor, the men were often laborers in the gold mines of South Africa. "So the women would stay behind and be the ones farming, tilling the lands, and rearing the children and all that," she observed. "So, it is a very hard-working group of people, and that's where I came from." Despite the hard work, however, these women maintained a positive attitude. "It was joyful nonetheless," she recalled. "People laugh loud. They speak...they enjoy and they share and meddle in each other's [lives], but pure hard work is the key that drives everything." WiSER Argentina attributes her rise to senior-level positions to this ingrained work ethic and the discipline of those early days which allowed her to face the challenges of future (professional) life.

Performing extremely well is the application of job related competencies and hard work resulting in success. "I've always taken my job seriously and...to the best of my ability," WiSER Stacy noted. "I do think that more opportunities will open up...if you show that you can execute and deliver on the job that you have." WiSER Erica had a similar experience. "By the time I was transferred on my first international assignment, I was managing a business with twelve countries reporting in," she said. "I knew the products. I understood the company, and I think they felt that it would be good for me to go to a bigger market with a different culture and a very different healthcare system. They were right. I learned a lot, became a better and stronger leader...it was a good experience." Likewise, WiSER Maria was selected for an expanded role because of her performance in the job she held. "I was recognized as a good performer also in the zones," she said. "Given that I was in a global role, most of the people from the six geographic zones that we have knew about me," she recalled. "They had had two or three different persons in the role without success, and when they heard I was available, they immediately jumped on it, because I had the perfect background."

2. *Follow your heart and follow through*

It is important to realize that career management is not just about securing promotions and climbing the career ladder. When setting professional goals, other factors, such as personal satisfaction, personal sensibilities, and personal values, should be taken into consideration. Once you've decided that you want to pursue an international career, follow your passion and don't give up. Know what you want, communicate it, and pursue it. Recognize, however, that risks will be involved. As WiSER Fiona revealed in the interview, she knows all about risks. Ultimately, she gave up everything to follow her dream to live and work abroad. While working for a Canadian company, she traveled over a four-month period to the UK, Germany, Switzerland, and Australia, in an effort to secure business partners for the firm. After returning to Canada, she decided that she would like to continue to work internationally. She gave her company a one-year notice and moved to Australia. "I thought that that would be an easy place to…get this kickstart again," she recalled.

Upon her arrival, however, she discovered there were certain formalities she had overlooked. "When I got there, the very kind officials at Sydney airport told me that I couldn't just arrive in a country and decide that I was going to live there," she explained. "I actually had to immigrate, and I had not bothered to actually think that through. They said I could stay on a visitor's visa, but I couldn't work — and of course, at this time, I had given up my career in Canada." This was not the half of it. WiSER Fiona had also left behind her husband and home — all in an effort to start a new life in Australia. "So, I couldn't really go back with my tail between my legs," she explained. Coincidentally, a friend of hers, who lived in Papua New Guinea, contacted her and offered her a job. While she initially had no idea where Papua New Guinea was located, she once again decided to take the plunge. "So, I got a ticket, and I went to Papua New Guinea," she said. "Sure enough, in the first week, I got a job; in the second week I got a place to live, and in the third week I got pregnant." At that point, she decided that she would be in Papua New Guinea for awhile. "And that was my first expatriate job," she added. Follow your heart and follow through, but remember that mapping out the course to your destination can help you avoid difficulties along the way.

3. *Plan your career*

It's never too early to begin setting professional goals and managing your career. Creating a career plan may seem daunting, but you can demystify the process with the help of an effective coach. Once you have created your career plan, leverage it to create visibility for your successes, and to promote the ways in which your work supports the organization in its efforts to achieve its goals. "I am very much the driver of my destiny," WiSER Faith revealed. "I have, for lack of more polite feminine language... plotted...every single piece of this—of where I'd go to graduate school, who I meet, what clubs I joined, what I need to do to get my promotions, where will I go next. It's a strength." WiSER Lindsay also emphasized the need to develop a career plan, and she revealed that, when she took her first HR director role, her boss insisted that she develop one. "What's a career plan?" she recalled thinking. "I found it really hard, and I clearly remember to this day going into my new management director's office and saying, 'Steve, I really need your help because I don't really know what I'm doing here.'" At that point her manager helped her plot out the plan on a whiteboard. The exercise helped her to consider her career aspirations. She started with a goal and reverse-engineered the path needed to get there. With her manager's help, she considered sectors, countries, roles, and experiences that she required, such as acquisition experience. "It's amazing," she said. "I could take that 'career plan' out of the cover and show it to you, and you could see I have ticked off everything that I said I would do." She added, "No, I haven't done it in the right order, but pretty much everything that I said I'd do, I've done during that time."

As noted, career management can also serve as a vehicle to increase your organizational visibility and promote your wins. "Something I absolutely insist on is that I always make sure I have goals every single year," said WiSER Laura. She added that these goals and performance objectives were always aligned to the organization and the manager she was supporting. Furthermore, she insisted that these goals and objectives were reviewed at least twice a year. Although she realizes that this approach is not "rocket science," she found it to work exceedingly well. "If my manager or whoever at that time wasn't willing to take the time to do that with me, I would do it," she said. "And I would religiously go through and say, 'Okay, this is what I've accomplished this year, this is what went well, and this is what didn't go well.'" She would then focus on two or three areas of potential improvement and develop a strategy to accomplish this. She indicated that this process went further when she sat with supervisors (and even managers above her supervisor) to carefully review goals, risks and accomplishments. "Even though some of the time I am sure these people would roll their eyes and say, 'Oh, it's her again'...

[I make] sure that they know I have a vision," she added. "I have a plan, and this is where I want to be."

4. *Speak up, make your intentions known*

The inability of many women to break through the glass ceiling, or the glass border, has much to do with their reluctance to speak up for themselves. A perennial problem for many women is their failure to let people know what they want. "I think that we don't necessarily do a good enough job of just saying, 'This is what I want,'" said WiSER Meredith. "I'm going to ask for it, and who cares that they say, 'no.' If an international assignment is what you think you want...go for it, explore it.... The worst thing that anyone can say is, 'no.'" While managers routinely assume that men will be interested in expatriate assignments, women generally have to ask about them if they want to be considered for these roles (Catalyst 2000). Furthermore, given that just over a quarter of organizations (28 percent) have a structured career management process in place and only 19 percent have a formal candidate pool, there is a good chance that viable candidates will be overlooked (Brookfield 2012, 23). This suggests that it is not in your interest to sit back and wait until you're noticed. You may be waiting a long, long time—or worse yet, you may never find yourself on the short list for an international opportunity.

It is best to be explicit about your goals, and to clarify what you need in order to be successful. "I think many people do not get where they want to be because they do not 'speak up,'" said WiSER Argentina. "They are too afraid to try. They do not want to take the risk of a 'no.'" In WiSER Argentina's case, she was willing to take that risk, and it led to her first international role. WiSER Nathalie K. followed a similar path. "I remember very clearly that there was an email sent to the whole company saying '[Our office in] Spain opens its doors,'" she recalled. "And I got butterflies in my stomach, and went to see the head of HR the following Monday, saying: 'I'd like to go, can we make that happen?' It took about six months to make it happen, but it did happen."

In taking a more assertive attitude at her organization, WiSER Nina said she followed the example of her male colleagues. "I realized that men are much better in saying what they want than women," she observed. "I also realized that you have to say what you want, and not assume others know." She recalled that, when she learned about an overseas assignment in London, she expressed an interest in the job. "I said that very early on, and everybody said, 'Oh, you are too young,'" she recalled. They pointed to her lack of experience and her lack of familiarity with the organization as a whole. "I said, 'Well, so what — I will learn,'" she said. "I said it several times, and then, I wrote a letter to our secretary general, and I said next time the job is available, I am interested." Eventually, she did get the coveted position in London.

The reluctance of women to assert themselves is also highlighted by a humorous anecdote that WiSER Tuulia shared. She recalled that she was talking to some friends about mountain climbing, and she asked them if they had reached a particular peak that was considered rather daunting. WiSER Tuulia noted that one woman, who had climbed that peak on two expeditions, only briefly mentioned this fact. At the same time, her male friend, who had climbed the peak just once, described the adventure in great detail and emphasized the risks involved. Finally, another person involved in the conversation began to laugh and said, "Did you notice the lady has been there twice, and the guy is just screaming about it?" The moral of the story is, if you want to be heard, you may need to occasionally raise your voice.

Although you may be committed to speaking up for yourself, this often proves challenging — and cultural norms sometimes get in the way. In some Eastern cultures, the view that a woman should be seen and not heard remains quite prevalent. As WiSER Alicia indicated, however, speaking up is a challenge that we can meet. "Growing up, I was very quiet, very reserved, so very, very shy," she told us. "I was a middle child; I wouldn't even speak to an adult, wouldn't do any public speaking, nothing. And to this day, I am much more reserved." In her professional life, however, she encountered strong managers who insisted she learn to express her views. "I would never speak up in meetings," she recalled. "I would go to them after the meeting, and I had one manager tell me, 'I'm not going to listen to you unless you have enough guts to say it in the meeting.'" While such experiences were uncomfortable, they pushed her to develop her ability to make herself heard, to the benefit of her career.

5. *Take creative paths to lasso your expatriate assignment*

Imagine stepping stones in a pond that lead to the other side. Some of us may prefer to cross by using the biggest, most visible, stones. Others may explore those stones that sit slightly below the surface, zigzagging across the pond, but they still manage to get to the other side. Meanwhile, some of us might be halfway across the pond when they realize that they need to backtrack and take a different path in order to get to the other side. As long as getting to the other side is your goal, there is no wrong way to get there. Keep your eyes on the prize.

Consider volunteering for an especially challenging assignment, perhaps a project or joining work streams, that is in great need of someone to spearhead success. Strong performance and the willingness to step up when others are not, will give you visibility, and could result in a fantastic international opportunity. Even when results aren't ideal, skills can still be learned. WiSER Kelli indicated that volunteering for certain tasks enabled her to gain experience that made her a viable candidate for promotion down the road. "It really wasn't even my responsibility and my role, but I stepped [in] and said…'I can work on that project,'" she said. "Then, when you've gotten some experience, of course, you are the one that they turn to then in the future."

WiSER Diana studied law and also secured a graduate degree in taxation in her home country of Columbia. She was with a global tax firm when they began to develop a practice that focused on expatriates. She was the only one asked to join the practice, because she was the only one who could speak English. As part of her work, she collaborated with one of the firm's partners in Florida and she helped him to update a tax law presentation. When he requested the same kind of assistance each year, WiSER Diana took it upon herself to help him out, even though it was above and beyond her job. This partner eventually turned out to be the one who offered her the opportunity to move to the US. Although Diana was a senior associate in the office in Columbia, she started her new role as a first year associate in order to learn about US taxes.

Another option includes accepting a short term international project in order to demonstrate your global agility. WiSER Tuulia revealed that she was originally offered a four-month assignment to use her expertise from the Finland office and apply it to the development of similar standards and processes in the German office. She accepted the four-month assignment and several years later still remains in Germany. Although it didn't start as an expatriate assignment, her successes over a brief period of time (four months) expanded the opportunity.

Some WiSER have gone so far as to accept a position below their current level to gain international experience. "I did very well for myself in my various jobs," recalled WiSER Janice. "I lived in Atlanta, and then, I decided I needed more international experience on my resume, because I didn't really have any. Even though my clients were big firms, I never had big international clients." Ultimately, WiSER Janice agreed to accept a position as a director even though she had already secured vice president status. Although the job was a step down in terms of position and proved to be a lateral move in terms of salary, it opened the door to an exciting overseas assignment in London within two years.

The important message the WiSER conveyed, is to be open to creative career pathing, especially when looking to work abroad. Otherwise, you severely limit your options. WiSER Andrea indicated that people who are too specific in their goals often get frustrated when they don't secure the position they want. "So I always try to also keep it very flexible," she added. By considering a wider variety of appropriate options, she found that she was more likely to find a position that was satisfying.

6. *It is never too late*

Research has indicated that the younger you move abroad, the more it benefits your career (Reiche 2011). In line with this conclusion, the majority of the women we interviewed (60 percent) were junior professionals when they first expatriated. That said, if you haven't been abroad before a certain age, it doesn't mean your chances are over.

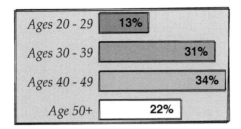

Average age of expatriates (2011)
Source: Brookfield Global Relocation Trends Survey 2012

There really is no age limit for a first international assignment. We have spoken with WiSER who began their international career after more than twenty years of experience in multiple organizations, and they went on to land great jobs.

In addition to this valuable career management advice, visit our website for The International Career Toolkit. This toolkit is focused on providing hands on tools to help you execute an international job search. It is filled with information on where to look for international jobs, how to make yourself an attractive candidate in the international sphere and how to brand and sell yourself.

It's a wrap!

While looking a the world map hanging in my den, I (Caroline) was thrilled to see all the places I've visited, which were marked with different colored stick pins. It was pretty easy to where I haven't visited yet, and I can easily determine where I would like to go over the next few years. Many of you may have a similar map. When you look at that map, do you know where you want to go? Do you know why you want to go there, and what you want to do when you arrive? Knowing what you want from your career, and working with intention toward achieving those goals, is the essence of active career management. As Jesse Owens once said, "We all have dreams, but in order to make dreams come into reality, it takes an awful lot of determination, dedication, self-discipline, and effort." Active career management can turn your dreams into reality.

Succeeding in your International Assignment

Section III

The Roller Coaster Ride

*"Life is not measured by the number of breaths we take,
but by the moments that take our breath away."*
~ Maya Angelou

*"I would never get homesick. But [as an expat] you definitely do,
and it's just part of it. Just realize that it's going to come and go
and come in times and places that you wouldn't expect.
Be ready to experience that and be okay with experiencing that."*
~ WiSER Meredith

Recently, we took a break from writing our book to visit a nearby amusement park with both of our families. The park featured many different styles of roller coasters; and as it turned out, Caroline preferred the more traditional wooden coasters, while Sapna opted for those with inverted tracks, on which you spend a portion of the ride upside down. Apart from these preferences, however, we were drawn to roller coasters for most of the same reasons — the anticipation of rising into the air, the exhilaration of plummeting to earth, and the oddly exciting feeling of being tossed around like a rag doll in a washing machine. It created an adrenaline rush that swept our bodies. In a way, an international assignment is much like the experience of riding a rolling coaster. You'll find that you're excited and anxious, all at once.

Similar to a roller coaster ride, expatriation involves ascending, descending, many winding tracks and finally, returning to where you began. There are three phases of the expatriation cycle:

- *Fasten your seatbelt.*
  It is time to prepare for your adventure. There are many things you can do once you've learned more about your assignment and where you'll be based. Prepare yourself as best you can before making the move to the host country.
- *Enjoy the ride.*
  You will arrive at your new destination to find a new home, a new job, a new language, a new culture, a new country, and new colleagues — but no friends. Everything is unfamiliar. It is important to remember, though, that most expatriates go through the same emotional stages as they struggle to adapt to their new environment. Once you start feeling comfortable with your new job and host country, it is important to ensure that you are not forgotten at the home office. The assignment may be coming to an end before you realize it, or an extension may be in the works.
- *Welcome back riders.*
  Your assignment is complete. Often, global work ends with a return home, which is often more of a challenge than leaving for an international assignment. Preparing for your repatriation can make the transition back home much easier.

There are many resources available to assist you with the logistics of your move abroad, including relocation officers. The issues you'll need to deal with include negotiating your expatriate contract, solving tax issues, finding a house, locating a school, identifying babysitters, etc. Please visit our website if you're interested in learning more about these topics. While logistics are extremely important, we will focus on broader aspects of your move. During the interview, WiSER Heidi provided an accurate description of the experience of expatriation. "When you make a move like that, everything is exciting, vibrant, and sparkling, with renewed enthusiasm and renewed excitement. I was very receptive to the move, and therefore people were very receptive to me. Excitement is infectious."

Fasten your seatbelt

The time between your acceptance of an assignment and the starting date can be as brief as a few weeks or as long as a few months, but regardless of how much time you have prior to your move, it's important to take advantage of that time to prepare for your adventure. When preparing for your international assignment, it's critical to find out as much as you can about your role, the place in which you will live, your host country's culture, your housing opportunities...well...the list goes on and on. You might be thinking to yourself, "Of course I would do that." Yet, we have spoken to very successful WiSER who revealed that they did not adequately prepare themselves. In some cases, they trusted that the company would take care of them. In other cases, they were so focused on managing their career move that they didn't think of anything else. And in other cases, they simply thought that the new opportunity wouldn't be that different. Well, things can be very different, and lack of preparation for such differences could lead to a failed assignment.

When thinking of the changes involved in an expatriate assignment, an old joke comes to mind. A woman dies and goes to heaven. When she encounters God, she is told, "Before you enter heaven, it is our policy that everyone spends one day in hell." The woman is confused. "Why would I want to spend one day in hell?" she says. God continues, "After twenty-four hours, you can let me know if you would prefer to enter heaven or stay in hell." At that point, God pushes a button and sends her down the elevator to hell. The doors open, and hell is magnificent. It is filled with beautiful people in beautiful clothes, all of them laughing and drinking. The woman engages in animated conversations with perfect strangers, and she is offered fine foods. After twenty-four hours, she takes the elevator back to God, and says, "I never thought that I would say this, but I would like to spend my eternity in hell." God sadly indicates that she's not the first person to choose hell over heaven. God then adds, "I'm sorry to see you go," and sends her back down the elevator. When the doors open, the woman is shocked by what she sees. The place is filled with fire and brimstone, and everything is permeated with the bitter smell of sulfur, while people in tattered rags stumble around, moaning in despair. She finds someone who looks familiar, and says: "I was just here yesterday, and it was nothing like this. I just asked God to let me spend the rest of eternity here. Am I in the right place?" The familiar face replies: "Oh, this is the same place alright. Pity, that no one told you yesterday was our recruiting day."

It's important to remember that this joke, while patently absurd, contains a kernel of truth that can be applied to many different situations. While not all expatriates have a "recruiting day" experience abroad, it's safe to say that the reality of living in an international location may be more challenging than your first impressions have led you to believe. WiSER Stacy shared a light-hearted story about some of the challenges that she faced. "When you are visiting an international location, especially as a senior manager, you're flying first class or business class," she said. "You are staying in a five-star hotel that caters to business travelers. You are being entertained by the site practically twenty-four/seven. It's not that they're trying to pull the wool over your eyes, but they understand that you are some place completely foreign, and so they are excited to share with you the good parts of their culture." The experience may be very different when you have actually relocated. "Of our various surprises, the funniest one [involved] the bed and the mattresses," she recalled. She noted that, when she stayed in a local hotel, the beds and mattresses were extremely comfortable, and she expected to find the same situation when she set up house. "When we moved, we had a forty-foot container that we could ship over," she explained. "We didn't send our beds or mattresses, because we just assumed that they would have the same kind that we have, based on our hotel experiences." The assumption turned out to be inaccurate. "We had very painful mattresses," she recalled. "They were like bricks. On one of our trips back to the US, we squished memory foam mattress layers into suitcases, so we could literally check it in and take it with us."

The following WiSER shared that there is a distinct difference between visiting a country as opposed to living there. They also shared that, although preparation is important, all the preparation in the world can only take you so far. WiSER Jolanda said: "That's what I realized when I came over to Switzerland really not knowing the Swiss at all. I mean I've been skiing on holidays but…that doesn't mean you get to know the Swiss…You prepare yourself that it will be different but you can never prepare for how different." WiSER Anna agreed that it's impossible to prepare yourself for all of the challenges involved in an overseas assignment. "You do have different working environments…. That was something I did find quite difficult," she said. "But I can't see how you can possibly prepare for that. You know it is something that you can only really experience by being there."

While it is impossible to "know" the unknown, tools such as the Internet, social media sites, websites that are dedicated to international relocation, and relevant books and blogs can help you boost your level of awareness. Cultural classes can be extremely beneficial and help you understand how and why "business as usual" is different in your host country. Equipped with such knowledge, you will have a deeper understanding of why people behave the way they do in your host country. The key to success is not to know everything, but rather to face new challenges and opportunities with an open mind and a degree of courage. What follows is an overview of tips, shared by WiSER, that will help you prepare as best you can for your assignment.

Tips to prepare for your international assignment

1. Learn about the job and the new organization

Although the idea of taking an international assignment may be intriguing, it is vital that you accept a job that you will enjoy, since you will have a variety of adjustments to make as well as challenges to overcome. Moreover, many of these will not be directly associated with your job. Therefore, you need to learn as much as possible about the organization for which you will be working, while also identifying potential support systems. Be sure to visit the site and the business before you go, and tour your workplace. Moving is an involved proposition, and it won't be easy to reverse your decision once you've already made your move. Start to establish a connection with your new workplace and meet everyone with whom you'll be working before moving. Contact your new manager so that you have a clearer understanding of the job, as well as the goals for the position. Have you been hired to change the organizational culture, to launch new initiatives, to bring in certain skills and expertise, to reorganize the organization and fire people, or perhaps to fill a managerial skills gap? WiSER Nathalie K. offered advice based on her own experience. "I think it's important to understand...[what] your role is, and what is expected of you within the organization," she explained. "And that may evolve as you are there, but it provides clarity not just for yourself, but for the people around you on what they can expect from you as well." Furthermore, permit yourself a "gut check" to determine if you truly support the decision you've made so that you can get excited about it.

2. *Learn about the host country*

Understanding the culture of the host country will yield clues about what makes them tick, why they behave the way they do, and how you can work with them. Language is the most valuable tool for gaining insight into a culture so we advise you try to learn the basics. Allow yourself to get excited. WiSER Emily told us that this is an essential part of preparing for relocation. "Know the country that you are going to," she said. "Learn about the culture; understand the history. It might not seem to be important knowledge, but it is important to them. And so it makes sense to spend that time and be interested in the places that you are in. I think... they make a difference in being successful."

If you have a partner and/or family, you are not the only one who will live and operate in the new culture. They will experience the differences as much as you will, and therefore, it is advisable to take steps to help prepare your family as well. While many organizations offer cross-cultural training to the expatriate manager, they do not always extend this service to their family. If, however, you can ensure that your family learns about the new culture and language prior to the move, this will reduce some of the stress once you've relocated. Therefore, if your organization does not offer this perk, don't hesitate to ask for it. A family's failure to adapt to a host country is a major reason that expatriate assignments fail. Take care of your family, and they will take care of you.

3. *Ask questions and ask for help*

WiSER Diana observed in the interview that she regretted not asking more questions about her assignment and its location. "Ah...maybe better communication, by myself or the employer, would have helped," she said. "For example, the company told me that I was going to have a driver. That was true. I had a driver. I understood that I would have a maid also, and other such luxuries.... But did you know that nobody told me that I would also have an apartment that was full of lizards?" Diana recalled taking a shower with ten lizards looking on. She was horrified and to her colleagues' great amusement (after all, she was staying in a tropical country), she went to HR for help. "They did try to put my concerns to rest by informing me that the lizards won't do me any harm," she recalled. "This was not a consolation. I know that the lizards are not going to do me any harm, but I don't want to take a shower with lizards in the shower." The importance of asking questions beforehand cannot be overestimated—and if you ask all the questions that come to mind and still find yourself in a sticky situation, ask for help. See our website for a list of smart questions to ask.

4. *Understand costs and benefits associated with expatriation*

Expatriation can be financially rewarding, but it can also be costly. If you receive an expatriate package and it is relatively comprehensive, you may feel as though you've hit the jackpot. After all, when is the last time someone paid for your rent or your children's education? Well, don't get too excited. Appearances can be deceiving. As an expatriate, you will incur costs that you typically wouldn't have or you would, but now they incur all at the same time. When WiSER Alicia moved to Germany, she found that cash flow became an immediate concern. "The biggest challenge we had was, quite frankly, the cash flow," she said. "They do give you a month's salary, but that goes really quickly when you have to buy all your appliances, pay down payments for rent, school deposit, and so forth." She added, "You had to have such a huge cash outlay for everything because this country does not operate on credit as you do in the US."

WiSER Maxine likened managing the cost of her move to project management. "When we moved to Germany, we had an Excel spreadsheet, which had 300 items on it—from how do you manage your life insurances, to your wills, to your legal jurisdiction with regard to whether your redundancy payment will pay out, to how you register your cars," she said. "It is a project management task. Do not underestimate the time that will take, and the cost of it." Maxine indicated that the cost of her move and the move back cost her family £50,000 of their own money over seven years. Therefore, whether you are self-initiating expatriation or supported by your organization, be aware of hidden costs and cost of living differentials.

Expatriation packages can be very comprehensive, dealing with many aspects related to your move. The typical relocation package elements you will want to understand include the following:

- Local compensation and benefits according to the role in the host country (car, grade, compensation etc.)

- Familiarization trip
- Removal and shipping
- Welcome package (induction to country, visits etc)
- Settling in service and language training
- Flights home
- Tax support
- Relocation allowances
- Cost of leaving allowance
- Housing
- Education

We recommend that you visit the web pages of groups such as Mercer, Towers Watson, Hewitt, or HSBC in order to learn more about expatriation packages.

5. Address dual career issues

As the saying goes, "behind every great man, there is a great woman". Among the WiSER, the situation can be inverse, in the sense that behind every "great woman" there is a "great man". The WiSER (with partners) clearly indicated that their partner's support was seminal to their success abroad. Many went on to share stories of how their partners, many of whom had a successful career in their home country, chose to stay at home or back burner their career for their duration abroad. Among WiSER with a trailing spouse, 58 percent reported that their partner worked in the host country (most often found on their own) , and 42 percent said that their partner either put his career on hold to take care of the family in the host country or did not find work.

If the organization has not, or cannot, facilitate a job for your partner, start to ask questions. Determine if there are different types of work that may be permitted within the host country. Sometimes it is difficult to get a work permit to work for a large organization, but you may be able to start a small business or do some consulting. Groups like the United Nations can sponsor workers in various nations because of their global status. Furthermore, your partner could work via the internet for a home country-based organization, like an online university. Dare to be creative!

As WiSER Joanne thoughtfully discussed, "We always made the decision on how the careers would go, which one we would follow, and whatever we choose...you have to have that constant conversation because it's very, very hard in most families for the male to take a second chair after they have been the first chair for all their lives. So, you have to just manage to have an open dialogue so that you maintain a good relationship in that conversation. Whether or not working in the host country for your trailing spouse is an option, the most important thing you can do is to ensure that behind you, there still is a "great man", who supports you.

6. *Discuss and understand a repatriation plan*

Ideally you will want a job upon return that builds upon the experience that you've acquired during your stay abroad. Bear in mind that a traditional assignment lasts three to five years. In most cases, neither you nor the organization knows what lies that far in the future. Some flexibility can, therefore, be beneficial to you and the organization. The ability to advance or postpone an assignment end-date based on available opportunities, needs of the organization or personal needs, could enhance repatriation opportunities, so be sure to keep this in mind. In addition, be aware of succession-planning discussions, and advertise your performance and goals to repatriate so that they are taken into consideration. There is a big difference between repatriating simply for the purpose of "going home" and returning to your home office with the intention of leveraging your new experience. You want to be able to build on your experience, which is the reason you sought an international assignment in the first place. Whether you stay with your current organization or self-initiate repatriation, be sure that you accept a job that you'll enjoy.

Enjoy the ride

When you arrive in the host country, be prepared to go through a roller-coaster of emotions. You will feel alternately happy and then sad. Even if you have learned to speak the language, or if you have been lucky enough to have had cross cultural training, your feelings will still fluctuate. This is called the expatriate cycle (Expat Explorer 2012). At first, everything seems new and exciting, and you find that there are many things to discover. This period is generally referred to as the "honeymoon phase." Within about three months, however, you will become sensitive to some of the differences between the host country and your home country, evidence that you have entered the "negotiation phase." Many of the differences you dislike become a source of annoyance and dissatisfaction, and in time, you may become homesick. WiSER Andrea described her experience of the first two phases. "The first time that you move...is the first time that you realize that you are basically on your own in a different country, that you don't have any kind of support system, that you have to build everything again from scratch, from zero," she said. "You have to build new friendships, you have to find...new doctors. You have to shop in a different place, and buy different things." This early period of adaptation can be an emotional roller coaster. "There is a huge learning curve, and it's always exactly the way they describe," she said. "In the beginning...you are happy. Then, after this two-to-three month period... comes the homesick time, when you start to compare everything, and you miss everyone and you miss everything in your daily life." It will take another few months to find yourself in the "adjustment phase." At this point, the host country starts to feel less foreign, and you feel more confident. You become familiar with the different routines and customs and start to understand the new culture and to accept the differences. In the end, you will feel comfortable in the new country. You will find your place in the local community and identify ways to combine the new culture with your own. This is called the "mastery phase."

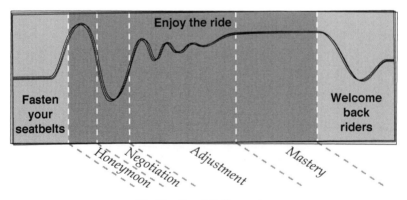

The Emotional Rollercoaster

Whether you have prepared in advance or not, moving to another country will always create enormous stress. During the negotiation and adjustment phases, you will experience shock at two levels. At a practical level, during your daily routine, you will experience "country shock." Meanwhile, as you struggle to adapt to unfamiliar behavior, you will experience "culture shock." To compound matters, this all happens during a period when you are making your first impression in a new job. In the next chapter, we explore ways to manage a successful entry, despite the onset of country and culture shock.

Country shock

When you move abroad, you will have to adjust to a new physical environment. This means getting used to a new climate, new faces, and a new currency—just to name a few. In addition, you are doing without many of the things to which you were accustomed to at home. If you have relocated to a developing country, you will face even more challenges, including a poor communication infrastructure, frequent electricity fall-out, fuel shortages, and substandard roads. Adapting to your new environment will involve setting up new routines and learning to find your way around a new city. Routines don't require energy, but when you have to think continually about the simplest tasks in life, it can drain the energy you normally reserve for "sophisticated' tasks." WiSER Pauline explained that you will usually have to factor in more time and planning for simple tasks. "You're not on your home turf," she said. "You have to assume that it's going to take longer, whether it's to get my car repaired, or my immigration papers, or my kids to go to a doctor, or whatever it may be. You need to factor in that little bit of extra level of complexity."

On more than a few occasions, you will feel incompetent and frustrated. You will find that you suddenly have to think about each and every daily activity—activities that normally required little, if any, thought. The difference, of course, is that you are operating in an environment that is new and unfamiliar. WiSER Emily shared a humorous story involving her own efforts to adapt to a new environment. "I remember when I moved to Hungary," she said. "Hungarian is a completely different language, and so there is just no way of understanding until you learn it. I think I had been there about a month and everything was going fine, but I had this whole nervous breakdown one night because I accidentally bought... what I thought was laundry detergent." In the absence of a washing machine or Laundromat, she had adopted the habit of washing her clothes in the sink, and she was shocked at the results when she poured the contents of the bottle on her clothes. "I threw all this bleach...onto my jeans, and I only brought...two suitcases with me," she recalled. "They were covered with these white streaks, and I ended up sobbing, and my roommate felt like, 'Why is she sobbing over some jeans?'" Her response to the incident, of course, was a reflection over her larger frustration with the language barrier. Meanwhile, WiSER Stacy got to use bleach in an unfamiliar manner. "I learned how to wash vegetables in bleach water," she said. "I'd never heard of that. I had thought [that] if you drink bleach, it would kill you." Overall, our advice is to maintain a sense of humor. It will get better!

Apart from the need to reestablish daily routines, your new job will require a good deal of your time and energy. Hence, the first months in your new host country are likely to be exhausting. This may seem disconcerting, but many of you have probably gone through similar adjustments before, whether in the course of simply changing jobs or moving to a new city in your home country. In all these situations, you had to get used to a new environment, find your way in a new city, build your social network from scratch, and so on. In the course of these moves and changes, you have already employed some of the skills that you will need to settle and succeed in another country. WiSER Supriya found that each move brought its own challenges and rewards. "Every move has been difficult," she recalled. "It's not very easy. Every move allowed me to move up; every change of assignment was something new and challenging. But it was also very difficult because you had to adjust your whole work life balance and commitments to your family."

Culture Shock

Culture is like an iceberg with some parts revealed and some concealed. How people interact with each other and their environment varies from culture to culture (see chapter 3). What we refer to as culture shock is brought on by stress resulting from losing cultural clues—the signs and symbols that guide social interaction. "These clues, which may be words, gestures, facial expressions, customs, or norms are acquired by all of us in the course of growing up and are as much a part of our culture, as the language we speak or the beliefs we accept. When an individual enters a strange culture, all or most of these familiar cues are removed. He or she is like a fish out of water" (Oberg 2012).

Adjustment to a new country is often complicated by the fact that that people tend to glorify certain aspects of their home country and view many aspects of the new country in a negative light. WiSER Erica observed that romanticizing the past limits your capacity to work with the people who are right in front of you. "Throughout my career I have heard a lot of people talk and reminisce about the past. They say things like 'Oh, when we had this, when we had that, we used to do it this way,' etc. etc. This is the worst thing to do," she noted. "This new country and this new group of people that you work with accepted you with open arms, and you need to be respectful and be positive... don't compare."

Making an effort to become integrated into your new community will help reduce culture shock and get you settled in more quickly. The WiSER engaged in activities such as participating in sports, taking language courses, going out socially with colleagues, etc. Even though your posting is temporary, treat it as if it was the rest of your life. Don't think that you are only there for three months or three years and make decisions based on that notion. Decisions based on the perception that your assignment is temporary could include renting a cheap apartment, failing to join clubs and other social organizations, and neglecting to reach out to neighbors. WiSER Andrea concurred. "For me, every time I go, I always think I could be here forever," she said. "So I [might] as well...get engaged in things, understand the local politics, learn the language, mix with the people — and that is something that makes you learn much more and enjoy much more than if you are just thinking of that as an assignment." Meanwhile, WiSER Sezin described how the simple act of buying furniture led her to become more engaged with her host country. "In Iraq, I couldn't carry my furniture, so what I did was I bought things," she said. "I colored things; I bought fabric; I made curtains; I covered the sofas. That process of setting up a home for me introduced me to the market...the people, introduced me to the homes. And by nesting, in a way, I got to accept the place. From that I learned, that's the way I settle into places." Once you become engaged in things, learn to understand the local politics, learn the language and mix with the people, you will integrate fluidly. Refer to chapter 3 to recognize and better understand different cultural behaviors and see tips on how to adapt to new cultures.

It should be noted, however, that efforts to engage in some countries as a single woman can be challenging. WiSER Claudia described an experience she had in Panama. "Prostitution is not a crime here, so there are a lot of prostitutes. So, going out at night was a problem.... I have 1.8 meters height and this causes attention when you go out. I'm a big person.... I could not go to a bar on a Friday night to make friends, because here it's impossible to do due to a cultural aspect." So, she concentrated on out-of-work activities that involved safe environments. "In the first week, I found out where I could go to receive dance classes, swimming classes, and I started having like three kinds of activities outside work," she recalled. "Maybe if I would be a guy, I could just go to a bar and make friends," she conceded. "Yes, it would be easier." Again, adjusting is not always easy, but engaging in activities that give you energy and put you in contact with like-minded people will make you feel at home before you realize it.

There are signs and symptoms that that can help you recognize when you or a loved one are experiencing country or culture shock.

Emotional signs	Symptoms
Sadness/ Depression	Headaches, pains, and allergies
Anger	Over-concern about your health
Vulnerability	Insomnia or sleeping too much
Irritability	Obsessed with cleanliness
Loneliness	Withdrawal
Shy/insecure	Idealizing your own culture
Homesickness	Trying too hard to fit in
Lost/confused	Smallest problems seem overwhelming
Boredom	Questioning your decision to move to this place
Frustration	Stereotyping of host nationals
Anxiety	Hostility toward host nationals

Overall signs and symptoms of culture and country shock

One of the WiSER told us that she was expecting to come home one day and see her husband and children on the couch, in a dark room, with arms crossed, saying that they were miserable and wanted to go home. Luckily for her this never happened. The key is to understand that country and culture shock are temporary conditions—not only for you, but also for your family. You will need to assist your family members during their adaptation period. "You are going to have an increased accountability to your family...[something] you don't feel in your home country, because your spouse and your kids are more independent in their home environment," WiSER Elsa I. advised. "You put them out of that [environment], and now you have—at least in my mind—an accountability to minimize the isolation they might feel, or smooth the transition for them."

Again, avoid idealizing home, attempt to integrate yourself and your family quickly by using the tips to adapt to a new culture (see chapter 3), in order to minimize country and culture shock.

Avoid being forgotten

At this point, you have adjusted to your new job and host country. You are starting to enjoy yourself, and just as you are getting comfortable, you need to start planning your next move. It would seem to be in the organization's best interest to fully exploit your acquired skills and competencies, to build on the lessons you have learned, and give you a satisfying job so that you will be inclined to stay with the organization. However, this doesn't always happen. Your career is further jeopardized by the fact that many expatriates find repatriating more difficult to manage than the expatriating process and end up leaving their organization. Imagine, after an organization invests all that money, or an individual uses thousands of dollars of personal savings to uproot and move themselves, the experience is not recognized or valued by the home country.

There are some basic reasons that this happens. Organizations hire expatriates for a variety of reasons—to staff openings with a diverse workforce, to establish a skills transfer, to bring expertise in-house, or to develop leadership skills. However, the majority of expatriates believe they were selected in order to develop themselves for the next bigger and better opportunity within the organization. Many feel as though they have made sacrifices in order to be an expatriate, and that they will be justly rewarded with promotions, raises, and recognition. This may be a feeling they share with those that serve their nation in the military and return home with amazing experiences—both good and bad—in which few people take much of an interest. WiSER Magi shared with us the feelings that she experienced when repatriating. "Most companies have a...lack of understanding [on] how to treat and take back the people they send," she said. "[However] what the people want when they come back home is [a] thank you...just to say 'thank you' or to present you with a piece of paper that says you've completed successfully this expatriate assignment.... Little things like that...would make [a] very large difference in how many people stay with the company after two years of being back."

One survey reports that 33 percent of repatriates are promoted, 58 percent of repatriates stay at the same level, and 9 percent are demoted after their return. Indeed, just 27 percent of expatriates are even guaranteed a position after they return from assignment, and most are expected to develop their own strategy for repatriation (Tyler 2006). This results in valuable talent not being preserved in home countries or within the organization, itself. An important reason for this could be that although many organizations (74 percent) have a written repatriation policy in place, only 16 percent of those organizations had that strategy linked to career management and retention (Brookfield 2012,16). This means that you will have to take the initiative when it comes to finding a challenging job upon your return. If you don't take the lead, you'll risk ending up with a job that may not leverage your international experience and could also involve less responsibility and autonomy than desired. You may even end up without a job at all, or find yourself waiting for an opening, which could take months. Any of these situations could easily occur, and they are among the reasons that expats leave organizations upon their return. Indeed, 12 percent of the international assignees leave their organizations (Brookfield 2012, 17). If organizations hope to retain their expatriates and capitalize on their experience (i.e., get some return on investment), they must structure their repatriation processes.

This trend underscores the vital importance of employing strategies that ensure you will be remembered at the home office. At the same time, you need to lay plans to integrate back into your previous home after completing an expatriate assignment. Recently, my family and I (Sapna) returned from a visit to the USA, and my husband met with some colleagues in the local offices. Meanwhile, I met with my former boss and former business partner. These reunions were eventful and enjoyable. It is always a wonderful thing to reconnect. Even our kids indicated that they wanted to make sure their friends hadn't forgotten them. This got us thinking. How can expatriates make sure that they aren't "forgotten" when they are on assignment?

According to a German legend, even the smallest of plants did not wish to be forgotten. Legend has it that, in medieval times, as a knight and his lady walked by a river, the knight picked some posies for the lady. Unfortunately, due to the weight of his armor, the knight fell into the river. As he drowned, he threw the posies to his beloved and shouted, "Forget-me-not." The flower was often worn by ladies as a sign of faithfulness and enduring love.

When one embarks on an expatriate assignment, there is a shared concern of being forgotten at the home office for other suitable opportunities, new assignments, or even promotions. As WiSER Pauline told us: "The advice I would give is to keep a connection back to your home organization" she said. "That is absolutely critical. You've got to keep your network up. You need to keep in touch with what's going on back home because the risk is that you can indeed be forgotten about. You're out of sight, out of mind as they say. Depending on what kind of talent management your company has, it is really important to keep that connection back to your base." When you are far away and forgotten, you will not be considered for new positions or promotion until you are almost due back. Shy of wearing a flower, how does an expatriate show his/her sign of "faithfulness" to the organization and home office and not be forgotten?

Tips to be remembered at home office
- Have a mentor/sponsor at the home office and try to have monthly one-on-one meetings with them. Ideally he or she looks out for your interests and keeps you informed of all important developments in the home organization.

- Foster two-way communication with people in the home office.

- Keep current on developments and changes in the home office.

- Follow "hot trends" and "cool news" in the geography of the home office.

- Take vacation time to visit the home office and, if possible, try to work from there a couple of days.

- Pro-actively inform people of your career aspirations and your interest to repatriate.

- Request HR formal interviews so that you can share your new experiences and acquired skills.

- Encourage HR to consider policies that require regular visits to the home office, a three-month notice prior to the end of the assignment, and flexibility in the duration of the assignment so expatriates — like other employees — can move for other opportunities prior to, or after, assignment end dates.

- Get involved in global work streams, task forces, and other organizational initiatives that will showcase your experience.

- Ensure that you will receive strong repatriation assistance for you and your family. Coming home can be terribly difficult, given that it is an international move that is not treated as one. Things may have changed significantly during your absence, or perhaps you are being moved to a different place in your home country, which is also brand new. You have to re-establish, or establish, everything you did on your expatriate assignment (Tyler 2006).

Although it is important that the home office is aware of your work — and your aspirations — it is also important to stay focused on the opportunity that's in front of you. Performing well on an international assignment will be a visible feather in your cap, as WiSER Stacy learned during an assignment in India. "When I moved to India, it was an offshore process, and...my manager was in the US," she recalled. I was sent there to help, get it back into shape. So clearly, I had a huge focus on India, at the time." Meanwhile, she noticed that her peers in the US were being assigned global projects, and she felt that her visibility at the home office was endangered. "I felt like I enjoyed great visibility when I was in the US and it just wasn't there anymore...everybody knew I had gone to India and knew what I was doing, but I just didn't have - I wasn't in front of the COO very often, which is what I used to enjoy." So she reached out to a senior manager who was in Hong Kong, that she had worked with and asked her for some mentoring. Much to her surprise, her mentor strongly recommended that she focus exclusively on the needs of her team in India and not worry about her visibility. "Because when you leave, you need to make sure that they can sustain themselves, and that's the visibility that you need," he mentor advised. "And part of being in this assignment is the recognition that it isn't about the special projects that everybody gets in the US, because you have one of the biggest projects right there." Succeeding in your expatriate assignment is the best advocate for you to create visibility. There is only one condition to it: let everybody know how successful you are and keep some lines open to the home office.

Welcome back riders

You have caught your stride, things are moving along well, and you may be looking at concluding the typical three-to-five year assignment. When you go back home, after having completed your international assignment, you might assume that settling back in a country where you've lived for so many years will be easy. Well, the opposite is true. Indeed, repatriation is often considered to be a more difficult process than expatriation. The problems you encounter when repatriating, the so-called reverse culture shock, are brought on by the fact that you simply don't expect that you will need to re-adapt to a place with which you are so familiar. Given that the difficulties involved with expatriation are primarily the result of cultural differences, you would expect the transition to your "cultural base" to be a smooth one. After all, you know the country, the culture, and possibly have personal relationships there. But during your absence, especially if you have been away for an extended period of time, your home environment will have changed. In addition, your international experience has changed you. Fitting in is therefore not as easy as you might expect it to be. Consequently, when returning home, you may experience many of the same emotions that you felt when you expatriated.

In the first few weeks it feels wonderful to be back home, visiting friends and family, being the center of attention, eating your favorite food, and doing all of the things that you missed so much while being abroad. About one month into your repatriation, however, reverse culture shock begins to set in. You have already shared stories of your adventures abroad, and now your regular routine begins. This is when you become acutely aware of the things that you don't particularly like back home, and you may find yourself glorifying everything about your international experience. You just don't feel "at home" in your home. The WiSER shared reasons why repatriating can be so unexpectedly difficult.

1. *Home office has changed*

If you are returning to the home office, you will notice that, of course, things have changed during your absence. Colleagues may have left or moved to another department. Management may have changed. Strategy and processes may have changed. In short, many things will be different than the way you remember them. You will have to recreate your network in order to learn about the new political and organizational environment.

2. *It is more difficult to build a social life*

Expat communities are known to be small, close and tied communities in which it is easy to integrate. All expatriates are in the same position: they arrive in the host country with zero relationships, zero network. Therefore, all expats who have been there for a while know how wonderful it is to be welcomed into that community and they take care of new families. Unfortunately, back home there is no such thing as a "repatriation community". WiSER Elsa L. described some of the challenges that she experienced during her return home. "It was much easier to go overseas and spend thirty years than it was to come back," she recalled. "I think when I first came back, people said to me, 'Well after thirty years of living overseas what do you like best about being back?' And I used to always say, 'Well, having electricity everyday and not having my water cut off for hours at a time,' because those were things that I lived with for the last ten years." She found, however, that the biggest challenge involved in returning was connecting with people. "One, people are very busy with their lives, and I think they tend to live more insular lives," Elsa L. observed. "I didn't know the people, there was no immediate community to become part of. People just drive into their garage, and then they go from the garage to their house. And then, when it's time to leave, they go into the garage, they get in the car, and they go. It isn't like you connect with people a lot on a personal level."

3. *People can't relate to your experiences*

Many people back home haven't had the kinds of exotic experiences you have, and they may not be able to relate to them. On top of that, there are only so many stories or slideshows they will be willing to tolerate. Over time, you may feel quite disconnected. WiSER Jacqueline shared with us some of the feelings of disconnectedness she experienced when she first came back from Africa. "I had fully prepared myself for how I would have to support my [Kenyan] husband coming to America for the first time, but I never had prepared myself for the re-entry adjustment it would take on me coming back to America," she acknowledged. "It was so difficult. I went through almost a year of depression, and I was in my own country." While people showed initial interest in her overseas experience, this interest often proved to be short-lived. "I talked to people and they would say, 'Oh, you were in Africa, what was it like?,'" she explained. "And I started telling, but within seconds they would ask, 'Oh, so how do you keep your garden so green?' It's like, I have seen Rwanda. I have seen Sudan. We had a staff murdered in Sudan, and I had to counsel and debrief my staff on that. I had seen so much, and then I came back, and no one had seen that with me." She noted that she did not begin to settle until she accepted a job that brought her into contact with other people with international experience. "Then, I started to understand more what I had been going through," she said. "But those two years prior to that experience...[were] pretty dark."

4. *You are not special anymore, nor is your environment*

WiSER Martha explained to us that you can develop an appetite for being an expatriate. "I think there is almost an addiction that comes from living overseas because you are always experiencing newness — new cultures, new languages, new people, new countries," she said. "And that becomes very easy to get wrapped up in. You don't want to go back to your home territory because it's dull.... You are not special anymore, and it's not special either...You get used to being different and people [being] interested in you because you are unique." She added that she had to come to terms with the fact that, when she came home, that was not the case anymore.

5. *Life can be less luxurious*

Particularly in less developed countries, expatriates tend to benefit from an extensive support structure. In many cases, you will enjoy the luxury of a driver, nanny, gardener, and cook. Upon your return, all of this support will disappear, and you will have to do everything by yourself once again. Millions of other women do as well — that's for sure. At this point, however, you are not used to handling these chores anymore. WiSER Martha discussed with us some of the challenges involved in readjusting to domestic chores upon her return. "Well, there is the practical side of it, which is the fact that we don't have the help anymore," she said. "I feel like the mountains of laundry never end, and the cooking, and the cleaning.... We're still grappling with that. Suddenly you realize: 'I had this very high-powered job overseas, but I had a lot of help. Now, I've got the same job actually, same expectations, same work load, and no help.' So, that's been tough."

6. *You have changed*

Last but not least, all those years living and working abroad have changed you as a person. "I find that the people I do connect with here…are people who have had international experiences, that have lived overseas or worked overseas, because others have a more limited view of the world," WiSER Elsa L. told us. "The very limited view of the world is something I don't have very much tolerance for." And that is one of the problems you will face coming home. You view the world from a different perspective, you have become the product of two different worlds. You will have to find the changed 'you' a new place in your own society.

Managing re-entry shock

Given all of the challenges that we have discussed, how can you manage your repatriation with style? For one thing, you can start while you are still in the host country. More than likely, you will have mixed feelings about your departure. Try to embrace the positive feelings you have about your upcoming adventure. Before leaving, create some sense of closure. Do the things you always wanted to do, but didn't have a chance to do. Visit the places you would like to see one last time, and take your time to say 'goodbye' to the people you will miss. Bear in mind that repatriating doesn't mean that you will never return, or that you will never see these friends again. After all, you are moving, not dying. Meanwhile, prepare yourself for the shock of re-entry so that it won't take you by surprise. And don't forget that you have been through transitions before, and you will manage this time as well (Storti 2001). Apart from the above, there are very practical things you can do to minimize reverse culture shock once you are back on your home turf.

Minimizing culture shock - tips

- Prepare your friends and family for what you will be going through so that they can take your feelings into account.

- Try to find other returnees with whom you can share your thoughts and challenges, and see what useful advice they can share.

- Identify an expatriate community or get in contact with other people who have international experience. You could do this by joining an international organization at home to maintain a flavor of the international environment.

- Continue practicing the language you learned with others.

- Get involved in global projects and initiatives.

- Accept all invitations for outings with colleagues, neighbors and friends as you begin to find your new niche.

- Stay in touch with the friends that you made during your expatriate assignment.

At some point, after three to eighteen months, the worst will be behind you. You will start to feel settled again. You will realize that you can readjust without having to let go of values and behaviors that you embraced during your international assignment.

It's a wrap!

To revisit our original analogy, an international assignment is very much like riding a roller coaster. There are multiple cycles involved in expatriation, including the three phases of the overall adventure and the four emotional phases of adjustment. In combination, these phases can create a dizzying experience that is filled with unexpected twists and turns, and loaded with thrills. You will probably scream, cry, and laugh along the way. We have tried to give you a balanced overview of what you can expect. After careful consideration, and much soul searching, you will need to ask yourself whether you are ready to purchase the ticket and jump on the ride.

Your Debut

"You never get a second chance to make a good first impression."
~ Will Rogers

"I didn't want to like her, but I ended up liking her. She is fantastic."
~ Male colleague of WiSER Alicia

It is time for your debut. As you consider your initial entrance to a new nation, culture, job and work team, you will be forced to fundamentally rediscover yourself and another culture simultaneously. Your debut will leave critics reeling only if you can operate at an optimal level immediately. In order to wow your audience, ensure you make a good first impression by effectively communicating with everyone you encounter and make sure that you make your first thirty days on the job count.

Achieving peak performance in a senior level international role will require you, not only to ramp up and perform well, but also to avoid pitfalls. During a recent conversation with the head of learning and development for one of the largest global employers, he shared the following observation with us: "Leaders trip on pebbles." Naturally, this comment intrigued us, and we asked him to explain it. He replied by noting that leaders, especially global leaders, have generally found themselves in that position because they are proven entities. They have shown that they possess the knowledge, skills, and abilities to fulfill their roles. If that's the case, why do these leaders sometimes fail? He noted that they don't fail because they've tripped over a boulder; they fail because they've tripped over pebbles. Regardless of what you trip over, there is a pursuant fall. In international roles, you are more likely to encounter "pebbles" than "boulders" given the complexities due to "concealed" cultural differences. As a female international leader, you will encounter even more "pebbles" due to the bell curve (see chapter 5).

As you make your debut, regardless of demands and challenges, remember you are "the chosen one" among many other talented professionals to take on a challenging international opportunity because your talents can help the organization meet its goals. It's your time to shine.

First impressions

The majority of the WiSER we interviewed indicated that the first month of a new assignment was the most challenging — and the most critical for success. The first thirty days are fraught with pebbles and will put you to the test. On the one hand, expatriate life is exciting and interesting. It allows people to cross-pollinate ideas and activities from around the world. On the other, you are quite vulnerable at this time. You are unfamiliar with your new role and the dynamics of your new group, and you have left much of your network. All of this is compounded by the fact that you are in a new country. Making a positive first impression as an expatriate is crucial. First impressions are made within thirty seconds of meeting someone. That is not much time at all! The good news is, you have thirty days to make a lasting impression. Within the first month, your colleagues are looking for the answers to several questions, with the often uncomfortable awareness that you are neither local nor a male. Are you competent? Are you trustworthy? Are you someone to approach or avoid? Do you have status and authority? Are you simply interested in upgrading your résumé, or are you someone who is genuinely interested in other people?

More than likely, you will join a warm, welcoming community of expatriates. At the same time, it is a community where you may go grocery shopping with the CEO's wife. Perhaps you will find yourself scheduling play dates and sleepovers between your children and those of your colleagues. It is even possible you will find yourself camping with colleagues who are also close friends. In short, you will be part of an intimate community where first impressions are doubly important, given that the community is both your professional and social network. "It is [crucial] to earn trust and credibility in your environment, particularly in an international environment," WiSER Hermie stressed. Considering that 31 percent of global organizations have more than 100 employees and 26 percent have more than 500 employees deployed as expatriates (Brookfield 2012, 16) — and bearing in mind that a portion of these are global nomads — there is a good chance that, after leaving your assignment, you will work with them again in a different role and country.

Expatriating involves challenging opportunities to build collaboration, to explain a strategy, to streamline processes, to communicate with teams that have different cultural and communication approaches — all with the goal of driving results. In an expatriate assignment, you will refine your problem-solving skills, communication skills, stress-management skills, and teamwork skills, while learning what is truly meant by adaptability. Imagine that you are part of a global work team in a country other than your own and that in this country, math is done as follows:

− means to multiply
÷ means to add
+ means to divide
x means to subtract

Although your math skills may be outstanding, you would need to retrain yourself in order to calculate effectively in this new country. This process is time-consuming, and it will require patience, adaptability and creativity. It goes without saying that the example presented is unreal, the effects, however, are very real. Your outstanding skills and knowledge, which were part of the reason why you got this international assignment, will be put to the test in your new environment. Look at it this way, you have been given a blank canvas, and it is time to start work on a masterpiece.

The power of words

Effective communication is the most obvious, and most important, way to create your first impression. Communication encompasses the way you present yourself, and the manner in which you express your ideas. Your ability to effectively communicate will be the basis upon which your new colleagues will develop an opinion about you. This is where cultural differences come into play. Communication is, to a great extent, shaped by cultural norms, and it is imperative to modify or adapt your communication styles in order to be understood (and to avoid being misunderstood) when working in different countries. "I absolutely modify my communication style depending upon the cultural context I am working in," noted WiSER Sandra.

In some cases, even a move back to your home country, after having spent many years abroad, can involve certain communication pitfalls. WiSER Pauline had this experience after repatriating to the USA following fifteen years in Europe. "It was the first time that I actually had to work a lot with North America[ns]," she recalled. "Actually, that was where I had a problem." She recalled that, about three months into the job, her vice president approached her and strongly recommended that she modify her communication style when dealing with [local] residents. Pauline was shocked and confused. She was an American, after all, and didn't expect there to be any issue. "Well…you're American, but you've worked in Western Europe for a long time, and people are more direct there," her boss responded. "You need to tone things down a little bit when you're talking to them." Evidently, her assumption that she would know how to deal with fellow Americans after a long period of expatriation turned out to be misguided.

Tips for effective cross-cultural communication

Communicating effectively in an international environment requires a mastery of a range of skills, including speaking, presenting, writing, and listening. In addition, you need to "read" the unspoken in various settings, ranging from one-on-one encounters to presentations before large audiences. Here is a list of tips to effectively communicate across cultures that were shared by the WiSER.

1. *Follow cultural protocol and preferences*

When communicating you need to consider cultural protocol and preferences. WiSER Martha observed that these include the manner in which you interact with superiors, and the way you greet people or initiate a conversation, which all have to do with respect. Likewise, WiSER Annette explained that modes of explanation that are effective in one culture may not work as well in another. "One thing I have learned is that [some] cultures like story-telling," she explained. "And by that I mean, when you are trying to...give an example...you say, 'I think you should do "X," and this reminds me of a project ... where we were looking at "Y," and we decided to do "A-B-C," and this turned out to be a good decision." She noted that this kind of storytelling worked well in the Middle East, where people preferred concrete examples that were based on personal experience. However, these long, personalized explanations tended to bore German workers, who were inclined to request that she get to the point and provide concise directions. Meanwhile, it is also important to take into account the company culture, which is often reflected in lingo and colloquialisms. We recommend that you familiarize yourself with these, but we also suggest that you use them sparingly to ensure that you keep things simple and clear.

2. *Practice active listening*

Listening should be treated as the "better half" of good communication. As the saying goes, God gave us two ears and one mouth because listening is twice as important, but twice as difficult. In an international environment—where there are different levels of knowledge of the language, different communication styles, accents, and body language—the importance of strong listening skills is even greater. "I don't think listening is an inherent talent that a lot of us have," WiSER Pauline said. "But I think listening becomes even more important when you're working in a multicultural environment." To be an effective listener involves listening without thinking about what you will say next—and remaining focused. It means to acknowledge the person you are listening to. Active listening will also make you more receptive to unspoken body language.

It is best to save judgments for later, after you have heard and understood what was said. You don't need to feel obligated, but keep an open mind toward the option that is being promoted. "I think that when I am flying into a country where I haven't worked a lot...I am very careful, that I don't think that I know what the answer is" WiSER Karin observed.

3. *Develop strong writing skills and follow writing 'protocols'*
Strong writing skills are crucial in an international environment, given that you will often communicate with people who speak English as a foreign

language, or that English is not your mother tongue. "Business writing, I think, is an important skill, and [it is] also very helpful in the international arena," WiSER Julie Anne said. "[P]eople may not understand your point when you're giving a speech, but if you are following it up with something in writing that's well written, they'll get it, even if it's not in their native language." Similarly, WiSER Emily stressed the need to write in a straightforward manner, given that you will often address people with an imperfect grasp of English.

No less important, however, is the need to be aware of writing protocols in your host country, and to make international colleagues aware of your native country's own protocols. "When you write an email to an American, and you put exclamation marks at the end of a sentence, that typically means that you are yelling at them. In Germany, it means important," WiSER Magi explained. She recalled that she took time to explain the difference to both her German and American colleagues because it had given rise to irritation and misunderstandings. "It was fun being able to teach both sides," she said.

4. *Listen to the unspoken*

Read between the lines and look for hidden messages. You also need to become adept at "reading" body language. Hearing what is not being said can serve as a valuable road map to understanding people in a country other than your own. It can also help you avoid miscommunications. "You have to have the ability to pick up on signals, to read between the lines, because the cues are certainly not what you're used to," WiSER Pauline explained. "The hidden messages are not what you grew up with. It's much, much more complex when you're working in an international environment."

WiSER Jolanda agrees that unspoken messages are often the most important. "If you get an email or letter from somebody from the UK, and it's more than four or five sentences long, it means there's something wrong because they're like the Japanese. They cannot say, 'no,'" she explained. "If they become long and windy, it means you're actually hitting them somewhere where they feel very uncomfortable, and they actually want to say to you, 'Don't do that.' But it doesn't really say that in that email."

In addition to reading signals or body language of others, find quiet moments and pay attention to what you are "hearing" from your own body. Does your body tighten up when you are dealing with certain issues? Remember that others are reading your unspoken signals as well.

5. *Be Clear*

Communicating in a different cultural setting may require that you take more time to discuss things. You may find it necessary to talk more slowly, and getting across an idea may involve drawing pictures or using hand signals—especially in cases where you speak the local language poorly, while few of your colleagues have a strong grasp of your language. It is never a mistake to repeat things in such situations, and it is better to take the risk of over-communicating rather than to under-communicate. "I am very conscious of making sure I try to explain myself so that people aren't misreading my actions because of their own personal cultural context," WiSER Sandra explained. "I had to learn to be more direct. While superficially, my international team seemed to have good English skills, they could speak better than they could understand. It was a real challenge in terms of actually learning to be very precise with words." Sandra had to learn to communicate in a manner that was concise and direct, despite the fact that this style of communication would have been considered rude in her native UK.

At the same time, however, it is important to avoid seeming as though you are simply barking orders. When language fails, resort to images, suggested WiSER Carrie. "I drew a lot of pictures and I used a lot of hand signals," she said. "I always had a whiteboard in my office, because you sometimes need to show people up or down or across or boxes or charts or something visual."

6. *Be more or less formal, more or less direct*

The directness and formality of language varies from culture to culture. Whether they use titles, operate on a first-name basis, write or speak casually or formally is directly informed by cultural norms. In the US, for example, you are likely to be on a first name basis with all your colleagues, including your superiors. In Germany, relationships are much more formal, requiring you to formally address not only your superiors, but also your peers, your secretary and even persons who are younger than you are, e.g. Mr. Zimmermann or Ms. Decker-Conradi.

Following is an example of how directness differs from culture to culture. WiSER Maria encountered this challenge when working in Canada. "Canadians avoid confrontation— let's say it like that," she noted. "Whenever they have to give a tough message, they give it in a very non-confrontational way." She observed that people in her native Belgium, on the other hand, tend to be far more direct. "It's not that we are impolite," she explained. "[It's] that we just give the messages in a more direct way, and when I speak English, or when I translate my Dutch to the English, I would be quite direct." While her style of communication discomfited many of her Canadian colleagues, none of them raised the issue in a conversation. "Nobody would ever tell me...I wasn't aware of that until I got that feedback on paper," she recalled. "Then, I realized that I had to adapt my communication style."

7. *Avoid sarcasm*

Sarcasm is typically a cutting remark that takes the form of humor, and humor differs nation to nation. Sarcasm is not considered an element of effective communication in domestic settings, and we discourage it altogether in an international environment. Rather than being considered as humor, a sarcastic remark can easily be interpreted as disrespectful, impolite, and insincere.

8. *Ask questions.*

If you want to improve your chances of soliciting honest feedback, enhancing team collaboration, and building good relationships, it is important to ask questions. It is not always easy to determine what the right questions are, but, if at first you fail, try again. WiSER Stacy indicated that she would occasionally throw out an idea and gauge the reception. At one point, she observed that everyone had been working hard and suggested that it might be a good idea to grant some "comp-time" as a reward. "Everyone said: 'Yes, yes. Great Idea,'" she recalled. Before the roll out, she asked a variety of questions. She asked about issues including time accrued and whether time off would be valued and looked upon as a reward. It was only when asking these questions that Stacy learned that many workers had so much time left, that they didn't need extra compensation time and wouldn't use it anyway, if they felt like they had to get their work done.

WiSER Sezin indicated that, in certain cultures, subordinates will not correct a supervisor if not explicitly asked to do so. In one case, she sent out a letter that included inaccurate information that her team had failed to point out. "The team...came back to me, screaming, saying 'How dare you do that?'" Sezin was stunned and told them that she thought they had agreed the content of the letter was correct. "If there was an inaccuracy, why didn't you tell me?" she asked them. They told her that they didn't say anything because she was the boss, and she should know. "So, since then, I actually drill and drill and drill and drill until I get to the bottom of things," she said.

9. *Avoid passing judgement*

Cross cultural communication is challenging. Communicating across cultures in a language different than your mother tongue creates more complexities. As WiSER Veronika advised: "Never judge people because of how they present something, how they actually talk over the phone, never judge anybody's competence or skills just due to this factor... Some very good technical people...just don't come across as good because they are not very good...in English. But it has nothing to do with that you are not good or bad, it's more about communication."

Effective communication is essential to create a positive and lasting first impression. They are essentially your paintbrushes, however, your canvas is still blank. It's time to paint!

Creating your masterpiece

You can impress others as you make your debut by adopting the appropriate mindset and taking the appropriate actions in your first month on the job. At this point, you will need more than just paintbrushes...it's time to take stock of all of your supplies, resources, and tools — your full arsenal. Moving abroad brings with it many changes in daily life. Culture (revealed and concealed) describes a society's norms and reflects its fundamental values and attitudes. These norms determine how members of a society prefer to interact and build relationships. These norms can differ greatly from your own cultural norms and it is important to decide which differences you will embrace, while staying true to yourself. Adapting to a new culture requires you to listen, observe and understand before you judge and, most importantly, respect other customs.

Don't let others paint their own impressions upon your canvas before you have a chance to do so. We strongly suggest that you develop your own opinions regarding your host country and new job based on objective information. "When I first began working with a global NGO, there was an experienced female professional who said to me, 'If you want to go far, avoid getting into the gossip group,'" WiSER Sezin told us. WiSER Lindsay agreed, and advised, "Work-wise, you have to be quite culturally open-minded, and not have negative biases or perceptions about people or stereotypes." Being open to the new culture is a prerequisite for being successful in an expatriate assignment. Spend time with the locals and show that you are genuinely interested in their different habits, ways of working, etc. Speaking the language, even haltingly, will play a big role in smoothing the path to your integration. You don't have to be fluent, but any effort you show to learn and speak the local language is much appreciated by the locals. This is a quick way to gain their admiration and support.

WiSER Jacqueline described her own efforts to learn everything she could about her host culture. "I didn't assume that I would be accepted in the culture," she explained. "So, I spent a lot of time on this. I think that I really did my homework before I left. I took time to understand what the culture would be like…. I kind of looked for anything that happened as an opportunity to learn and to grow." When she was invited to dine with a local family, she recalled, she asked about the food and learned many of the local recipes. "I love cooking, and so I learned how to prepare all the local dishes," she said. "I started learning Swahili. Whatever occasion I had, I would try to speak even though it was broken…at least I made the effort." These activities had personal as well as professional benefits. "I think all of those things together added to the richness of experience," she added.

As the saying goes, "different strokes for different folks." In an effort to adapt yourself to your new culture, you will carefully have to consider what changes you need to make in order to be effective. Be conscientious of the effectiveness of your leadership style during the first month on the assignment, and don't hesitate to modify your leadership approach, if you find that your approach is ineffective. "I think that, [in] the first weeks or the first month, I was really surprised and confused, because I realized that the way I used to lead in Denmark just didn't work at all in the UK," WiSER Karin recalled. "I always used the open door approach — you just come and we discuss. I gave this introduction speech, and I wanted all of us to work together." Despite this blanket invitation, she found that no one took her up on her offer for a personal consultation. "I got back to my office for a week and a half, and no one came," she said. "I was very confused, and I felt that I may have gotten into something that I [couldn't] manage because I really didn't know what to do." At that point, she contacted some friends and asked them what she was doing wrong. She soon discovered that employees in the UK won't stop to consult with a superior unless they are personally invited. "I said, 'Okay, if it's that easy then I'll just invite them,'" she recalled.

When modifying your approach ensure that you feel authentic and that others continue to perceive you as being authentic. WiSER Martine noted that, when she first took a position in the USA, she realized that positive feedback and rewards were doled out generously for good performance. She recognized this and began to do the same. Yet, she soon received responses that she needed to provide even more positive feedback. This struck her as amusing because, in her native Netherlands, the amount of positive reinforcement she had been giving out would have been perceived as lavish, perhaps even insincere. Don't be afraid to make changes within the framework of "best of both worlds" (see chapter 3).

"Surviving the first few months of being abroad, being away from your family, from friends, that's difficult because it's very challenging," WiSER Argentina observed. "We don't know our surroundings, and then, the language is different. The habits are different." To make matters worse, she found herself alone and isolated on most weekends. "I cried many times in those days," she said. "I think that my boss kept saying: 'No, no, no, it's okay. It's normal.'" At some point, when her boss found her particularly upset, she said: "Well, if you are about to cry I have many things to cry about, we can both cry. But if you want, we can also have fun. We can go out — and I was coming here to invite you to come out."

The exchange ended in laughter, and those kinds of supportive friends helped her get through the first few months of her assignment. While you face a plethora of challenges during the adjustment period, bear in mind that what you stand to gain from an international assignment far outweighs the challenges and hardships you may feel intensely upon your arrival.

The first month is a crucial time to "show off" your talents. The most effective way to do this is to win the respect of local and expatriate colleagues by demonstrating that you are skilled and competent. Identify "low-hanging fruit" in order to gain early "wins" that will help you to establish your credibility with your new superiors, colleagues and subordinates during your first month on the job. "I think the competency in your field becomes more critical because it helps people overcome any particular assumptions they may make of you because of a cultural background or the fact that you're an American, or whatever," WiSER Pauline stated. "As soon as you show your competency in the given field, people stop talking. I mean, at the end of the day, people are rewarded for performance. People are respected for the results they deliver, and if you deliver, most people will park any other questions." As in your home country, however, you will most likely have to prove a little more than your male colleagues. "I think that, as a woman, you do have to prove yourself," WiSER Anne contended. "You do have to work a little bit harder. You do have to be a little bit more. You do have to get a little bit more prepared…. I definitely think so."

Refining your masterpiece

Your technical skills may help you get the job done, but showing off your global leadership competencies, will allow you to get the job done well. Competencies are a combination of knowledge, skills, and job engagement demonstrated through observable and measurable behavior, and they can be developed or fine-tuned if you believe you need to do so. As a female expatriate, mastering WiSER competencies—self-awareness, conscious imbalance, operating outside your comfort zone, and active career management—will enable you to get the job done with flying colors.

Self-awareness is knowing your strengths and weaknesses, likes and dislikes—which are all based on your values—and using this knowledge to make critical decisions. It will also help you to manage other's perception of you. The first month of your new expatriate role will be filled with professional and personal decisions, ranging from selecting a staff to selecting a house. Getting the job done is just one piece of the pie. Getting the job done, while understanding and showcasing your strengths, is what will inspire others to perceive you as a leader.

Conscious imbalance is tipping the scales towards what gives you energy and fulfillment with the realization that the scales will need to be rebalanced on a regular basis. The first month is usually the most difficult period in an international assignment. So, it is important to recognize the situation that you're walking into. Certain sacrifices may be necessary during this initial period, but "overtipping" the scales temporarily in order to fulfill your desire to succeed in your expatriate assignment should not leave you riddled with guilt. "When the children [were] younger, I [felt] that I just ran my life by guilt," WiSER Alexis recalled. "I constantly felt guilty for not being at work, or guilty for not being at home when the children were sick or…I missed some important event at school." Despite such challenges, however, she added, "I would do it all again—five times over."

Operating outside of your comfort zone is the ability to embrace challenges coming from new experiences by tolerating ambiguity and remaining calm. It goes beyond a willingness to take risk and global agility, which are essential for any expat. The first month of your expatriate assignment will bring a high level of stress. When you combine relocation, with starting a new job, and then sprinkle in pre-existing notions or stereotypes about your nationality and gender, you can easily find yourself in an explosive situation. Therefore, you need to be prepared to stretch yourself in ways that may strike you as unprecedented, and you will have little, if any, downtime. "The first month, you are on the go 24/7, whether it's work or getting yourself and your family settled," WiSER Joanne warned. "The first year is hard," WiSER Erica agreed. "Stay positive, because that's the year when you learn about the new company, meet new people, learn new ways of doing things…it is probably one of the most stressful things you will do", so it is imperative that you focus on integrating and settling [yourself and] your family as quickly as possible." She added, "If they are happy, you will also be happy — and successful."

During this remarkably stressful period, we recommend that you immediately identify one, two, or three healthy habits that you enjoy and will engage in regularly in order to better manage stress. These are habits that will bring discipline into your life, and it is essential that you be able to engage in these habits without having to rely on anyone else. "I always kept reminding myself of what I wanted to be or to achieve," WiSER Argentina noted. "Also, I use three things that really help me stay focused. I exercise between two to four times per week. I pray. I read a lot. I enjoy reading books that will teach me something."

Active career management is knowing what you want from your career and working with intention to achieve those goals. Building a new network quickly is essential to grab the "low hanging fruit" in your first month. Professional relationships with superiors, peers, teams, and clients are the building blocks for navigating through the international landscape and gaining a grasp of the subtleties and nuances. It is critical to understand team dynamics, the political environment, and various competing agendas. "You have to understand the dynamics in teams, in power, in authority, so that you understand how you can be effective and address issues while being respectful…of the way things are," WiSER Diane observed. Likewise, WiSER Gillian recommended that you learn as much as you can about the new landscape. "Culturally and politically, I had to learn how to work differently," she recalled. "I had to understand where the key sensitivities were, and who the key stakeholders were." She added: "So, I had to learn to work with the politics…check out and try to find out what the rituals are at work, what things are said, how they are said, and find out who the key players are."

You may not frequently find yourself surrounded by other female expats, but if they are there, it's a good idea to get to know them — not only those in your organization but also those working in other organizations. This opens up the enriching possibility of sharing experiences. Over time, you can mentor each other, and help each other. As WiSER Alexis noted: "At the start, particularly, you lose that network of working women that you've stored up over many, many years, and you can actually feel quite lonely for the first month." This experience brought with it certain benefits, however. "I have realized how strong I am as an individual and, actually, that I can cope, working by myself," she added. "And [I learned] that I am able to network and develop new relationships quite successfully." Expatriating will test your networking abilities, but it is necessary for success on your assignment. In the longer term, that same network will help you make sound decisions and achieve career goals.

You will have plenty of opportunities to develop and demonstrate WiSER and other global leadership competencies due to your accelerated learning curve in the first month. In a metaphorical sense, be prepared to drink from a fire hose. That fact is, you will be absorbing a lot of information very quickly. Your first month is bound to include many mistakes — some small and others not so small. Not only should you allow yourself to make mistakes, but you should also forgive yourself in advance. You are in an intense and entirely new situation. As WiSER Martha told us: "...I think [you should] just go for it and be willing to make mistakes and to acknowledge those mistakes." The key to dealing with mistakes is to manage them. Inform the appropriate parties when a mistake is likely to affect them, take steps to remedy the error, ask for assistance to "fix it", and finally, learn from your mistakes. They will undoubtedly lead to good things.

In order to keep mistakes to a minimum and performance at a maximum, remember that there are various characteristics that predispose women to higher EQ and cultural adjustment. You should harness all of these skills and use them to your advantage during your first month on the new job. "Particularly as a female in a leadership role, I would say, leverage your unique strengths," advised WiSER Hermie. "If you have…more sensitivity and perceptive skills, as some women tend to, in addition to skills that are similar to other leaders…leverage these strengths and unique skills." WiSER Diane observed that her knack for building relationships proved to be an asset during an assignment in the USA. "In the US, I was well received, I think, because I…was interested in people," she said. "And they were hungry for some focus on the human dynamics within the organization."

Although you should leverage your female factor, some of you may find that you are the first female leader in the local organization. If you are the first, or one of the very few, female (expatriate) leaders in a host country, chances are that your gender will be a topic of discussion, at least at the outset. The bell curve illustrates this and other complicating factors only female leaders face in an international assignment. During your first few months on the job, bear in mind these factors, as they can influence the degree to which your assignment is successful. WiSER Alicia found herself in a host country with a relatively conservative business environment that featured rather formal rules of engagement. She prepared by researching the culture in advance. "So, I was a lot more conscious about it than I would be at home," she noted. She was especially conscious of the fact that many of the organization's customers and suppliers did not particularly enjoy dealing with Americans, let alone American women. "So, I have personally stepped out of certain conversations and negotiations…where I would be too much of a distraction," she explained. So, I'm cognizant of it." Interestingly, WiSER Emily derived a degree of humor from the patriarchal values she encountered during an assignment in Eastern Europe. "When I was in Budapest, my deputy was a man," she recalled. "And we'd often travel together in the Former Soviet Union, and almost inevitably, they would think, he is the boss." She added: "We used to laugh about it…see how long it [would] take them to figure out who was…the boss."

It's a wrap

First impressions are made within thirty seconds:

- "I can't believe they hired a woman. How did she get this job?"
- "She doesn't even speak my language? How stupid."
- "She seems tough."
- "Boy, she's pretty. Is she smart as well?"
- "She's all in the details; she's not a visionary."
- "She is into all that soft stuff. How is she going to execute the strategy?"
- "She is very nice. I hope the board will take her seriously."

In an international assignment, your first thirty days will be filled with a series of thirty-second first impressions, so you need to make them count. As noted, communication is the primary means of making such first impressions. Therefore, cross-cultural communication requires a mastery of speaking, presenting, writing, and listening across a wide spectrum of technologies as well as good old fashioned presentations and papers. Furthermore, you must be attentive to spoken and unspoken cultural signs and signals, in the course of everything from one-on-one interactions to large audience presentations.

We recommend that you always leverage humor to your advantage throughout the expatriation experience. Whether you are preparing to depart, entering your new experience, well into an assignment, or preparing to return, we know that laughter and objectivity will allow you to enjoy your expatriate experience more. While you may feel overwhelmed in the first month, which is filled with demands and challenges, don't forget to enjoy the "honeymoon" period where everything is new and exciting. Although you may experience some homesickness, you will adjust and start to feel comfortable in your new role and new venue. Think of yourself as a modern-day Frida Kahlo or Adelaide Labille-Guiard. All eyes will be upon you, as you make your debut. We are confident that your painting will be a masterpiece!

Epilogue

"If I have seen further, it is by standing on the shoulders of giants."
~ Sir Isaac Newton

*"Who you are today is a reflection of your experience.
Who you will be tomorrow will depend on the experiences
you are yet to choose."*
~ Caroline and Sapna

We hope you enjoyed joining us in the circle by the fire. Now, the fire is dwindling, the air is cooling off, and the stars are fading as dawn approaches. As great oral tradition goes, you are now bequeathed with knowledge and information passed on to you through the experts. You now hold information about bells and whistles to recognize and overcome. You also know about WiSER competencies to practice in order to perform well in an international role. You were an integral part of completing our circle.

As you sit at the tipping point, where the face of global employment is changing, and demand for talented female leaders in the international sphere is growing, you couldn't ask for a better time to expatriate and grow through your international assignment(s). Ninety-five percent of the WiSER shared that their expatriate experience enriched both their professional and personal lives, with the rewards far outweighing the risks. If you join the ranks of the modern day female explorer on a journey to an enriching professional life through expatriation, please share your stories on how *Worldly Women* helped you decide if an international move was for you, helped you pursue it and which tips you used to be successful in your international role.

Worldly Women your time is now!

Bibliography

Altman, Y. and S. Shortland. 2008. Women and international assignments: taking stock: A 25-year review. *Human Resource Management* 47 (2): 199-216.

American Management Association 2008. Expatriate assignments are on the rise. http://www.amanet.org/training/articles/expatriate-assignments-are-on-the-rise.aspx. Accessed November 25, 2012.

Anderson, S. and J. Cavanaugh. 2000. Top 200: The rise of corporate global power. Institute for Policy Studies. http://www.ips-dc.org/reports/top_200_the_rise_of_corporate_global_power. Accessed October 31, 2012.

Andors, A. 2010. Happy returns: The success of repatriating expatriate employees requires forethought and effective management. SHRM 55 (3): 3-10. http://www.shrm.org/Publications/hrmagazine/EditorialContent/2010/0310/Pages/0310agenda_relocation.aspx. Accessed November 21, 2012.

Audia, P. 2009. A new b-school specialty: Self-awareness. Forbes.com. http://www.forbes.com/2009/12/04/tuck-self-awareness-leadership-careers-education.html. Accessed November 21, 2012.

Bhargava R. 2012.Likeonomics: *The Unexpected Truth Behind Earning Trust, Influencing Behavior, and Inspriting Action.* Hoboken, New Jersey: John Wiley & Sons

Berard, J. 2012. Power of self-awareness. Global Knowledge. http://blog.globalknowledge.co.uk/2012/08/24/the-power-of-self-awareness. Accessed November 21, 2012.

Boatman, J. and R.S. Wellins. 2011. Global leadership forecast 2011. DDI World. http://www.ddiworld.com/glf2011. Accessed November 21, 2012.

Bradberry T. and J. Greaves. 2005. *The Emotional Intelligence Quickbook: Everything You Need to Know to Put Your EQ to Work.* New York: Simon & Schuster.

Brookfield Global Relocation Services. 2012. The 2012 global relocation trends survey report highlights. http://knowledge.brookfieldgrs.com/content/insights_ideas-2012_GRTS. Accessed November 21, 2012.

Buckingham, M. 2009. *Find your strongest Life: What the happiest and most successful women do differently.* Nashville, TN: Thomas Nelson.

Caliper. 2005. The qualities that distinguish women leaders. http://www.caliper.com.au/womenstudy/WomenLeaderWhitePaper.pdf. Accessed November 21, 2012.

Carter, N.M. and C. Silva. 2011. The myth of the ideal worker: Does doing all the right things really get women ahead? Catalyst. http://www.catalyst.org/file/523/the_myth_of_the_ideal_worker_does_doing_all_the right_things_really_get_women_ahead.pdf. Accessed November 19, 2012.

Catalyst. 2000. Passport to opportunity: US women in global business. http://www.catalyst.org/publication/78/passport-to-opportunity-us-women-in-global-business. Accessed November 21, 2012.

_____. 2013. Women CEOs of the Fortune 1000. http://www.catalyst.org/knowledge/women-ceos-fortune-1000. Accessed January 28, 2013.

CIA. 2011. World Factbook, 2011. https://www.cia.gov/library/publications/the-world-factbook/rankorder/2003rank.html. Accessed November 2, 2012.

Collins J. 2001. *Good to Great.* New York: HarperCollins Publishers

Credit Suisse. 2012. Gender diversity and corporate performance. https://infocus.credit-suisse.com/data/_product_documents/_shop/360145/csri_gender_diversity_and_corporate_performance.pdf. Accessed January 22, 2013.

Cross R.; A. Cowen, L. Vertucci, and R. Thomas. Leading in a connected world: How effective leaders drive results through networks. University of Virginia. http://www.robcross.org/pdf/research/leading_in_connected_world.pdf. Accessed December 10, 2012.

DOL (Department of Labor). 2011. Women's employment during the recovery. http://www.dol.gov/_sec/media/reports/FemaleLaborForce/FemaleLaborForce.pdf. Accessed March 17, 2010.

Dulworth, Michael. 2008. *The Connect Effect.* San Francisco, California: Berett-Koehler Publishers, Inc.

Economist Intelligence Unit Ltd. 2010. Up or Out. Next Moves for the Modern Expatriate. *The Economist.* http://graphics.eiu.com/upload/eb/LON_PL_Regus_WEB2.pdf.

Ernst & Young. 2012. Global marketing effectiveness survey 2011. http://emergingmarkets.ey.com/global-mobility-effectiveness-survey-2011/. Accessed November 21, 2012.

Europa. 2011. EU justice commissioner Viviane Reding meeting European business leaders to push for more women in boardrooms. Press release, January 3. http://europa.eu/rapid/press-release_IP-11-242_en.htm. Accessed November 21, 2012.

Expat Explorer. 2012. What is culture shock? April 24. http://expatexplorer.blogspot.co.uk/2012/04/what-is-culture-shock.html. Accessed November 21, 2012.

Expatica. 2008. Women on assignment: An evolutionary perspective. http://www.expatica.com/pt/employment/employment_information/Women-assignment_-An-evolutionary-perspective_11545.html. Accessed November 21, 2012.

Federal Glass Ceiling Commission. 1995. A solid investment: making full use of the nation's human capital. http://www.dol.gov/oasam/programs/history/reich/reports/ceiling2.pdf. Accessed January 8, 2013.

Foust-Cummings, H.; S. Dinolfo, and J. Kohler. 2011. Sponsoring women to success. Catalyst. http://www.catalyst.org/file/497/sponsoring_women_to_success.pdf. Accessed November 19, 2012.

George, B. 2011. Leadership skills start with self-awareness. Star Tribune, February 26. http://www.startribune.com/business/116923928.html?refer=y. Accessed November 21, 2012.

Gladwell M. 2002. *The tipping point: How little things can make a big difference.* New York: Little, Brown and Company.

Goldin, Claudia and Rouse, Cecelia. 1997. Orchestrating Impartiality: The Impact of "Blind" Auditionson Female Musicians. National Bureau of Economic Research. http://www.nber.org/papers/w5903. Accessed January 13, 2013.

Goleman, D. 2005. *Emotional intelligence: Why it can matter more than IQ.* New York: Bantam Books.

Gundling, E; T. Hogan, and K Cvitkovich. 2011. *What is global leadership? 10 key behaviors that define great global leaders.* Boston/London: Nicholas Brealey Publishing.

Hallowell, W. and C. Grove. 1997. Female assignees: Lessons learned. Runzheimer International. http://www.grovewell.com/pub-expat-females.html. Accessed November 20, 2012.

_____. 1997. Guidelines for women expatriates. InterMedia Solutions, Inc. http://www.grovewell.com/pub-expat-women.html. Accessed November 20, 2012.

Handwerk B. 2002. The Sherpas of Mount Everest. National Geographic. May 10, 2002. http://news.nationalgeographic.com/news/2002/05/0507_020507_sherpas.html. Accessed January 13, 2013.

Haslberger, A. 2007. Gender differences in expatriate adjustment. Paper, presented at the 67th Annual Meeting of the Academy of Management, Philadelphia, August 6-8.

Hogan, T. 2009. Global talent management and global mobility. Mobility. http://www.worldwideerc.org/Resources/MOBILITYarticles/Pages/0209hogan.aspx. Accessed November 20, 2012.

Howe, M.; J. W. Davidson, and J.A. Sloboda. 1998. Innate talents: Reality or myth. *Behavioral and Brain Sciences* 21: 399-442.

Hyslop, L. 2012. Number of expatriate postings likely to increase. *The Telegraph,* November 1, 2012.

Ibarra, H.; N. M. Carter and C. Silva. 2010. Why men still get more promotions than women. Harvard Business Review. http://hbr.org/2010/09/why-men-still-get-more-promotions-than-women/ar/1. Accessed November 19, 2012.

Iowa State University. 2012 Self-Awareness: The essence of effective leadership. http://blogs.extension.iastate.edu/hr/2012/04/16/self-awareness-the-essence-of-effective-leadership/. Accessed November 21, 2012.

Javidan, M.; M. Teagarden, F. Babrinde, K. Walch, N. Lynton, C. Pearson, D. Bowen, and A. Cabrera. 2007. Global mindset defined: Expat success strategy. Mobility. http://www.worldwideerc.org/Foundation/Documents/global_mindset.pdf. Accessed November 19, 2012.

Javidan, M.; M. Teagarden and D. Bowen. 2010. Making it overseas. *Harvard Business Review.* http://www.asaecenter.org/files/FileDownloads/HandOuts/2011International/Making%20it%20Overseas%20-%20HBR%20-%20Thunderbird%20University%20-%20provided%20by%20StrategicStraits%20Inc..pdf. Accessed November 19, 2012.

Javidan, M. 2010. Bringing the global mindset to leadership. HBR Blog Network. http://blogs.hbr.org/imagining-the-future-of-leadership/2010/05/bringing-the-global-mindset-to.html. Accessed November 21, 2012.

_____. 2010. The Skills you need to lead overseas. Interview. HBR IdeaCast, March 25. http://blogs.hbr.org/ideacast/2010/03/the-skills-you-need-to-lead-ov.html. Accessed November 21, 2012.

Jobvite. 2011. Jobvite survey: Social job seeker survey 2011. http://recruiting.jobvite.com/resources/social-recruiting-reports-and-trends/. Accessed November 21, 2012.

Jordan, J. and S. Cartwright. 1998. Selecting expatriate managers: Key traits and competencies. *Leadership & Organization Development Journal* 19 (2): 89-96.

Karajkov, R. 2007. The Power of N.G.O.'s: They're Big, But How Big? Worldpress. http://www.worldpress.org/Americas/2864.cfm. Accessed November 1, 2012.

Kelly, M. 2011. *Off balance: Getting beyond the work-life balance myth to personal and professional satisfaction.* New York: Hudson Street Press.

Keys, D. T. and R. S. Wellins. 2008. DNA of a global leader: There is a certain strategy that needs to be addressed to create global leaders. T+D. http://66.179.232.89/pdf/T+Dreprint_March08.pdf. Accessed November 21, 2012.

Keys T. and T. W. McKnight 2010. Corporate Clout: The influence of the world's largest 100 economic entities. Global trends.com http://www.globaltrends.com/knowledge-center/features/shapers-and-influencers/66-corporate-clout-the-influence-of-the-worlds-largest-100-economic-entities. Accessed January 13, 2013.

Kohls, L. R. 2001. *Survival kit for overseas living: For Americans planning to work and live abroad.* Boston/ London: Nicholas Brealey Publishing.

Krell, Eric. 2005. Evaluating returns on expatriates. *HR Magazine* vol 50, no.3.

Linehan, M. and H. Scullion. 2001. European female expatriate careers: Critical success factors. *Journal of European Industrial Training* 25 (8): 392-418.

_____. 2008. The development of female global managers: The role of mentoring and networking. *Journal of Business Ethics* 83: 29–40

Loehr, J. and T. Schwartz. 2003. *The power of full engagement.* New York: The Free Press.

Maertz, C. P.; A. Hassan, and P. Magnusson. 2009. When learning is not enough: A process model of expatriate adjustment as cultural cognitive dissonance reduction. Organizational Behaviors and Human Decision Processes 108 (1): 66-78.

McKinsey & Company. 2007. Women matter: Gender diversity, a corporate performance driver. http://www.mckinsey.de/downloads/publikation/women_matter/Women_Matter_1_brochure.pdf. Accessed November 21, 2012.

_____.2010. Women at the top of corporations: Making it happen. http://www.mckinsey.com/features/women_matter. Accessed November 21, 2012.

_____. 2012. The world at work: Job, pay and skills for 3.5 billion people. http://www.mckinsey.com/insights/mgi/research/labor_markets/the_world_at_work. Accessed November 21, 2012.

Mercer. 2008. Companies increase number of expats. October 27, 2008. Global HR. http://www.globalhrnews.com/story.asp?sid=1149. Accessed October 15, 2012.

Mercer. 2012. Press release Mercer's 2011/2012 Benefits survey for expatriates and internationally mobile employees. http://www.mercer.com/press-releases/Expatriate-Benefits-Survey. Accessed November 4, 2012.

Migration Policy Institute. 2009. BBC News. http://www.migrationpolicy.org/pubs/mpi-bbcreport-sept09.pdf. Accessed January 24, 2013.

Moore, T. 2010. In Germany, a quota for female managers. Time, March 22. http://www.time.com/time/business/article/0,8599,1974109,00.html#ixzz1ZL0Yi38M. Accessed October 31, 2012.

Mo, H. and J. M. Xia. 2010. A preliminary research on self-initiated expatriation as compared to assigned expatriation. *Canadian Social Science* 6 (5): 169-177.

Musselwhite, C. 2007. Self Awareness and the Effective Leader. Inc.com. http://www.inc.com/resources/leadership/articles/20071001/musselwhite.html. Accessed November 21, 2012.

NWLink. 2012. 70-20-10: Is it a viable learning model? http://www.nwlink.com/~donclark/hrd/media/70-20-10.html. Accessed January 23, 2013.

Oberg, L. Culture shock and the problem of adjustment to new cultural environments. Worldwide Classroom. http://www.worldwide.edu/travel_planner/culture_shock.html. Accessed November 19, 2012.

Peters, H. and R. Kabacoff. 1998/2010. A new look at the glass ceiling: The perspective from the top. Workinfo.com. http://www.workinfo.com/free/downloads/136.htm. Accessed October 31, 2012.

PriceWaterhouseCoopers. 2007. Women's economic participation: Enablers, barriers, responses. http://www.pwc.com/en_GX/gx/women-at-pwc/assets/pwc_genesis_park_report.pdf. Accessed November 21, 2012.

_____. 2010. Talent mobility 2020: PwC report investigates the future of international work. The forum for Expatriate Management. http://www.articles.totallyexpatcom/talent-mobility-2020-pwc-report. Accesssed November 15, 2011.

Pucik V. and T. Saba. 1998. Selecting and developing the global versus the expatriate manager: A review of the state of the art. *Human Resource Planning* 21 (4): 40.

Reed J. and R. Cook. Women in the global business world: Identifying the myths. Global Excellence. http://www.global-excellence.com/women-expatriates.php. Accessed November 21, 2012.

_____. Women and safety in a global business world: Deconstructing myth 2. Global Excellence. http://www.global-excellence.com/women-expatriates.php. Accessed November 21, 2012.

_____. Can women expatriates handle work and family abroad? Deconstructing myth 3. Global Excellence. http://www.global-excellence.com/women-expatriates.php. Accessed November 21, 2012.

Reiche S. 2011. Do international assignments add value to your career?. IESE. http://blog.iese.edu/expatriatus/2011/08/23/do-international-assignments-add-value-to-your-career/. Accessed November 21, 2012.

Rock, D. 2009. Managing with the brain in mind. strategy+business. http://www.davidrock.net/files/ManagingWBrainInMind.pdf. Accessed November 20, 2012.

Schachter, H. 2011. Why mindset can trump skill set. Globe and Mail, July 4. http://www.theglobeandmail.com/report-on-business/careers/management/why-mindset-can-trump-skill-set/article615652/. Accessed November 21, 2012.

Shaffer, M. A.; D. A. Harrison, H. Gregersen, J. S. Black, and L. A. Ferzandi. 2006. You can take it with you: Individual differences and expatriate effectiveness. *Journal of Applied Psychology* 91 (1): 109-125.

Schoemaker, P. J. H. 2011. *Brilliant mistakes: Finding success in the far side of failure.* Philadelphia: Wharton Digital Press.

Scivicque, C. Career management: Defining the process and purpose. Careerealism. http://www.careerealism.com/career-management-defining-process-purpose/. Accessed November 13, 2012.

Shortland, S. and Y. Altman. 2011. What do we really know about corporate career women expatriates? *European International Management* 5 (3): 209-234.

Smith, J. J., 2006. Areas identified where expats have most difficulty succeeding. HR Disciplines. http://www.shrm.org/hrdisciplines/global/Articles/Pages/CMS_018746.aspx. Accessed November 21, 2012.

_____. 2007. Expats average 13.4 more work hours per week over home location. http://www.shrm.org/hrdisciplines/global/Articles/Pages/Cms_023198.aspx. Accessed February 22, 2012.

Shorto, R. 2008. No Babies? The New York Times Magazine. http://www.nytimes.com/2008/06/29/magazine/29Birth-t.html?pagewanted=all&_r=0. Accessed October 16, 2011.

SHRM (Society for Human Resource Management). 2004. Emerging trends in global mobility: the assignee perspective. 2004 Worldwide Benchmark Study. http://www.shrm.org/Research/SurveyFindings/Documents/Emerging%20Trends%20in%20Global%20Mobility%20-%20A%20Study%20by%20SHRM%20and%20Willamette%20University.pdf. Accessed November 21, 2012.

_____. 2008. Selected cross-cultural factors in human resource management. SHRM Research Quarterly. Third Quarter. http://www.shrm.org/Research/Articles/Documents/September%202008%20Research%20Quarterly%20-%20Selected%20Cross-Cultural%20Factors%20in%20Human%20Resource%20Management.pdf. Accessed November 21, 2012.

_____. 2008. Leadership competencies. http://www.shrm.org/Research/Articles/Articles/PagesLeadershipCompetencies.aspx. Accessed January 9, 2013.

Spencer, S. T. 2011. Briefcase essentials for women in business. Knowledge@ Wharton, May 19. http://knowledge.wharton.upenn.edu/article.cfm?articleid=2782. Accessed November 21, 2012.

Storti, C., 2001. *The art of coming home*. London: Nicholas Brealey Publishing.

_____. 2007. *The art of crossing cultures*. 2nd Ed. Boston/London: Nicholas Brealey Publishing.

Tessman, D. and R. Wellins. 2008. DNA of a Global Leader. ASTD. http://www.astd.org/Publications/Magazines/TD/TD-Archive/2008/03/DNA-of-a-Global-Leader. Accessed January 22, 2013.

Thunderbird School of Global Management. 2012. GMI for executives and corporation. http://globalmindset.thunderbird.edu/home/global-mindset-inventory/assessment-executives-corporations. Accessed November 21, 2012.

Thurmon, D. 2010. *Off balance on purpose*. Austin, TX: Greenleaf Book Group Press.

Trompenaars, F. and C. Hampden-Turner. 2006. *Riding the waves of culture: Understanding cultural diversity in business*. London: Nicholas Brealey Publishing.

Tull, M. 2009. Risk-taking. About.com. http://ptsd.about.com/od/glossary/g/risktaking.htm. Accessed November 21, 2012.

Tung, R. L. 2005. Can women succeed as global managers? Executive Education, China Europe International Business School E-Newsletter iDEA. http://www.ceibs.edu/pdf/execed/e.inspire1.womensc.pdf. Accessed October 31. 2012.

Tungli, Z. and M. Peiperl. 2008. Expatriate practices in German, Japanese, UK and US multinational companies: A comparative survey of changes. *Human Resource Management* 48 (1): 153–171.

Tyler, K. 2001. Don't fence her in: Outdated assumptions about spouses, safety and culture may prompt managers to pass over women for international jobs. HR Magazine. http://www.shrm.org/Publications/hrmagazine/EditorialContent/0301/Pages/0301tyler.aspx. Accessed October 31, 2012.

_____. 2006. Retraining repatriates. HR Magazine. http://www.shrm.org/publications/hrmagazine/editorialcontent/pages/0306agenda_global.aspx. Accessed October 31, 2012.

Vance C., McNulty Y., Chauderlot F. 2011. Unpublished Manuscript. A comparison of female and male strategies for securing and enduring expatriate career development experiences.

Wanberg, C.; J. Zhu, D. Harrison, E. and Diehn. 2011. Crossing cultures: Unpacking the expatriate learning and adjustment process. SHRM Foundation. http://www.shrm.org/about/foundation/research/Documents/Wanberg%20Exec%20Summary%206-11.pdf. Accessed November 21, 2012.

White, A. K. 2009. *From comfort zone to performance management*. La Houlette, Belgium.

Woodward, Nancy H.. February 26, 2009. Expats still essential, but recession changes their roles. http://www.shrm.org/Publications/HRNews/Pages/ExpatsChangesRoles.aspx. Accessed January 7, 2013.

World Economic Forum. 2011. Global Talent Risk – Seven Responses.

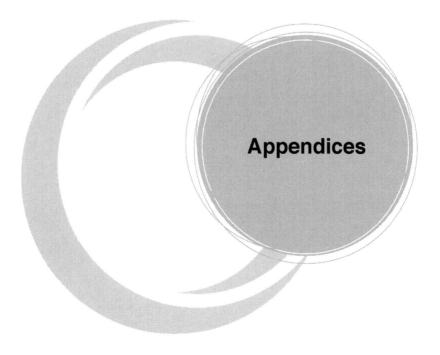

Appendices

Appendix A: Research details

1. *Research hypotheses*

We started our research with two hypotheses:

a. *There are shared global leader competencies among WiSER.*

As we began our research, we measured and coded for six competencies which we thought would be prevalent among WiSER based on initial interviews. Those competencies were:

- ability to operate outside of comfort zone,
- active career management,
- conscious imbalance,
- energy management,
- self-awareness,
- creativity.

b. *An international assignment will enhance your professional career.*

2. *Research method*

We interviewed 62 women who all held a C-level, executive, or emerging executive role. The WiSER lived and worked abroad for at least one year. Interviews were conducted during the period February 2011 - February 2012, either over the phone or in person and lasted approximately between 60-90 minutes. All interviews were audio-recorded and transcribed by a third party. The WiSER also completed an online survey to capture demographic data relating to personal and professional life and specific to their expatriate assignment(s).

3. *Data analysis*

A researcher (Dr. Zachary Kalinoski) compiled the transcribed interviews and online survey data. The principal investigators (authors) and researcher set up a coding scheme of variables that they considered important (the code book). In particular, they were interested in coding for the following variables and were determined a priori: mother and father's profession, mentor/sponsor, mentor gender, desire to live abroad, life status of first international exposure (e.g., child, young adult, professional), professional status of first international assignment (i.e., intern, junior professional, senior professional), husband/partner at time of international assignment (e.g., husband worked in country, husband did not relocate), marital status, children, self-initiated vs. company-initiated expatriation, assignment location, career enhancement, ability to operate outside of comfort zone, active career management, conscious imbalance, energy management, self-awareness, and creativity. In addition, the investigators were interested in coding some more open-ended questions that later were content-analyzed, including advice to other women, important skills/competencies for expatriation, modifications to communication and work styles, and miscellaneous quotes.

The researcher coded all 62 interviews based on the coding criteria set forth and agreed to by all parties. To ensure reliability of the coding system, the researcher employed the two principal investigators to code a sub-set of the interviews to gauge inter-rater agreement. Failing to account for agreement would assume that all of the variance in the ratings could be due to within-rater idiosyncrasies or conceptions of the data rather than a shared understanding of what the data actually suggests are present. Therefore, each investigator coded separate interviews (one who coded one set and the other coded a different set) to be compared against these same interviews that the researcher coded. The responses were compared to each other and percent agreement was calculated for every variable and then averaged to ascertain the overall level of agreement between coders. The researcher and the principal investigators met together each individually to discuss any discrepancies and to ensure that there was a mutual understanding about the concepts being coded.

In addition, the researcher content-analyzed the open-ended questions. The researcher combined any examples that were retrieved by all three coders and deleted redundant examples (e.g., same quote from same interviewee). Next, the researcher began categorizing each example into related themes for each of the four open-ended questions. After all of the examples were categorized for each question, the researcher created a definition for each category. Once this process was completed, the categories and their associated definitions were separated from the example items. To ensure the reliability of the coding system, these separate documents were given to the two principal investigators to re-sort into their designated categories. If the categories and their definitions reflect what the data says, then two independent individuals should be able to re-sort the items back into their original category distinctions. This was a shared task in that both investigators collaborated on the sorting task.

To assess the reliability of the coding system for both the interviews and the sorting task, the researcher assessed inter-rater agreement between researcher and the two principal investigators. The metric used to assess inter-rater agreement was the percentage of agreement displayed between two coders. The percent agreement metric is viewed as a more liberal form of assessing inter-rater agreement and the literature would recommend using a more conservative, secondary metric in addition to percent agreement. However, this study is exploratory in nature and thus this metric is adequate for these purposes.

Inter-Rater Agreement

5 of 18 variables	Researcher and Coder 1	Research and Coder 2
Career Enhancement	90%	70%
Self-Awareness	62%	60%
Conscious Imbalance	71%	40%
Operating Outside Comfort Zone	80%	70%
Active Career Management	90%	80%
Based on all 18 variables		
Mean	82%	76%
Standard Deviation	13%	18%
Median	80%	80%

4. Research results

The qualitative analysis of the data revealed that four competencies were observable at a greater and significant percentage. Those are the WiSER competencies explored in this book.

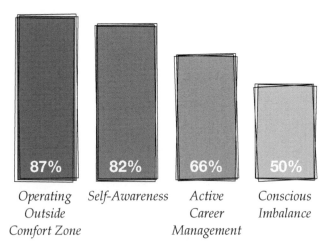

WiSER competencies

When asked, 95% of WiSER answered that an international assignment enhanced their career.

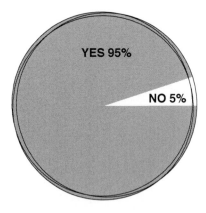

Was career enhanced by international assignment?

Appendix B: WiSER profile

Life-related demographics

The WiSER were single, married or divorced; with and without children; aged between 25 and 60; representing six of the seven continents, with only Antarctica not represented.

Countries of origin
- Australia (1), Belgium (2), Brazil (2), Canada (3), Denmark (1), Egypt (1), Finland (1), Germany (5), Holland (5), India (3), Ireland (1), Israel (1), Italy (1), Jamaica (1), Macedonia (1), Northern Ireland (1), South Africa (1), Sweden (1), Turkey (1), UK (5), USA (17), not reported (7)

Nationalities
- Australia (1), Belgium (2), Brazil (2), Canada (1), Denmark (1), Finland (1), Germany (4), Holland (5), India (1), Ireland (1), Israel (1), Italy (1), Singapore (1), South Africa (1), Sweden (2), Turkey (1), UK (3), USA (19), dual citizenship (7), not reported (7)

Age at time of interview
- WiSER's age ranged from 25 - 60
- 13% were between ages of 30-39
- 42% were between ages of 40-49
- 24% were between ages of 50-59
- 3% were 60 and over
- 18% did not report their age

Civil status

Marital status at time of interview
- 81% were either married or in a serious relationship
- 5% were single, never married
- 11% were either divorced or widowed
- 3% not evident

Family status at time of expatriate assignment
- 63% had children while on international assignment
- 34% did not have children either before or during their international assignment(s)
- 3% did not report
- Twice as many women had children while on international assignment than those who did not have children
- 56% were married/in a serious relationship and had children while on an international assignment

Partner information at time of international assignment (based on 50 WiSER who had a partner at the time of their assignment)
- 58% of partners worked in the host country
- 18% of partners did not work in host country
- 10% of partners did not relocate to host country
- 14% not evident

Miscellaneous
- 45% had first international experience as child or teenager
- 77% expressed desire to live abroad before their first international assignment
- 34% of all WiSER (regardless of SIE or OIE) had one or both parents who were immigrants

Work-related demographics

The WiSER have a wealth of experience but also a variety of experience in multiple organizations. We validated their seniority based on various criteria, including but not limited to title, span of control (number of staff and geographical responsibility), salary and budget managed. The level of expertise in this sample was high and reputable.

Expat experience

Expat locations
- A total of 150 international assignments spread among the 62 WiSER
- Countries of expat locations: Australia (3), Austria (1), Bangladesh (1), Belgium (3), Burundi (1), Cambodia (1), Cameroon (1), Canada (3), China (4), Czech Republic (4), Ecuador (1), Egypt (1), El Salvador (1), Finland (3), France (3), Germany (16), Hong Kong (4) UK (14), Hungary (1), India (3), Indonesia (2), Iraq (1), Italy (3), Japan (2), Kenya (4), Liberia (1), Malaysia (2), Mali (1), Mexico (3), Monaco (1), Mongolia (3), Mozambique (1), Nepal (1), Netherlands (3), Nicaragua (1), Panama (2), Papua New Guinea (1), Paraguay (1), Peru (1), Poland (2), Romania (1), Russia (2), Singapore (6), Slovakia (1), Somalia (1), South Africa (2), South Korea (2), Spain (3), Sudan (1), Switzerland (6), Taiwan (1), Thailand (1), UAE (2), USA (14), Venezuela (1), Yemen (1)

Expatriate experience
- 21% had 5 or more international assignments
- 29% had 3-4 international assignments
- 50% had 1-2 international assignments
- 60% had first international assignment when junior professional
- 27% had first international assignment as senior professional
- 11% got first international assignment as intern
- 2% not evident
- 71% were expatriated through organization (OIE)
- 26% self-initiated their expatriation (SIE)
- 3% had both experiences

Selection for first expatriate assignment (based on 56 responses; multiple answers were possible)
- 23% actively selected to work for a global employer in the hope of an international opportunity
- 11% only applied for international opportunities
- 34% actively informed my employer of my interest in international opportunities
- 36% were presented with an international opportunity by employer
- 23% were recruited for an international opportunity

Length of expatriate experience
- 45% 1-3 years
- 29% 4-6 years
- 21% 7-12 years
- 5% 13+ years

Length of time in organization prior to obtaining most recent expatriate assignment (based on 30 responses)
- 33% worked in organization 1-3 years
- 30% worked in organization 4-6 years
- 17% worked in organization 7-9 years
- 20% worked in organization 10+ years

General experience

General work experience at time of interview
- 9% had less than 12 years of experience
- 16% had 13-16 years of experience
- 16% had 17-19 years of experience
- 59% had 20 + years of experience

Function at time of most recent international assignment
- 19% had a cross-functional position
- 24% worked in the area of human resources
- WiSER represented 11 different functional areas. In addition to HR, the following functional areas were represented: business development, communications, finance, information technology, insurance, legal, manufacturing, marketing, operations, research.

Mentors/sponsors at time of interview
- 85% had one or more mentors/sponsors in their career
- 40% of mentors/sponsors were male
- 14% had female mentors/sponsors
- 23% had had both male and female mentors/sponsors
- 23% not evident if WiSER had only male, only female or both male and female mentors/sponsors

Seniority

Salary in USD

Only includes base pay and bonus. Health benefits, stock options, housing allowance, COLA, school tuitions, and other fringe benefits are not included.

- 18% earned $75,000 - $125,000
- 41% earned $125,000 - $225,000
- 26% earned $225,000 - $300,000
- 15% earned >$300,000

Job level (based on 49 answers to the question, how many levels down was the job from a chief level position?)
- 20% were C-level (0 levels down)
- 51% were executive (1 to 3 levels down)
- 29% were emerging executive (4 to 6 levels down)

Budget responsibility
- 53% = <$15M
- 6% = $15.1M - $100M
- 15% = $101M - $500M
- 18% = $501M - $1B
- 9% = >$1.1B

Appendix C: Organization profile

Sector at time of interview
- 69% worked for for-profit organization
- 15% worked for non-profit organization
- 13% worked for a governmental organization
- 3% were self-employed

Industry at time of most recent international assignment
- WiSER worked in 19 different industries

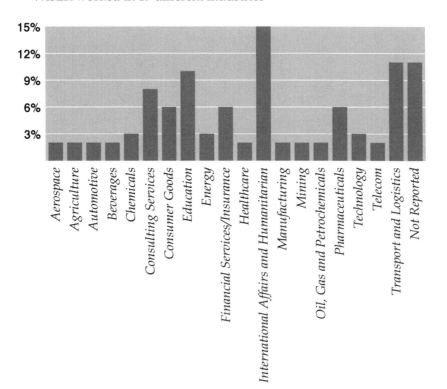

Organizations

Sample set of world class organizations WiSER are (or were) employed with:

- Adecco
- Added Value
- Arthur Anderson
- Association for the Advancement of International Education (AAIE)
- Astra Zeneca
- Baxter
- Bayer
- Brio International
- CGIAR
- ChildFund International
- Coca Cola
- Deloitte & Touche
- Deutsche Telekom
- Deutsche Post - DHL
- Dow Chemical
- Dow Corning
- Dow Jones
- Eli Lilly
- Fairtrade International
- General Electric
- General Motors
- Have Faith In Your Brand
- ING
- Johnson & Johnson
- The ISTAR Group
- Kuehne+Nagel
- LEGO
- Lloyds of London
- Medtronic
- Mylanda
- NASA
- Open Society Foundations
- Orrekel English
- Pfizer
- Procter & Gamble
- Randstad
- Rio Tinto
- Russell Reynolds
- Samsung
- Shell
- Siemens
- Sommer Consulting
- United Nations

Appendix D: Interview questions

Questions for one-on-one interview for Qualitative Study Women in Senior-level Expatriate Roles

1. Please describe your family and the atmosphere of your household. How many children were in your immediate family? Where did your parents work? What was common advice given?

2. Please describe an episode from your childhood that helped to inspire your career choice.

3. What college level class professor or experience had the most impact on you and why?

4. Did you have/do you have a sponsor or mentor who played/plays a critical role in your professional life? Please describe an episode that sheds light on your relationship with this individual.

5. Please describe a few major professional or personal milestones (positive and negative).

6. Please describe how you actively managed your career to achieve your success.

7. Please describe some of the challenges you have encountered in balancing your career with your personal life. Can you share some specific examples of challenges and how you navigated them?

8. Please describe the ways in which your priorities have changed over the years, if at all.

9. Please describe the ways your career and social life intersect. How do you network and socialize?

10. Describe the circumstances that led to your first international experience. How did you feel about the possibility of being abroad?

11. Describe the reception you received as a female organizational leader working in another country.

12. Please describe any modifications you made to your work or communication style when you entered the workforce of another country.

13. What advice would you give to women considering international roles?

14. What skills and competencies do you consider critical to be successful in an expatriate assignment?

15. What did you gain from your international experience? What did it bring you?

Appendix E: Two promising paths

There are two main ways to obtain an international job:

- you are sent abroad by the organization you're working for — the organization induced expatriation (OIE)
- you find a job in another country on your own — the self-initiated expatriation (SIE)

	Organization Induced Expatriation(OIE)	Self-Initiated Expatriation(SIE)
Being considered as a candidate	Expatriate selection processes often not well structured Less accessible to women because of home country barriers	Good way to overcome home country barriers
Moment of expatriation	10-15 years to be considered Companies are looking for alternatives to expensive expats	You can determine your own timeline.
Networking	Active career management within the organization (known territory)	Active networking in the intended host country (unknown territory)
Regulatory environment	Organization sponsors work permits, visas, tax equalization etc.	Manage on your own Host country employer has to justify international hire
Level of support	Greater security and organizational support	No security and no support
Mobility	Build career within the organization	Mobile across organizations
Period of assignment	Assignment for a specific period of time Repatriation is taken care of	Assignment for an unknown period of time Repatriation has to be self-managed
Cultural adaptation	Takes more conscious effort	Facilitated because of intensive interaction with host country nationals and because of country of choice

Characteristics of Organization-Induced Expatriation (OIE)
and Self-Initiated Expatriation (SIE)
Source: Vance, McNulty & Chauderlot 2011, and Hu Mo & Xia Jian-Ming 2010

If you're seeking to define yourself as a leader of tomorrow, international assignments, both short and long, can serve as a fast track (Hogan 2009). Given that only 17-20 percent of all expatriate roles are held by women, more and more women are taking the initiative to find international roles on their own. Whether you pursue an international opportunity through your employer or on your own, you are bound to encounter your share of advantages and disadvantages.

Appendix F: Acknowledgments

This book would not have been possible without the support of many. We are especially grateful to our spouses for their continuous support and encouragement, and for giving us the time to write this book. To John, my great man, thank you for taking our family on this wonderful international experience, which led to me co-authoring this book. Your belief in me, your enthusiasm and your commitment to help me realize my professional ambition, mean more to me than you know (Caroline). To Bob, thank you for helping me reach the finish line. You have always been my rock and I cannot thank you enough for sharing your critical eye, creative thoughts, and professional ideas with me as I wrote this book (Sapna). We thank our parents for opening our eyes to the world. We would also like to thank the WiSER for being open, honest and generous with their time and insights. Thank you to many friends, for giving us the confidence to complete this book. A special mention to Samira for introducing us to one another, to Katie Pintar and Tanya Talbot for proof-reading the script, and to Dr. Maren Weber for reviewing the survey format and questions.

A warm thank you to the various subject matter experts: to Dr. Zachary Kalinoski for his superior data analysis and reporting skills, Dr. Thomas Welsh for his editing expertise, Janet Hannah for creating all the beautiful graphs and lay-out, and to Patricia Mensinga for designing the inspiring book cover.

Worldly Women is a result of our personal expatriate experience, and professional experience with many inspiring managers in world class organizations such as Deloitte & Touche, KPMG, JPMC and Coopers & Lybrand. We are so pleased to have had the opportunity to co-author with one another, and explore the evolving role of women in the global workforce.

Appendix G: About the authors

Sapna Welsh

Sapna Welsh is a Partner of Leverage HR, LLC. Leverage HR LLC helps professionals sustain success through international career coaching & skill building. For the past twenty years, Sapna has helped individuals improve their performance through professional coaching, training, mentoring, skills assessment, and performance management. Coaching currently includes cross-cultural preparation of managers as they prepare to expatriate to the US. She has worked in various sectors including: banking, insurance, public accounting, manufacturing, logistics, non-profit, academia, and start-ups.

Sapna holds a Masters degree in Labor and Human Resources from The Ohio State University, a BBA in International Business from The George Washington University, and licensure as a Professional in Human Resources and Registered Corporate Coach. She previously served as an HR adjunct faculty member at Franklin University and also served on the Human Resources curriculum advisory board.

Sapna is married and lives in Bonn, Germany, with her husband and three children.

Caroline Kersten

Caroline Kersten has twenty years of experience, first as a business strategy consultant followed by tenure as a Human Resources manager in both profit and non/profit organizations. In 2008 she started her own consulting business, Kersten HR Consulting, advising and supporting businesses in HR and organization development. In August 2011, she started a partnership with Leverage HR. She is an experienced consultant in the areas of HR strategy, change management, personal development, competency management and performance management. Caroline currently teaches "Managing People & Organizations" to American university exchange students, at the Akademie für Internationale Bildung in Bonn. She has worked in various sectors including: government, automotive, consumer electronics, and leasing.

Caroline holds a Masters degree in European Studies and a Masters Degree in Dutch Law from the University of Amsterdam, as well as an LL.M. in European Law from the College of Europe Bruges. She is fluent in four languages (English, Dutch, German and French).

Caroline is married and lives in Bonn, Germany, with her husband and two daughters.

About LeverageHR

We met at our children's school through a mutual friend. We hit it off immediately. We began talking about our professional backgrounds, international experiences, and needless to say our families. We talked about potential opportunities to continue to offer professional services from Germany and both of us shared passion around understanding the role of professional women in the international sector.

So we embarked on a two year project to better understand women in the global workforce, positioning ourselves as experts in the field of female expatriate leadership. We share over forty years of combined HR experience in world class organizations such as Deloitte & Touche, KPMG, JPMC and Coopers & Lybrand.

We believe that expatriate experience is crucial for future leaders. We build on our expertise and personal expatriate experience to help professionals pursue expatriate opportunities, develop competencies to reduce ramp up time and perform well in an expatriate position, and repatriate smoothly. Expatriate development is no longer a luxury, it is an absolute necessity for individuals and organizations that want to survive, thrive, innovate and grow.

In addition to keynote presentations, we provide coaching and training, targeting women pursuing an international career through the following services:

- Global Peak Performance Coaching
- Global Expatriation and Repatriation Coaching
- International Candidate Assessment
- International Expatriate Policies

For more information we invite you to visit our website www.LeverageHR.com.

Printed in Germany
by Amazon Distribution
GmbH, Leipzig